Social Work Theory and Methods

This gateway text lays the foundations for a thorough knowledge of the theory and methods that social workers need. Pulling together the work of a team of experts, this book uses the innovative "theorizing practice" approach, rather than the traditional "applying theory to practice" approach, thereby providing a much more satisfactory basis for understanding the relationship between theory and practice and making it easier for practitioners to employ theory in practice.

Part I sets the scene by examining the relationship between theory and practice, how research can be used to inform practice, and the important role of policy and organizational factors. Part II provides 14 chapters, each exploring a different theoretical approach. All in all, this book provides the ideal introduction to using social work theory and methods in practice.

Neil Thompson, PhD, DLitt, is an independent writer and educator specializing in online learning. His books include the bestselling *Anti-Discriminatory Practice, Understanding Social Work: Preparing for Practice*, and *People Skills* (all published by Palgrave). He is a sought-after consultant and conference speaker. His website and blog are at www. neilthompson.info.

Paul Stepney, PhD, is Adjunct Professor of Social Work at the University of Tampere, Finland and visiting professor at two other Finnish universities. Prior to this he has taught at four UK universities and worked as a hospital social worker. Paul's research interests are in critical practice and prevention, and he is co-author of two books on social work.

An excellent resource that truly grounds practical application with foundational knowledge and research in a variety of contexts and approaches. This book is a gem for not only social workers, but any practitioner in the helping professions. The unique way that the authors and contributors seamlessly blend together research, theory, and practice provides a book that is relevant, readable, and eminently useful to all aspects of service sector work.

Darcy Harris, *PhD, FT, King's University College, London, Canada*

This is a terrific book for social work students at all levels. In all my years in social work education, I have always used theory in teaching but never taught a course specifically about theories. This book makes me want to do just that. The authors conclude that the end of the book is the beginning of a journey of deeper learning for the reader. I felt that myself and look forward to the expedition.

Susan Cadell, *Professor, Renison University College – University of Waterloo, Canada*

The coming together of Neil Thompson and Paul Stepney to co-edit a book on *Social Work Theory and Methods* provides a mouth-watering prospect of fresh insights and richly innovative writing for a social work audience. Social work theory will always be indispensable to critically minded practitioners.

Stephen A. Webb, *Glasgow Caledonian University, Scotland*

Social Work Theory and Methods

The Essentials

Edited by
Neil Thompson and Paul Stepney

Routledge
Taylor & Francis Group

NEW YORK AND LONDON

First published 2018
by Routledge
711 Third Avenue, New York, NY 10017

and by Routledge
2 Park Square, Milton Park, Abingdon, Oxon, OX14 4RN

Routledge is an imprint of the Taylor & Francis Group, an informa business

© 2018 Taylor & Francis

Library of Congress Cataloging in Publication Data
A catalog record for this book has been requested

ISBN: 978-1-138-62976-9 (hbk)
ISBN: 978-1-138-62978-3 (pbk)
ISBN: 978-1-315-21022-3 (ebk)

Typeset in Adobe Caslon Pro
by Sunrise Setting Ltd, Brixham, UK

Dedicated to our social work sisters and brothers across the globe

CONTENTS

FOREWORD

Social work has always contended that context matters. One of the distinctions that sets social work apart from some of the other psychological and therapeutic modalities is that we use a "person-in-environment" perspective, viewing the client within his or her physical and social environment (Barker, 2014).

In *Social Work Theory and Methods: The Essentials*, edited by Neil Thompson and Paul Stepney, a more apt descriptor may be "person-in-situation." This approach builds on Thompson's prior thought-provoking work on "theorizing practice" (Thompson, 2017) where theory and practice are not separate, but fused.

Thompson's model helps the practitioner draw conclusions about the interrelated factors contributing to the client's problems, and it allows the selection of the best interventions for alleviating those problems. Those social workers with good practice experience—meaning those who are more experienced—begin with the problem presented and then weave in theory and methods as needed and useful.

As an example, my first professional social work role was that of a social worker in the emergency room of a large university hospital. While I had a good grasp of crisis theory, the needs of the individuals I saw presented with more than the medical crises that brought them there. Some were living with serious and persistent mental health problems; others were the victims of domestic violence or substance abuse. Some were homeless. Some patients were accompanied by police officers because they had been arrested for a criminal act. Still others were in a terminal phase of illness, and there was disagreement among family members regarding treatment options. Tenets of many therapy models could be applicable. Brief therapy, family mediation, group dynamics, negotiation, advocacy, cognitive-behavioral therapy, and solution-focused therapy were potentially helpful.

While not all social work settings are as varied as an emergency unit, many social workers do deal with a wide spectrum of issues, no matter where they practice, and many would characterize their clinical approach as eclectic. What may not be clear though, is how the theory, empirical data, and technical procedures are linked together (Borden, 2009). Grounding in the fundamental theoretical approaches is the first step. This provides the practitioner with a range of ideas and methods to draw upon, as needed, for a particular situation in a particular therapy setting, and allows the social worker to better address the real-life issues of their clients.

In daily practice, social workers make judgments and decisions that can, and do, impact upon the lives of others. Caring and compassion are both important, but social work intervention cannot be based on feelings or a "best guess." Social work practice requires critical thinking, excellent clinical observation, and a good understanding of basic social work theories and methods that can be used therapeutically.

This is easier said than done. In *Social Workers' Desk Reference* (Roberts, 2009), the section on "Theoretical Foundations and Treatment Approaches in Clinical Social Work" contains twenty different chapters; "Community Practice" contains ten. I do not use this example as a negative. As a social worker, I am proud of the various contributions that social work is making across all levels of practice, and the expansion of social work methods and intervention techniques reflects exciting developments in our field. This growth, however, demonstrates how complex the social work profession has become, with divergent specialties and conceptual orientations. The variety of theoretical perspectives in use, even within a specific practice area, is specialized. The breadth of our profession today results from the continued opportunity social workers have to practice within new contexts.

Given these factors, especially the abundance of theory choices, a social worker just entering the profession needs a starting point. That is the intent and purpose of this text. In addition to overview chapters for theory, research, and policy written by the editors, 14 outstanding authors provide a compact introduction to the essentials of theoretical approaches that can provide important insights for practice.

In some ways, Thompson's idea of theorizing practice stands theory on its head. Instead of basing interventions on our usual (and perhaps favorite or comfortable) theory, and trying to impose that theory, or force it to fit the situation, this approach starts with the situation and allows the situation to point to the useful theory. For this to work, social workers must have a good foundational grasp of theory. They need to recognize that theory is not simply something studied in the classroom and then disregarded. Instead, it is theory that provides the tools necessary for critical thinking and for determining rationales for our interventions.

Because social work is a practice profession, the integration of theory and practice is critical. To keep our profession viable, social work practices must remain theory based. At the same time, we need our theories to be practice informed. The careful observations made by social workers in their work settings are what practice adds to this equation. That is why this textbook is an important addition to the social work literature. It will help students and those just entering the profession better understand the linkage of theory and practice, and it will assist them in becoming better-grounded social work practitioners.

Elizabeth J. Clark, PhD, MSW
Former Chief Executive Officer
National Association of Social Workers, USA

References

Barker, R. L. (Ed.). (2014). *The social work dictionary* (6th Edn). Washington DC: NASW Press.

Borden, W. (2009). Comparative therapies. In A. Roberts (Ed.). *Social workers' desk reference* (2nd Edn). New York: Oxford University Press, pp. 259–64.

Roberts, A. R. (Ed.). (2009). *Social workers' desk reference* (2nd Edn). New York: Oxford University Press.

Thompson, N. (2017). *Theorizing practice* (2nd Edn). London: Palgrave.

PREFACE

Social work is not a simple, monolithic enterprise. It is practiced in various ways according to the setting, the organizational context, the national policy context, the client group, the style and approach of the individual practitioner and, of course the particular case circumstances. However, underpinning this diversity is a set of theoretical understandings and a set of "practice modalities" commonly referred to as "methods." This book seeks to capture some of the key elements of that underlying knowledge base.

Drawing on the experience and expertise of a range of internationally acclaimed social work authors, this book offers insights into a number of important theoretical approaches and associated methods to serve as a vitally important repertoire of professional knowledge and resources. Of course, given the wide scope of social work theory and methods, not all possible approaches are covered, but what does feature will be more than sufficient to offer an excellent foundation for high-quality, informed practice and for continued learning and development.

Traditionally social work education and professional training have been premised on the idea of "applying theory to practice," an idea uncritically accepted for decades. However, one of the important contributions of this book is to present a challenge to that notion, with its assumption that we should begin with theory and then seek to relate it to practice. In its place, we offer the proposal that we should begin with the specifics of practice and then draw on the relevant aspects of the theory base to make sense of it as we engage with the challenges of that particular situation. This is what is known as "theorizing practice" (Thompson, 2017a). What appears initially to be a simple change of terminology actually makes a huge difference to how we conceptualize the relationship between theory and practice and the role of social work methods.

"Theorizing practice" is also intended to help us find creative solutions to the many demanding and messy problems we encounter in practice. Given that inequality and discrimination are at the root of so many social problems, such an integrative approach can promote practice in ways that combine effectiveness with a commitment to social justice (Stepney, 2012; Thompson, 2017b).

This book has been developed with a view to it serving as a first step into the world of social work theory and methods for students and will therefore serve well as a teaching tool for everyone involved in social work education. Our aim is for it to be used in social work classrooms to promote a solid foundation of understanding of social work theory and methods and point the way to the further and more advanced literature.

However, it is not only students who can gain from this wide-ranging text. It should also serve well as a basic reference source for newly qualified practitioners and for more seasoned professionals wanting to revisit their roots.

Overall, then, what you will find in this book is a fresh approach to social work theory and methods and a sound foundation of knowledge encompassing a number of essential social work theories and methods. We trust you will find it of value and we wish you well in your efforts to benefit from the important insights it offers. We invite you to join us in our journey into the world of theorizing social work practice.

References

Stepney, P. (2012). An introduction to social work theory, practice and research. In P. Stepney and D. Ford (Eds) *Social work models, methods and theories* (2nd Edn). Lyme Regis, UK: Russell House Publishing, pp. 20–35.

Thompson, N. (2017a). *Theorizing practice* (2nd Edn). London: Palgrave.

Thompson, N. (2017b). *Social problems and social justice*. London: Palgrave.

ACKNOWLEDGMENTS

First of all, we would like to thank the contributors for producing such helpful guides to their particular area of expertise. Having contributions from such a diverse range of people has no doubt enriched the book considerably.

We are also grateful to Elizabeth J. Clark for providing such a helpful Foreword and for getting across so clearly what the book is all about. We must also thank Samantha Barbaro and her team at the publishers for their support and for having faith in us to be able to deliver a quality text.

Neil would like to thank his wife, Dr. Sue Thompson, not only for the moral and practical support that she so readily and ably provides, but also for bringing her extensive social work expertise to bear in commenting on an earlier draft.

Paul would like to thank his wife, Monique, for making *iedere dag een bijzondere dag,* and for the invaluable support of his three children Natasha, Rowland, and Melissa. He would also like to thank colleagues from the University of Tampere in Finland for their helpful suggestions and comments, especially Dr. Anna Metteri from the School of Social Sciences and Humanities, Professor Eero Ropo from the School of Education, and Emeritus Professor Jorma Sipilä from the Institute of Advanced Social Research.

Finally, we would both like to thank those people far too numerous to mention by name who have contributed in one or more ways to our knowledge and understanding of social work theory and methods and our passion for affirming the value of social work as a contribution to developing humane and compassionate communities and societies.

THE EDITORS AND CONTRIBUTORS

The Editors

Neil Thompson, PhD, DLitt, is an independent writer and online tutor. He has held full or honorary professorships at four UK universities. He is currently visiting professor at Wrexham Glyndŵr University in Wales where he is involved in running the MSc Advanced Practice in Human Services online program. He has 40 years' experience in the helping professions as a practitioner, manager, educator and consultant.

He has 39 books to his name. These include: *The Critically Reflective Practitioner* (with Sue Thompson, Palgrave Macmillan, 2008), *Effective Communication* (Palgrave Macmillan, 2nd edn, 2011), *People Management* (Palgrave Macmillan, 2013), *People Skills* (Palgrave, 4th edn, 2015), *Understanding Social Work* (Palgrave, 4th edn, 2015), *The Authentic Leader* (Palgrave, 2016), *Anti-discriminatory Practice* (Palgrave, 6th edn, 2016), *The Professional Social Worker* (Palgrave, 2nd edn, 2016), *The Palgrave Social Work Companion* (with Sue Thompson, Palgrave, 2nd edn, 2016), *Social Problems and Social Justice* (Palgrave, 2017), *Theorizing Practice* (Palgrave, 2017) and *Promoting Equality: Working with Diversity and Difference* (Palgrave, 4th edn, 2018). His latest writing project is the *Social Worker's Practice Manual,* a hands-on guide to social work practice (www.socialworkfocus.com). He also has a growing number of e-books to his name, including *A Career in Social Work* and *How to Do Social Work* (www. avenuemediasolutons.com).

He is a Fellow of the Chartered Institute of Personnel and Development and the Higher Education Academy and a Life Fellow of the Royal Society of Arts and the Institute of Welsh Affairs. In addition, he is a sought-after conference speaker who has presented in the UK, Ireland, Italy, Spain, Greece, Norway, the Netherlands, the Czech Republic, Turkey, India, Hong Kong, Canada, the United States and Australia. In 2011 he was presented with a Lifetime Achievement Award by BASW Cymru (the Wales branch of the British Association of Social Workers). In 2014 he was presented with the Dr. Robert Fulton award for excellence in the field of Death, Dying and Bereavement from the Center for Death Education and Bioethics at the University of Wisconsin-La Crosse.

He has qualifications in social work; training and development; mediation and alternative dispute resolution; and management (MBA), as well as a first-class honors degree, a doctorate (PhD) and a higher doctorate (DLitt).

Dr. Paul Stepney is Adjunct Professor of Social Work at the University of Tampere in Finland and visiting professor at two other Finnish universities. Prior to this he has taught both social work and social policy at a number of UK universities, including Hull, Manchester, Exeter and Wolverhampton. He has also been an Open University tutor and contributed to the development of Open University Health and Social Welfare course material.

Paul is a qualified social worker with experience of adult social care, child protection, and mental health in both fieldwork and hospital settings. During the 1990s he combined teaching at Exeter University with a hospital social work post.

Paul's current research interests are in the areas of critical practice and prevention and he has had a number of articles published in peer-reviewed international journals. He has recently undertaken cross-national research with practitioners in two European cities to examine the role of prevention in mainstream social services. The research has highlighted how particular strategies of prevention can assist practitioners to find the most effective ways of managing risk, enhancing the well-being of vulnerable clients and protecting the public. He is currently supporting practitioners to develop a well-being Alliance and evaluating the effectiveness of mental health services in one NHS Mental Health Trust in the West of England.

He is the co-author of two books. Co-editor with Deirdre Ford (2012) of *Social Work Models, Methods and Theories: A Framework for Practice* (2nd Edn), Russell House Publishing and co-author with Keith Popple (2008) of *Social Work and the Community: A Critical Context for Practice*, Palgrave Macmillan.

He is a respected international conference speaker and has recently given both keynote addresses and papers at conferences in the Czech Republic, Croatia, Finland, Hungary and the UK. He has appeared on television as well as radio phone-in programs to discuss social policy reforms and social work practice issues in both Finland and the UK.

He has qualifications in sociology and social policy (BA Hons), social and community work studies (MA), social work (Postgraduate Diploma and CQSW) and a doctorate (PhD).

The Contributors

Donna Baines is Professor and Chair of Social Work and Policy Studies, University of Sydney. She teaches anti-oppressive theory and practice, restructuring and paid and unpaid care work in the neoliberal context and social justice and social change. Baines has published recently in the *British Journal of Social Work*, the *Journal of Industrial Relations* and *Critical Social Policy*.

Wing Hong Chui is Professor in the Department of Applied Social Sciences, City University of Hong Kong. He worked as a youth outreach social worker in Hong Kong after qualifying as a Registered Social Worker. He then taught social work and criminology at the University of Exeter, University of Queensland and University of Hong Kong. His areas of interest include youth studies, social work, criminology and criminal justice. He serves on the editorial board of a number of academic journals, such as *Australian Social Work*, *Child & Family Social Work* and *Social Work Education: An International Journal*.

Paul Davis has worked as a partnership manager for the Avon and Wiltshire Mental Health trust for the past 15 years, having previously worked as a social worker for 20 years. He completed a PGCE and obtained an MSc in Community Care from Bristol University in 2001. His focus has been on partnership and collaboration and, following his involvement in further education, he came to see adult learning as a suitable and inclusive framework for community development. He has published his research on mental health, inclusion and the green agenda in the US *Journal of Social Work in Health Care*, and is currently taking a lead in the development of a Wellbeing Alliance in North Somerset, UK.

Suki Desai has had a varied career in social work and social work education. She has worked as Regional Director for the Mental Health Act Commission, now part of the Care Quality Commission, responsible for the regulation of health and care services in England and Wales. She has also sat on Mental Health Review Tribunals responsible for reviewing the detention of those people compulsorily admitted to hospital under mental health legislation. Suki is currently undertaking a PhD at the University of Hull in the UK, looking at the Impact of CCTV within mental health wards.

Mark Doel, CQSW, MA (Oxon), PhD, is Professor Emeritus in the Centre for Health and Social Care Research at Sheffield Hallam University, UK. For 20 years he was a practicing social worker, then social work academic, writer and researcher. Mark continues to lead training workshops, largely in the fields of practice education and group work in which he has an international reputation. He is the Vice-President of the International Association for Social Work with Groups (IASWG). Mark has extensive experience in eastern Europe and he is Honorary Professor at Tbilisi State University, Georgia. Mark has published 21 books, most recently *Social Work in 42 Objects (and More)* and *Rights and Wrongs in Social Work: Ethical and Practice Dilemmas*. See www.shu.ac.uk/research/hsc/about-us/mark-doel.

Juha Hämäläinen is Professor of Social Work, especially Social Pedagogy, at the University of Eastern Finland. His research has focused particularly on the history and theory of child protection and child welfare policy, and more generally on the history of social work, social care and social welfare. He has published on the concept and theory of social pedagogy and has examined the interconnections of social work and social policy, with a particular focus on historical aspects, as well as methodology of comparative research of social welfare and social work. In addition, he has distinguished himself in parenthood, family and youth research.

Dr. Louise Harms is Professor and Deputy Head in the Department of Social Work and is the Associate Dean (Equity, Diversity and Staff Development) for the Faculty of Medicine, Dentistry and Health Sciences at the University of Melbourne in Australia. She is also the Director of the Trauma Recovery and Resilience Research Program, undertaking research relating to people affected by a range of traumatic life experiences with a focus on understanding the interactions of stress, trauma and loss responses with resilience and growth responses. This draws on her previous practice experience as a social worker in hospital and education settings.

Aila-Leena Matthies, PhD in Social Sciences, is Professor of Social Work at the University of Jyväskylä, Kokkola University Consortium. She has been publishing on ecosocial perspectives on social work in Finnish, German and English since the late 1980s. Her most recent publication on this research is: Matthies, A-L. and Närhi, K. (eds.) *Ecosocial Transition of Society: The Contribution of Social Work and Social Policy* (Routledge, 2017). Her other research focus is citizen participation and welfare service systems. She has edited a book with Lars Uggerhoej: *Participation, Marginalisation and Welfare Services: Concepts, Politics and Practices Across European Countries* (Ashgate, 2014).

Kati Närhi, PhD in Social Work, is Professor of Social Work in the Department of Social Sciences and Philosophy, University of Jyväskylä, Finland. Närhi is internationally involved and nationally one of the leading figures in the ecosocial approach to social work, with Professor Aila-Leena Matthies. Her other research interests are ecosocial transition, community social work, structural social work, action research, participation and user involvement. Recent publications are Matthies, A-L. and Närhi, K. (eds.) *Ecosocial Transition of Society: Contribution of Social Work and Social Policy* (Routledge, 2017) and Närhi, K. and Matthies, A-L. The ecosocial approach in social work as a framework for structural social work, in *International Social Work*. Prepublished June 14, 2016.

Malcolm Payne is Emeritus Professor, Manchester Metropolitan University, Honorary Professor, Kingston University and Docent in Social Work, Helsinki University. He has also recently held academic posts in Opole University, Poland and Comenius University, Bratislava, Slovakia. He is author of *Modern Social Work Theory* (4th edition, Palgrave Macmillan, 2014), *Older Citizens and End-of-Life Care* (Routledge, 2017), *Humanistic Social Work* (Palgrave Macmillan, 2011) and, with Margaret Reith, *Social Work in End-of-Life and Palliative Care* (Policy Press, 2009). He was Director, Psycho-social and Spiritual Care, and Policy and Development Adviser, St Christopher's Hospice, London, 2003–2012.

Ronald Rooney, PhD, is Professor Emeritus, School of Social Work, University of Minnesota. Dr. Rooney is the author of *Strategies for Work with Involuntary Clients* (1992, 2009) with the 3rd edition in press. He is also an author of *Direct Social Work Practice,* now in its 10th edition, with Dean Hepworth, Glenda Dewberry Rooney and Kim Strom-Gottfried (2016). Dr. Rooney is a licensed clinical social worker. He has provided training and consultation throughout the United States, Canada, Great Britain, Holland, Korea and Australia. His areas of practice are child welfare, family-based services and work with involuntary clients.

Robert Taibbi is the author of ten books on family and couple therapy, clinical supervision and clinical practice. He has also published over 300 articles, writes an online column for *Psychology Today* entitled "Fixing Families," and has received three national awards for Best Consumer Health Writing. He does training in the areas of family, couple, brief therapy and clinical supervision nationally, and is currently in private practice in Charlottesville, Virginia. He can be reached at bobtaibbi.com.

Emma Tseris is a lecturer in social work and policy studies at the University of Sydney, where her research and teaching areas include: social work practice in mental health settings; mental health experiences in relation to gender inequality; feminism and trauma theory; and alternative understandings of mental health beyond a biomedical framework. Emma is interested in creative and narrative-based approaches to research and teaching that aim to challenge conventional ideas about mental illness and learn from the perspectives of clients.

Fran Waugh is Professor in Social Work and Associate Dean, International in the Faculty of Arts and Social Sciences at the University of Sydney. She is passionate about field education (practice learning) being core to the integration of students' learning. Fran's research interests include higher education pedagogy to optimize students' education experiences and knowledge building in social work practice to enhance evidence-informed practice.

INTRODUCTION

This volume brings together insights from various nations, specialisms, and approaches. This diversity reflects the diversity of our profession and of the social world and its problems that social work exists to address. However, this diversity is underpinned by common principles and values and a shared commitment to making a positive difference in supporting, caring for, and empowering those individuals, groups, and communities which, for a variety of reasons, have need of what social work can offer.

For social work to achieve its full potential, its practitioners need a sound basis of understanding in order to be equipped to deal with the complex challenges and dilemmas involved. We are fortunate to have a significant literature base extolling various theoretical understandings, a large foundation of empirical research and accounts of the learning to be gained from actual practice in a variety of settings. This book is intended in some ways as a gateway to some aspects of that professional knowledge base, particularly those elements that generally go under the heading of "theory and methods."

We are focusing on these elements in particular, for three reasons:

1. We are aware that there is a lot of confusion about what is a theory, what is a method and what is the relationship between the two. There is therefore much to be gained by clarifying these issues.

2. Social work practice needs to be *informed* practice (theory) and can benefit from specific tools (methods) to achieve its goals. A good knowledge of theory and methods can help to bolster confidence and reinforce a sense of professionalism (Thompson, 2016).

3. We are aware that there is a significant literature base relating to theory and methods. Our aim is not to replace or displace that literature base, but, rather, to offer a gateway to them – hence the subtitle of "The Essentials." Our discussions with students and early-career practitioners confirmed for us that there is very much a need for a text such as this.

So, with this rationale in mind, we have put together a set of essays that have been carefully selected to present a coherent and accessible basic introduction to social work theories and methods. Of course, the text is not comprehensive – we would need a series of thick volumes to do that, and would probably still be criticized by proponents of one or more approaches that had escaped our attention. Our aim is the more modest one of providing a first-step introduction to the world of social work theories and methods. It is our intention to: (i) provide a foundation for understanding what theory and methods (and related matters of policy and research) are all about; (ii) provide a short introduction to a range of important approaches; and (iii) show the value (and indeed necessity) of a sound foundation of knowledge of theory and methods with a view to generating a degree of enthusiasm for finding out more (hence the notion of this being a "gateway" text). In other words, it will not tell you everything you need to know, but it should give you a reasonable grasp of the basics and motivate you to find out more about those areas that are of particular interest to you.

In this regard, the subtitle, "The Essentials," is significant. We are well aware that what we offer here is just the beginning of a journey of understanding, basic foundations for you to build on, leading, for example, to much fuller texts, such as Corcoran and Roberts (2015), de Mönnink (2017), Payne (2014), and Thompson and Thompson (2016), and beyond to the primary sources for each of the theoretical approaches.

The book is in two parts. The first part has as its focus the broader context of social work theory and methods, with each of the three chapters concentrating on a particular aspect of that context. In the first chapter Neil Thompson explores the relationship between theory and practice. He challenges the traditional notion of "applying theory to practice" and proposes in its place a process of "theorizing practice." This involves replacing the idea of beginning with theory and trying to fit it into real practice situations with one of beginning with practice and drawing on our professional knowledge base as appropriate to the specific circumstances. This is presented in the context of critically reflective practice.

Chapter 2, by Paul Stepney and Neil Thompson, presents a good case for ensuring that, as far as possible, our practice should be informed by the best available research evidence. A key message of this book is that our practice needs to be *informed* practice – and that includes the various ways in which research can provide us with important elements of understanding.

In Chapter 3 Paul Stepney provides an overview of the policy and organizational context in which social work activities take place. This helps to "ground" the discussion of theory and methods by providing a clear picture of how policy and organizational concerns influence and constrain what actually happens in practice.

Part II comprises a set of 14 chapters, each of which provides a basic introduction to a particular theoretical approach. In Chapter 4, Malcolm Payne discusses how the skills and understanding deriving from psychodynamic theory can be of value in a variety of social work contexts.

Chapter 5 invites us to consider how cognitive-behavioral work can also be a helpful source of understanding in tackling a range of problems that are commonly encountered in social work. Paul Davis and Paul Stepney introduce us to the approach and provide us with a good foundation for learning more.

In Chapter 6, Ronald Rooney presents a summary of the key ideas underpinning task-centered practice. This approach has a long and successful track record and, as such, is an approach well worth knowing about. It offers a structured and systematic approach that can be especially helpful in situations characterized by a degree of chaos or disorganization.

Crisis intervention is the focus for Chapter 7. Neil Thompson gives us a clear picture of how, in the right circumstances, this method and the crisis theory on which it is based can be a highly productive approach that can help to bring about very positive results in a short period of time.

Louise Harms highlights for us, in Chapter 8, what narrative approaches can contribute to our repertoire of methods. We build our lives around the stories we tell ourselves. Sometimes those stories are unhelpful and can benefit from being rewritten, which is precisely what this approach is all about.

Chapter 9 presents an account of how existentialism can be used as an important foundation of theoretical understanding. Neil Thompson highlights some of the key concepts of this complex philosophy and gives us a picture of how the ideas can be drawn upon in practice – that is, how it can be used to "theorize" practice.

Suki Desai adds solution-focused practice to our repertoire in Chapter 10. Her account shows how focusing on strengths and resilience factors can provide a strong platform for promoting empowerment. This approach has much to commend it and is a very worthwhile method to be able to draw upon.

Conflict is a common feature of social work practice. It is in recognition of this that Chapter 11 covers the topic of mediation. This method, clearly explained by Wing Hong Chui, provides a structured approach to conflict resolution. With its high success rate, it is certainly an approach that is worth exploring.

In Chapter 12 our focus is on social pedagogy, a method that blends elements of social work with an educational approach. Juha Hämäläinen highlights what is involved and gives a helpful picture of its benefits and appeal. Traditionally used with young people, it is now increasingly being used across the age spectrum.

Family therapy is a long-standing and well-established social work method. In Chapter 13 Robert Taibbi spells out what is involved by explaining some of the core ideas that inform this approach. Given that so many of the problems social workers are called upon to deal with are located in family settings, this is a method that can offer important insights and practice guidance.

In Chapter 14 Mark Doel sets out a clear rationale for including group work as a method we can draw upon. Bringing people together to support one another and learn together has tremendous potential for bringing about positive changes. A skilled group worker can be effective in shaping group dynamics that are positive and constructive.

Eco-systems theory is our concern in Chapter 15. Aila-Leena Matthies and Kati Närhi help us to look more holistically at the situations we encounter by setting them in their wider context. While social work traditionally focuses on individuals, eco-systems theory can help us broaden our focus without losing sight of the individual.

Chapter 16 also has a broad focus, this time exploring how advocacy, rights work, and campaigning have an important role to play in complementing other approaches. Donna Baines, Emma Tseris and Fran Waugh set out an informative overview of the key ideas involved and lay the foundations for incorporating this aspect of practice into our professional role set.

In the final chapter. Paul Stepney provides an introduction to community social work. Communities can be the source of problems at times, but also a source of solutions. Developing supportive, empowered, and empowering communities is not a simple or straightforward matter, but it is an undertaking that can certainly repay the effort involved.

So, all in all, this book should give a sound foundation of the context in which social work theories and methods are pressed into service (Part I) and an introduction to a wide (but not exhaustive) range of approaches that can be drawn up on as we "theorize" practice – that is, as we draw upon various aspects of our professional knowledge base in an effort to ensure that our practice is *informed* practice.

References

Corcoran, K. and Roberts, A. R. (Eds.) (2015). *Social workers' desk reference* (3rd Edn.). New York: Oxford University Press.

Mönnink, H. de (2017). *The social workers' toolbox*. London: Routledge.

Payne, M. (2014). *Modern social work theory* (4th Edn.). Basingstoke, UK: Palgrave Macmillan.

Thompson, N. (2016). *The professional social worker* (2nd Edn.). London: Palgrave.

Thompson, N. and Thompson, S. (2016). *The social work companion* (2nd Edn.). London: Palgrave.

PART I
SOCIAL WORK THEORY AND METHODS IN CONTEXT
INTRODUCTION

If we are to get the best use out of the theory base available to us and its associated methods and tools, then we need to understand that theory base in context, to see the bigger picture, so that we have a fuller understanding of what we are dealing with. In Part I we explore three aspects of that broader context.

First, in Chapter 1, we look at the relationship between theory and practice and relate this to the idea of "theorizing practice" – that is, the process of beginning with practice and then drawing on our professional knowledge base as required (in contrast to the traditional idea of "applying theory to practice").

In Chapter 2 we explore the role of research in informing our practice. We look at how the idea of evidence-based practice has evolved into research-informed, evidence-enriched practice. The core message is that, while research is not the only thing that should be informing our practice, we would be wise to draw on the best research knowledge available where possible.

In Chapter 3, the final chapter of Part I, we consider the significant role of the policy and organizational context – that is, we explore how (i) social policy; and (ii) the characteristics of the organization we work in will have a significant bearing on our practice and how we relate to the challenges we face. It demonstrates how important it is to have an understanding of these contextual factors.

These three chapters do not provide a comprehensive or exhaustive account of the wider context in which theory and methods are used, but they should provide a useful foundation of understanding so that we are better equipped to make sense of our role in the social work world. This lays the foundations for the accounts, in Part II, of specific theoretical perspectives and associated methods.

1

THEORY AND METHODS IN A PRACTICE CONTEXT
THEORIZING PRACTICE
Neil Thompson

Introduction

This chapter has been written to lay the foundations for the chapters in Part II that focus on a particular theoretical approach and/or method. Its task is to present a clear platform of understanding of: the nature, role and importance of theory; the relationship between theories and methods; the role of critically reflective practice; and the idea of "theorizing practice," as distinct from the traditional (and, as we see it, flawed) notion of "applying theory to practice."

What Do We Mean by Theory?

The word "theory" derives from the Greek word "θεωρία" (theoria) which means contemplation (in the sense of how we look or reflect upon the world). It has come to have two main meanings in modern usage. First, it can be used to refer to a specific theory (for example, Einstein's theory of relativity), that involves one or more propositions that can be empirically tested through experimentation or other forms of research. Second, it can be used in a more general sense to refer to an underlying professional knowledge base (social work theory, nursing theory, counseling theory and so on). It is this latter sense that we tend to adopt when we refer to "theory and practice," and indeed it is in this sense that it is used throughout this book.

In effect, the term "theory" refers to attempts to explain a phenomenon or set of phenomena – it is a basis of understanding. For example, attachment theory seeks to make sense of the significance of parent-child (or significant adult-child) attachment patterns and their implications in terms of both child development and subsequent adult life. It has been developed to help us develop our understanding of important aspects of human experience. That understanding can then inform the practice of various professionals – including social workers – in working with children and young people (and indeed, with adults whose difficulties may stem in part from their childhood attachment experiences).

In this respect, social work is informed by a wide range of theoretical underpinnings. Consider the following.

Society

The fact that the term social worker begins with the word "social" is no coincidence. The very idea of social work is rooted in an understanding of society as something that has its problems as well as its strengths. Where we have large numbers of people living together, sharing physical and emotional space, there will inevitably be difficulties and challenges – and these are often important factors that contribute to the problems that social workers are called upon to address. If we were to simply see people as individuals and have no conception of society as an entity that has a logic of its own ("sui generis," to use Durkheim's technical term – Durkheim, 1982), it would be difficult if not impossible to have any conception of social work. So, whether we are directly aware of them or not, social work is underpinned by a set of theoretical understandings of society that have developed over a long period of time. We therefore need to recognize that *sociology* is an important contributor to our professional knowledge base – to our *theory* base.

Social Policy

Social work is not, of course, just a group of uncoordinated individuals seeking to make a positive difference in their own way. It is underpinned by a set of formal governmental policies (whether nationally or on a more regional or local basis) that are, in turn, underpinned by a legislative base – that is, a body of relevant laws that give social workers certain powers (what we are allowed to do) and certain duties (what we must do). Social policy is, to a large extent, a society's way of addressing the social problems it recognizes (Thompson, 2017a) by setting up various services, projects and schemes. Social work is therefore very much part of the wider field of social policy, as will be clarified in Chapter 3. Consequently, it is important to recognize that theoretical understandings of social problems and potential ways of addressing them are part of the social work knowledge base.

Psychology

What makes individuals tick? What is happening when individuals interact? What difference do groups make to the people within them? These are just some of the questions that psychology seeks to provide answers for. Of course, much of the knowledge and understanding that psychology has produced can be very useful in informing social work practice. How problems develop, how individuals, families, groups and communities respond to those problems and how they respond to social workers and others who are trying to help them with those problems are all topics that psychology can cast some degree of light on.

This does not mean that social workers need to be psychology experts, but we need to have at least some reasonable degree of understanding of relevant psychological issues if we are to be tackling our work on an informed basis. Without the understanding that psychology brings we would be very ill-equipped to engage meaningfully and constructively with large elements of social work practice.

Philosophy

There are (at least) three aspects to this:

1. There are philosophical questions of values, ethics and morality that are never far away in social work. We shall return to the question of values below.
2. At the heart of social work is the "human encounter," the meaningful and constructive interaction of people in all their

humanity – the human-to-human connection, as I have called it before (Thompson, 2015). While technical knowledge from sociology, social policy and psychology can be very helpful, it needs to be set in a context of understanding what it means to be human (see Chapter 9 which focuses on existentialism).

For this reason, spirituality is an aspect of social work that is receiving increasing attention (see, for example, Holloway and Moss, 2010). Although spirituality is firmly wedded to religion in many people's minds, it is important to recognize that spirituality (our sense of who we are and how we fit into the world, our quest for meaning, purpose and direction) is a key issue in its own right for people of all faiths and none. An understanding of existential and spiritual issues is therefore a further important part of our professional knowledge, our theory base.

3. Philosophy is rooted in critical analysis and reflection on our world and our specific circumstances. This is essential for social work practice, as we shall note below when we explore critically reflective practice.

This is not a comprehensive list, but it should be enough to make the point that social work rests on a diverse and significant theory base. We have significant foundations of knowledge that we can draw upon as and when required. However, despite this, it is still sadly the case that some people in the social work world reject the value of theory. "Forget that college nonsense, you're in the real world now;" "I'm not interested in theory, I prefer to stick to practice;" and "It's all just common sense really" are comments that I and various colleagues have heard time and time again. Clearly, people who make such comments have lost sight of just how much knowledge day-to-day practice draws upon. We shall return to this important point below when we discuss "theorizing practice."

What Do We Mean by Methods?

For a long time it has been the norm in some quarters for the terms "theories" and "methods" to be used interchangeably. This is confusing because, although the two are closely linked, they are in fact different.

As we have seen, theory, in the sense we are using it in this book, is an attempt to explain, it is a basis of understanding that can be used to guide and inform practice. The focus is on *understanding*, albeit generally with a view to influencing practice. A method, by contrast, is a form of offshoot from a theory. The understanding on which it is based derives from a theoretical perspective, but it is not intended to offer any understanding in its own right. Rather, the purpose of a method is to facilitate the use of the theoretical knowledge in actual practice. The focus is not on the understanding, but on the *use in practice* of that understanding.

A clear example of this would be crisis intervention (see Chapter 7). There is a long-standing body of theoretical work that has been developed to cast light on people's experiences of crisis – that is, of significant turning points in their life. Crisis intervention is the related method, a framework for making use of the theoretical knowledge in practice situations. Another example would be group work. Group work, as Chapter 14 illustrates, is an approach to working constructively with groups of people who share similar problems or have other significant connections. As such, it is a method, a framework for guiding practice. However, it is rooted in group dynamics theory – that is, in psychological and sociological understandings of how groups work, how they can be developed and how they can go awry.

In a way, a method is a bridge between theory and practice. It is an established procedure (or set of procedures) that can be drawn upon and adapted to suit the particular circumstances. It is not intended that they should be used in a mechanistic, unthinking way (see the discussion of critically reflective practice below). Rather, a method is a structured, but flexible, guide to how particular theoretical ideas can be drawn upon. Another term for method that is sometimes used is that of "practice modality," and that captures well the notion of a framework to guide practice. For example, understanding how family dynamics work and how "family scripts" develop can cast important light on social work with families, and that is a positive thing in its own right. However, family therapy as a method goes beyond this knowledge by giving a set of guidelines for how such insights can be used in practice situations. But, family therapy, as we shall see in Chapter 13, is not a prescriptive, directive

approach to working with families. It is a framework of guidance, like any
other method, that then needs to be adapted to the situation concerned.
In a sense, a method is a form of tool. The hammer does not knock the
nail into the wood. You knock the nail into the wood by using the facil-
ity the hammer offers. The same rationale can be applied to social work
methods as tools.

Generally, there will be a direct relationship between a theoretical
approach and its associated method (as in the case of the three examples
I have given here). However, there will also be aspects of our professional knowledge base that will not necessarily have a directly associated
method ("contextual" knowledge from social policy and sociology, for
example), but will none the less still be valuable knowledge that we need
to bear in mind. Likewise, there will be methods or tools that have their
origins in a wide range of theoretical perspectives, a veritable stew of theoretical ingredients mixed together. My book, *The People Solutions Sourcebook* (Thompson, 2012a), contains 88 practical tools that social workers
and other people professionals can draw upon. Before the book was published, one of the publisher's readers suggested that I should explain the
theoretical background of each of the tools. Clearly, they had not thought
that comment through, as that would have been a major work and would
have at least trebled the length of the book. It would also have missed the
point of the book.

When considering theory and methods, we can usefully draw a parallel with science and technology. Science refers to the development of a
reliable knowledge base, while technology refers to creating mechanisms
and systems for making the best use of the knowledge that science makes
available. In this parallel, theory is the equivalent of science (a source of
understanding) and methods are the equivalent of technology (strategies
for making use of that knowledge in practice).

What this analogy also helps us to appreciate is that methods involve
skills. Using technology requires a set of relevant skills – for example,
IT skills for making best use of computer technology. Likewise, using a
social work method is not simply a matter of following a set procedure.
Instead, it is a matter of developing and using the skills required for that
particular technology/method.

What Do We Mean by Theorizing Practice?

The traditional approach in social work education (and, indeed, other professional disciplines) has been to encourage students to "apply theory to practice." This implies starting with theory (the professional knowledge base) and applying it to practice – that is, exploring how the ideas can be used in practice. However, on closer inspection, we can see that this is the wrong way round. It is far more helpful to begin with a practice situation and then draw on the professional knowledge base as and when required (Thompson, 2017b). This fits with Schön's (1984) notion of the reflective practitioner as a "tailor" of knowledge – as practitioners, we should not expect theory to give us "off-the-peg" solutions to the practice situations we encounter. Rather, they should be using the "cloth" provided by the professional knowledge base to tailor a "garment" (solution or basis of understanding) that fits the specific circumstances.

I have many years' experience of working with students and social workers in an education and training context and a recurring theme from these experiences when discussing the relationship between theory and practice is that people find it very confusing to "apply theory to practice:" Which theory? How does it apply? What does "apply" actually mean in this context? These are just some of the reflections of the confusion and lack of understanding relating to this traditional notion of "applying theory to practice." When, by contrast, I have explained the alternative notion of "theorizing practice," the unanimous response has been one of finding it a much more helpful and meaningful conception of the relationship between theory and practice. "That makes much more sense" has been a very common response.

This is not just playing with words. It actually makes a big difference in terms of how practitioners relate to theory and how effectively they use it in practice. Consider this example of how theorizing practice works:

> Andrea is allocated the case of Nia, a 7-year-old girl whose behavior is causing concern. There is no previous information on file about the girl or her family. So, Andrea is starting from scratch, or is she? Her understanding of human growth and development will give her a knowledge base in terms of what to expect when it comes to a 7-year-old's behavior.

But what Andrea actually finds is that Nia's level of development is more like that of a 3-year-old. She therefore recognizes that she is dealing with a case of developmental delay. She has "theorized" this, based on her knowledge of human psychology in general and child development in particular.

She subsequently "theorizes" that this developmental delay may be due to abuse, as her professional knowledge base tells her that abuse is a common cause of developmental delay. This leads her to consider indicators of abuse. She therefore draws on her knowledge of abuse and its indicators and "theorizes" that Nia does indeed seem to have been abused. She then draws on her knowledge of child protection procedures and reports the matter to the appropriate safeguarding body for her area. Once again she has drawn on her professional knowledge base to guide her practice, and has done so in a way that fits the particular situation she is involved in – she has "tailored" the knowledge to create a bespoke response to the situation.

It subsequently emerges that Nia has in fact been abused, and this makes Andrea wonder whether Nia has been traumatized by the abuse (which would largely explain the behavioral difficulties that led to the referral in the first place). She therefore draws on her knowledge of childhood trauma (theorizing once again) and comes to the conclusion that this is highly likely. So, once again, her practice is guided by her processes of theorizing practice.

This example illustrates the basic idea of theorizing practice by drawing on the underlying knowledge base as appropriate, as demanded by the circumstances of the case. The example is not exhaustive, of course. What if Nia were black? There would presumably have been consideration of needs associated with her ethnicity and the potential or actual role of racism in the situation. Again, it comes down to using knowledge in action, and that is precisely what is meant by theorizing practice (and precisely why the chapters in Part II highlight the key ideas of their respective approach and offer some guidance on how these can be used in practice).

In a very real sense, all actions are based on a degree of understanding, however basic or flawed. However, a key question would be: How adequate is that understanding? For example, someone who has had no training or experience in working with children could have approached Nia's case as a matter of her misbehaving and focused therefore on a punishment regime to keep her in line. This could potentially have not only failed to recognize the abuse, but actually exacerbated it, especially if it were physical abuse.

In an earlier work (Thompson, 2000) I introduced the concept of "the fallacy of theoryless practice," by which I meant the misguided view that we can simply "get on with practice" without using any theoretical understanding. As I have already indicated, all action is based on a degree of understanding, on our "picture" of the situation, however distorted, misleading or problematic that understanding might be. Of course, our professional knowledge base is not infallible. It is developing all the time, and previously cherished ideas can come to be abandoned (as in the case of the long-standing fallacy that people grieve in stages – Thompson, 2012b). However, by drawing on our professional knowledge base as it stands, we are making use of the best available evidence and therefore minimizing the chances of a misreading of the situation based on flawed understanding.

One of the dangers of the fallacy of theoryless practice is that it can mean that practitioners are basing their understanding (and therefore their actions) on stereotypes and discriminatory assumptions that can produce oppressive and counterproductive outcomes. Social work is premised on a commitment to social justice, and so a significant part of our professional knowledge base revolves around an understanding of how subtle processes of discrimination can lead to oppression (Thompson, 2016). For example, a practitioner who relies on "common sense" understandings of gender roles and expectations may be unwittingly reinforcing oppressive gender stereotypes.

It is therefore essential that practitioners are aware that: (i) it is a fallacy that we can "just get on with the job" without having a foundation of understanding; and (ii) if that understanding is based on untested assumptions, rather than the best knowledge our professional theory base can currently offer, there is considerable potential for that practice to be harmful. Theorizing practice therefore involves embracing and valuing our professional knowledge base and drawing on it in critically reflective ways, a point to which we shall return later.

Theory, Methods and Values

Whatever theoretical perspective(s) we adopt, whatever methods or tools we utilize, our practice needs to be rooted in social work values. No knowledge base is value free, nor is any form of practice (Moss, 2007). It is therefore important that we are aware of the values that influence our thoughts and actions and ensure that we are acting with integrity (that is, in ways that are consistent with those values).

It can be helpful to understand two categories of social work values. There are the traditional values, such as confidentiality, respect for persons and self-determination that have a long history in social work internationally. There are also more recent developments in social work values that I have referred to as "emancipatory" values (Thompson, 2015). By this I mean a commitment to challenging discrimination and oppression and promoting equality.

For many years social work's focus was on the individual and/or family and relatively little attention was paid to wider social factors. A key value was that of respecting the uniqueness of the individual. However, over time the individualistic psychological foundations of social work have been extended by the adoption of a complementary sociological perspective. We are all unique individuals and need to be respected as such. However, we are all unique individuals in a social context. And, to do justice to the complexity of human experience, we need to take account of both the uniqueness and the social context, with its influences and constraints.

Developing partly from the seeds of community work and partly from the influence of wider political movements, such as feminism, civil rights and the social model of disability, contemporary social work draws heavily on sociological as well as psychological insights. This has been reflected in the development of the value base, which now recognizes the promotion of equality and the challenging of oppression as core value considerations.

These considerations take the form of being aware of how unfair and oppressive processes of discrimination, marginalization and exclusion operate in society and being committed to challenging these wherever and however possible (Thompson, 2016). The clientele of social work is predominantly drawn from the most socially disadvantaged and vulnerable sectors of our communities, and so it would be naïve (and potentially dangerous) to disregard the impact and significance of discrimination and oppression. In some cases, the problems that bring people to the attention of a social worker may be rooted in oppression; in other cases, there may be other causes or factors, but these may be exacerbated by oppression; and in some cases it may even be the intervention of the social worker that is oppressive in its consequences (for example, in relation to gender stereotypes, as mentioned above; colluding with racism, unwittingly or otherwise; making disempowering ageist assumptions based on "common sense" conceptions of old age; and so on).

At the heart of emancipatory values is a commitment to social justice, recognizing the need to have a foundation of fairness, equality and empowerment underpinning our actions (and the theories and methods that undergird those actions). Equality, it should be noted, does not mean treating everybody the same (as that simply reinforces existing inequalities); it means treating everyone with equal fairness, hence the link with social justice.

It is important to recognize that emancipatory values are intended to complement traditional values, rather than replace them (just as sociological insights are intended to complement psychological ones, not to displace them).

One of the reasons values are so important in social work is that, as professionals, we are: (i) exercising power (even though bureaucratic and other restrictions may often make us feel less than powerful); and (ii) often working with people who are relatively powerless and vulnerable. We are therefore duty bound as professionals to exercise that power ethically and responsibly and make sure that the consequences of our actions contribute to clients having more control over their lives and circumstances (empowerment), rather than less (oppression).

This is why we need to have a good understanding of issues relating to discrimination and oppression, as a lack of awareness of such matters is likely to lead to, at best, our condoning discrimination and, at worst, reinforcing it. Consider, for example, someone who unthinkingly adopts a medical model of disability and fails to recognize the discriminatory implications of doing so (Oliver, 2009). They may feel that they are being kind and helpful when in reality they are contributing to marginalization and disempowerment.

One way of enhancing our understanding of discrimination and oppression is to draw on the PCS analysis framework I have developed in my earlier work (Thompson, 2016; 2018). It is called PCS analysis because it involves appreciating that discrimination operates at three connected levels, personal, cultural and structural:

- The **P** level is the personal level of beliefs, attitudes and, potentially at least, prejudices.
- The **C** level is the cultural level. This relates to the way in which stereotypes and other discriminatory assumptions are passed from generation to generation and come to influence individuals without their realizing it. The **P** level is embedded within the **C** level in the sense that our personal attitudes and beliefs are strongly influenced by the culture(s) in which we have grown up and in which we are now operating.
- The **S** level relates to the structure of society and the fact that it is not a level playing field. Social inequalities, based on social divisions, such as class, race/ethnicity, gender, disability, age, language groups, sexuality, religion and so on, are "sewn in" to the structure of society. Just as the **P** level is embedded in the **C** level, in turn the **C** level is embedded in the **S** level, in the sense that the ideas and beliefs that are a key part of the cultural level both reflect and reinforce structural relations of inequality and power.

PCS analysis can be used as an analytical framework for making sense of discrimination. It can be used, for example, to make sure that we are not adopting too narrow or superficial a view of discrimination. It helps us to appreciate the different dimensions of discrimination and establishes the need to look at the issues involved holistically. This is in contrast to a common approach that focuses narrowly on personal prejudice (the **P** level), without considering the powerful role of wider cultural influences and the even wider structural factors that play such an important part.

It is therefore worth re-emphasizing my earlier point that our understanding and use of theory and methods need to be underpinned by an appreciation of, and commitment to, a set of core values. This value base needs to encompass both traditional, person-centered values and the sociologically informed emancipatory values if we are to ensure that we are practicing ethically and safely.

Critically Reflective Practice

The work of Schön (1984) has been recognized as a major contribution to our understanding of how knowledge is used in practice. He was critical of the notion of "technical rationality," with its assumption that professional practice can be reduced to following a set of instructions or technical procedures. Although he did not invent the concept of "reflective practice," he played a major role in developing it and spreading its influence. The reflective practitioner, according to Schön, is someone who develops an understanding of the field they are working in and reflects on it accordingly. This reflection can be at the moment of practice (reflection-in-action) or thereafter to review what happened (reflection-on-action).

From this has developed the idea of reflective practice as intelligent, thoughtful practice rooted in an understanding of our professional knowledge base, that knowledge base comprising elements of formal theory; research; "practice wisdom" developed over time; plus our own personal, experience-based understandings of the situations we encounter. This is as opposed to practice based on habit, uninformed guesswork, copying others, mindlessly following procedures and/or reacting to anxiety (our own or other people's).

This conception makes it a good foundation for theorizing practice. We begin with practice and then draw – reflectively – on our professional knowledge base in order to develop a clear and helpful picture of the challenges we face and potential strategies for rising to them. It is this that makes it intelligent, informed practice, and therefore suitable as a basis for professionalism, rather than simply a bureaucratic approach that relies on technical rationality and the mechanistic following of procedures or application of tools and methods.

This brings us back to the questions of skills. Having the knowledge base is an essential prerequisite, but we then need the skills of being able to use that knowledge in practice, to "operationalize" it, to use the technical term. These skills include (but are not limited to):

- *Creativity skills.* As I have explained many times in my teaching and training work, social work is not a matter of "painting by numbers." As England (1986) acknowledged long ago, social work involves an element of artistry; it is a craft that requires us – if we are to achieve optimal levels of practice – to use and develop our creativity skills.
- *Analytical skills.* Social work involves managing complexity, having to make sense of complex, multi-dimensional situations, and so well-developed analytical skills are a distinct advantage. To be able to theorize practice effectively we need at least basic analytical skills, but the more well developed those skills are, the more effective we can be.
- *Self-management skills.* If we are chaotic and disorganized, if we are unfocused and easily "lose the plot" in terms of what we are trying to achieve, we will struggle to be effective in general, but particularly when it comes to reflective practice in the form of theorizing that practice. No one is perfect in terms of self-management skills; we all get things wrong from time to time. However, we need at least a basic level of competence in terms of being able to manage ourselves, our pressures, tasks, roles and responsibilities.
- *Interpersonal skills.* An extensive knowledge base plus excellence in the skills mentioned above will be of very little value if we do not have the interpersonal skills to relate effectively to people. Everyday interpersonal skills are a good start, of course, but as professionals we need to take our skills to a much higher level. Consider, for example, nonverbal communication skills. Unless we have a visual impairment or a condition like autism, we learn the basics of nonverbal communication (recognizing "signals" and transmitting such signals effectively) from a relatively early age. However, these and other interpersonal skills need to be taken to a more advanced level if we are to achieve the best results in our work.

Reflective practice can therefore be seen to be a highly skilled undertaking. Anyone with fairly basic skills can follow procedures mechanistically, fill in forms and just "get on with the job." However, good professional practice needs to be reflective practice. It needs to operate on a firm basis of knowledge, skills and values.

Although Schön's work has proven to be both influential and helpful, it also has limitations. It is therefore important to go beyond Schön, in the sense of seeing his work as foundational, while also recognizing the need to build on those foundations. One aspect of this is particularly important, namely developing a more holistic version of reflective practice that is consistent with: (i) a sociological outlook (Schön's work remains at the level of the individual and does not adequately address wider social issues, such as power relations, gender dynamics and so on); and (ii) social work values, especially the emancipatory values associated with tackling discrimination and oppression. In other words, Schön's work offers us a good start, but it does not take us far enough.

In particular, it is important to recognize the crucial role of *critically* reflective practice. A critical approach is one that questions the status quo and does not take existing social arrangements for granted. It is one that is sensitive to power relations and how these can be associated with discriminatory processes that result in oppression (see the discussion of PCS analysis above). In this regard, a critical approach to reflective practice is one that is premised on a commitment to social justice and which therefore involves exploring the subtle issues involved – something that Schön's work did not do.

Thompson and Thompson (2018), in their detailed examination of critically reflective practice, highlight the importance of critical breadth and critical depth. Critical breadth refers to the need to look more holistically at the situation, to take account of the sociological issues as well as the psychological ones, and therefore to be tuned in to issues of social inequality, disempowerment and marginalization.

Critical depth refers to the ability to look beneath the surface, to not take situations at face value. This relates to the traditional social work idea of addressing the underlying problem(s), rather than focusing superficially on the presenting problem(s). It involves being prepared to question and explore and thereby open the door to a critical breadth approach.

The two dimensions, critical breadth and critical depth are therefore closely interlinked.

Critically reflective practice is therefore not a rejection of the now traditional role of reflective practice in Schön's sense. Rather, it is an extension and development of it. It is geared towards making practice not only intelligent, thoughtful and underpinned by professional knowledge, skills and values, but also closely attuned to the need to promote social justice by adopting a more questioning and holistic approach – that is, a critical, progressive one.

Conclusion

This chapter has covered a lot of ground in a relatively short time. It should therefore be helpful for me to sum up the key points I have wanted to convey. It is particularly important that these points should "hit home," not only because of their general relevance to social work, but also because they "set the scene" for the exploration of specific theories and methods in the chapters that form Part II.

1. *Theory seeks to explain.* It provides a platform of understanding that is more reliable than our everyday understanding of people and their problems offers. People who say they have no interest in theory are therefore saying that they are happy to practice in a largely uninformed, uncritical way.

2. *Methods are bridges between theory and practice.* A method is not a set of steps to be followed mechanistically or unthinkingly, but, within a context of reflective practice, they can be used as helpful frameworks to guide practice. They are related to one or more theoretical perspectives, but can be adapted to suit the specific circumstances.

3. *Theorizing practice makes more sense than applying theory to practice.* The traditional idea of applying theory to practice produces confusion by creating the impression that we should begin with theory and somehow fit it into practice. Theorizing practice, by contrast, advocates beginning with practice and then drawing on our professional theory base as appropriate, depending on the circumstances, parallel with Schön's analogy of the reflective

practitioner as a tailor of the knowledge base to produce a bespoke understanding as a basis for practice.

4. *Theories and methods need to be underpinned by values.* As social workers we occupy positions of power, influence and authority and we work mainly with disadvantaged, vulnerable groups of people. We are therefore duty bound to act ethically and that includes working within our professional values, both the traditional ones and the emancipatory ones geared towards promoting social justice.

5. *Our practice needs to be critically reflective.* We begin with Schön's basic framework that leads us to an understanding of reflective practice as intelligent, thoughtful and informed practice and add to that our understanding of the need for a *critical* perspective – that is, one that focuses on both critical breadth and critical depth.

These points, important though they are, do not tell the whole story, of course, but they should be enough to provide a sound foundation on which to build over time.

References

Durkheim, E. (1982). *The rules of sociological method.* New York: The Free Press.
England, H. (1986). *Social work as art: Making sense for practice.* New York: HarperCollins.
Holloway, M. and Moss, B. (2010). *Spirituality and social work.* Basingstoke, UK: Palgrave Macmillan.
Moss, B. (2007). *Values.* Lyme Regis, UK: Russell House Publishing.
Oliver, M. (2009). *Understanding disability: From theory to practice* (2nd Edn.). Basingstoke, UK: Palgrave Macmillan.
Schön, D. (1984). *The reflective practitioner.* New York: Basic Books.
Thompson, N. (2000). *Theory and practice in the human services* (2nd Edn.). Buckingham, UK: Open University Press.
Thompson, N. (2012a). *The people solutions sourcebook* (2nd Edn.). Basingstoke, UK: Palgrave Macmillan.
Thompson, N. (2012b). *Grief and its challenges.* Basingstoke, UK: Palgrave Macmillan.
Thompson, N. (2015). *Understanding social work: Preparing for practice* (4th Edn.). London: Palgrave.
Thompson, N. (2016). *Anti-discriminatory practice* (6th Edn.). London: Palgrave.
Thompson, N. (2017a). *Social problems and social justice.* London: Palgrave.
Thompson, N. (2017b). *Theorizing practice* (2nd Edn.). London: Palgrave.
Thompson, N. (2018). *Promoting equality: Working with diversity and difference* (4th Edn.). London: Palgrave.
Thompson, S. and Thompson, N. (2018). *The critically reflective practitioner* (2nd Edn.). London: Palgrave.

2

THEORY AND METHODS IN AN INTELLECTUAL CONTEXT

USING RESEARCH

Paul Stepney and Neil Thompson

Introduction

We have already noted in Chapter 1 the importance of drawing on theory, of making use of the professional knowledge base. Part of that knowledge base comes from research that has been carried out over the years, formal research undertaken in universities and research centers, that can help to cast further light on various aspects of the social work world. In this chapter, we discuss the importance of making use of that research base, explore the limitations of relying on research, and examine what is involved in developing research-informed, evidence-enriched practice. A key question will be: How can research help us know whether what we are doing is effective and therefore worth doing?

Social work knowledge, including the theory and methods underpinning practice, is more contested than in many other human service professions, such as medicine, nursing and teaching. This uncertainty is reflected in social work's professional culture and collective representation of itself, which molds its status and standing in the world. This, in turn, influences what it is like to be a social worker, how others view the profession and the work we do.

Contemporary social work is confronted with a fundamental dilemma, that remains as relevant today as when it was first posed by Geoffrey

Pearson more than 40 years ago, namely: "whether it is an agency which enlarges human freedom or restricts it, and whether it is relevant to the problems it confronts or irrelevant" (Pearson, 1975, p. 126). One of the difficulties in resolving such important issues is deciding whether social work's theory and methods have a sound evidential base, supported by good research findings, or amount to little more than "practice wisdom" and common sense dressed up. In this chapter, we show how research can provide convincing and helpful ways of responding to such difficult questions and, in the process, demonstrate the value of promoting research-informed and evidence-enriched practice.

In whatever country or international setting one looks, North America, Australasia, Europe and the Far East, social work is under constant pressure to be more cost effective, protect vulnerable people, defend human rights and find solutions to many pressing social problems. Social workers are aware of this context and the expectations placed upon them, but find it difficult to articulate exactly how social work can reconcile its commitment to its clients alongside its obligations to society. In so doing, it may miss the point of its own professional vision by reducing the problems of its clients, who are among the most marginalized, disaffected and oppressed in society, to those that it can tackle – protection, rather than prevention; risk management, rather than empowerment.

As with all professional groups, social work's professional culture attempts to make the world less troublesome. It claims to see the world as it is and "start where the client is at," but, in an age of high workloads and restricted resources, this can quickly be reduced to seeing the world as it wants it to be. Such problems reveal the awkward nature of the terrain that social work inhabits and, significantly, they are at the heart of the debate about the relationship between research and practice. It follows, therefore, that we need to explore the "research question" in a little more depth.

What is Research? Different Theories of Knowledge and Competing Views of Reality

At its simplest, research is concerned with: "seeking knowledge for a purpose" (D'Cruz and Jones, 2004, p. 5). It does this by searching for answers to specific questions and more generally offering new insights and explanations about contemporary problems. What makes research distinct from, say, interviewing a client, is that it is done in a: "systematic, disciplined and rigorous way ... making use of appropriate research methods and designs" (Becker and Bryman, 2004, p. 14). The choice of research methods will be influenced by what counts as knowledge (from the Greek term, "epistemology") and embrace different views of reality (what researchers call "ontology"). It is important for us to try and understand these concepts, even if they appear rather abstract and highbrow, as they also underpin the various social work theories and methods presented in Part II. If we can make progress with this, then we will be in a much better position to see how research might inform and, in turn, enrich social work practice.

The early approaches to research came from the natural sciences and became known as "positivism" (basically, scientific experiments were used to try and find general laws based upon "social facts" or "natural truths" that could explain an "objective reality"). However, Thomas Kuhn and Karl Popper challenged this view that knowledge could be based on "facts" as absolute truths. Scientific knowledge, they said, could not achieve absolute certainty or "truth," because scientific methods and observation are theory driven, value laden and are influenced by culture and social context (Kuhn, 1970; Popper, 1959). Whether research is conducted in the laboratory or out in the field, the assumptions of the researcher about what topic or problem to research, how to carry it out, who to collaborate with and who is most likely to benefit from the research are all value laden issues that cannot be stripped of their social and cultural significance.

This threw the scientific community into sharp division, especially in the emerging social sciences, between the *positivists* on the one hand, and their critics on the other, who became broadly known as *interpretivists*. The *interpretivists* argued that all knowledge is probabilistic and provisional – what is known about the world today will probably have to be modified and refined tomorrow. Our understanding of the world and our theories of knowledge or *epistemology* are mediated through a social lens. And this lens is infused with theory, values and ideology, and, what is more, we cannot remove the lens like a pair of spectacles. The implication of this is that, if we accept that certain truth is not possible, then we have to acknowledge that our understanding is mediated through different theories and paradigms (clusters of theories).

In the social sciences, the interpretivist approach has flourished and this has had a number of important *ontological* consequences. For example, the sociologists Berger and Luckmann (1971) suggested that there is no one objective reality, but a number of competing realities based on people's subjective knowledge and experience (see also Gergen, 2009). Furthermore, such multiple realities have to be actively constructed. For example, the subjective experience of a family struggling to survive on welfare benefits or a black single mother living in a run-down inner city neighborhood will be very different from wealthier citizens in middle-class areas or the super rich in their gated enclosures. How people internalize and understand their experiences and life chances is not a passive, one-off, taken-for-granted activity, but an active process of making sense of the world around them and their place in it. Hence, in the social sciences the social construction of reality became an important idea in the interpretivist perspective.

This approach became influential within social work because it stressed the uniqueness of human understanding and experience, something that was consistent with social work values. Consequently, interpretation became the order of the day, rather than "positivist" facts. The emphasis shifted to what Weber (1864–1920) called "Verstehen," which means understanding. This involved recognizing that, as far as social life is concerned, aiming for objective certainty is too ambitious. Even the natural sciences are now less committed to the pursuit of "scientific objectivity," with quantum mechanics recognizing that probability, rather than certainty, is the best that can be hoped for (Kumar, 2009).

In terms of ontology, interpretivist positions, of which there are many, are seen as relativist in contrast with the objectivist position of positivism. Relativism is a philosophical term premised on the idea that, if people's subjective experience creates a number of different realities, rather than one "objective truth," then any view can be perceived to be just as valid as any other, and "science" therefore ceases to have any advantage over other, less rigorous approaches. However, the pragmatist philosopher, Richard Rorty, argues that all views have to be in relation to a particular perspective; that is inescapable (Rorty, 1991). However, the rigorous and systematic nature of interpretivist social science means that it offers advantages over everyday, non-scientific views. So, while complete objectivity is not possible, scientific rigor none the less offers a more fruitful understanding – it takes us back to Weber's notion of "Verstehen."

Finally, just to muddy the water a little more, if we move back towards the positivist end of the spectrum we find another approach called realism. This is set out in Figure 2.1.

Realism is seen as something of a middle way, combining elements of the other two positions. For example, it adopts the positivist view that there is one objective reality (rather than multiple versions) and that this reality is independent of our understanding and influence on it (Sayer, 2000). Realist research also believes in the use of scientific methods of inquiry similar to the natural sciences. However, unlike positivism, it takes an interpretivist view of people's experience, seeing these as contested and complex. What this means is that when it comes to interpreting people's experience realism can take up a more critical position and situate knowledge, based upon both subjective experience and more objective evidence, within its appropriate social context. This brings into play the existing social and economic structures, divisions and institutions within the society. Hence, critical realism: "seeks to be sensitive to the multiple realities of subjective experience, but views these within the context of dominant social structures" (Stepney, 2009, p. 18). For a

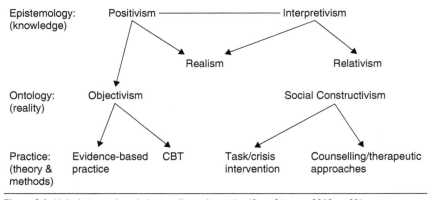

Figure 2.1 Links between knowledge, reality and practice (from Stepney, 2012, p. 23).

fuller and more elaborate account of the influence of realism in the social sciences, see Sayer (2000).

This all means that what counts as knowledge and our views of reality (to use the language of the researcher, our epistemological and ontological position) will influence our choice of theory and methods. Furthermore, it will impinge on how we see the relationship between research and practice, and how we try to develop research-informed and evidence-enriched practice. However, before proceeding, we need to be entirely clear about what is meant by research-informed and evidence-enriched practice, and there are also some underlying lessons that we should pause to explore.

Research-Informed and Evidence-Enriched Practice

The term, "research-informed and evidence-enriched practice" has emerged in recent years, as a result of various "push and pull" factors. The push signaled an attempt by both researchers and practitioners to move away from the limitations of medicalized versions of evidence-based practice (more on this later). The pull was an attempt to encapsulate a number of positive developments that were identified in the Joseph Rowntree Foundation (2015) report, *Developing Evidence-Enriched Practice in Health and Social Care with Older People*, including:

- A focus on "things that matter" to clients and caregivers;
- The value of drawing upon a range of evidence, not just research findings, but also practitioner knowledge, agency knowledge and the voice of clients and caregivers;
- A desire to adopt a strengths-based approach that is constructively critical;
- Ensure evidence is presented in an engaging and accessible format;
- Securing support from senior managers;
- Facilitating the active use of evidence for learning and service development;
- Recognizing organizational realities and overcoming obstacles; and
- Acknowledge the ongoing need for experimentation and learning, including learning from mistakes (adapted from Joseph Rowntree Foundation, 2015, pp. 6–10).

Practice Focus 2.1

At the end of the children and families team meeting, once all new referrals had finally been allocated, there was a general open discussion about common issues and problems. Hilary, one of the more experienced social workers, commented on the gradual increase in the number of child neglect referrals coming to the team. Others agreed and there was a short discussion about possible causes. Lisa, a new member of the team, said: "Yes, and because these cases are often seen as low risk, we don't have much opportunity to do anything about it, which is a great pity."

At this point, Sue, the team manager, said: "Look, this is clearly an important issue and I wonder if other teams have noticed this and if this is a national trend? Before deciding the best thing to do, we need some research evidence on this. And while we're doing this, it might be a good idea to look at what the research evidence says about the best way of tackling this problem."

This really enthused the team and led to a number of staff agreeing that it was a good idea to look at what they could learn from research.

This project gathered evidence from five sites in Wales and one in Scotland and focused on the health and social care needs of older people, caregivers, local practitioners and managers, as well as the views of researchers. One of its key findings was that using a wide range of contextual evidence wisely brought many benefits, greater well-being to clients and caregivers, and was a sound basis for service development. Although the focus was on older people, the findings are clearly applicable to other client groups, as Practice Focus 2.1 illustrates.

Five Mutual Lessons to Guide the Development of Research-Informed and Evidence-Enriched Practice

In a highly original contribution to the debate, Martyn Jones (2012) asks two fundamental questions: What can research learn from social work practice? and, vice versa: What can social work learn from research? He identifies five important lessons for both, and these are worth briefly summarizing. Let us start first with the lessons for research.

What Can Research Learn from Social Work?

The first lesson is to start where the social worker is at, and acknowledge the various contexts and pressures that impinge upon practice: policy, legal powers and duties, agency requirements, professional ethics and so on. The second lesson is to recognize that research is only one influence on practice among many, and hitherto it has not really been a major or significant one. The third lesson concerns understanding the centrality of values, in particular social work's commitment to anti-discriminatory practice, promoting human rights and working for social justice. The fourth lesson is about recognizing the power that is vested in professional social workers and the expectation that they will use it carefully and wisely. Researchers hold similar power and authority, and so this is something that applies equally to them. The fifth lesson for research is to recognize the intrinsic demands and rewards of the job. Jones neatly sums it up when he says that: "social work is controversial, under-resourced, overstretched, emotionally and intellectually exhausting but immensely fulfilling, inspiring and passionate" (Jones, 2012, p. 274). If these are the lessons for research, let us turn this around and look at the lessons for social work.

What Can Social Work Learn from Research?

The first lesson is to recognize the diversity and different traditions within research and the need to create some time and space to do this – it will be well worth the effort. Lesson two is about seeing the similarity in the way researchers go about their work: engaging with people, constructing good research questions, processing information and analyzing it – all in the pursuit of knowledge. So, in this way research can assist the practitioner to develop the core skills involved in doing the job and doing it well. The third lesson is to recognize that research typically gets involved in the same messy issues and dilemmas that the practitioner grapples with, and, in so doing, "get its hands dirty" (Jones, 2012, p. 275). The fourth lesson is that research can assist the practitioner by using its status and position to open doors and increase access to information and people of influence. The fifth lesson is that research can support social work to achieve its wider social mission by working in partnership "for the greater good" (Jones, 2012, p. 275).

These lessons are helpful and will need to be borne in mind if we are going to develop a culture of partnership and collaboration between research and social work (see Jones, 2012, pp. 273–6). Furthermore, they create a sound foundation and enabling conditions conducive to the development of research-informed and evidence-enriched practice. Although there are many different approaches to research methods in social work, an overview of these is beyond the scope of this chapter (for two good introductory texts, see Bernard, 2013; Rubin and Babbie, 2015). However, we do need to look more closely at evidence-enriched practice and the research tradition that has developed and underpins it. How did this come about and what exactly does this involve?

What is Evidence-Enriched Practice?

In a highly influential contribution, Richard Hugman (2005) surveys the contemporary international social work landscape and identifies two alternative responses to the dilemmas we posed in the introduction. Here Pearson (1975) asked: "whether social work represents a personal counselling service ... or mopping up operation for society's dregs" (p. 130). Hugman notes, on the one hand, the growth and popularity of postmodernist ideas, and depicts these as a "search for uncertainty." On the other hand is the rise of evidence-based practice (EBP), which can be portrayed as a "search for certainty" in increasingly troubled times and an "age of uncertainty." In the US, UK, Australia, Canada and in many European countries, EBP has become increasingly influential and seen as complementary to the modernization of social services and the management of risk (see Chapter 3 in this volume). So, what is EBP and how is this different from evidence-enriched practice?

Good practice in all the human services, including social work, comes from an objective and systematic assessment of the available evidence and this, it is argued, will lead to practitioners taking the most appropriate course of action (Newman et al., 2005). Although the complexity of decision making and the nature of external influences are not always fully acknowledged, EBP is the approach where: "there is the most clear and robust evidence of effectiveness" (Hugman, 2005, p. 615).

The concept of EBP derived from the natural sciences, particularly medicine, through the Cochrane Collaboration. Evidence-based medicine is informed by a neo-positivist approach to knowledge based upon scientific measurement and observation. In this medicalized version of EBP the most favored research methodologies are random controlled trials (RCTs) where one group receives the treatment and various outcomes are compared with those from a statistically similar control group. RCTs and systematic reviews published in international journals have become the gold standard in research (Sheldon, 2011).

In social work a pluralist version of EBP has developed (Trinder, 2000), which adopts a more diverse range of methodologies. This has led in social work to the favoring of practice theories and methods that have proved to be effective in the short term (Webb, 2006), such as cognitive-behavioral therapy (see Chapter 5 in this volume) and task-centered practice (see Chapter 6). One of the criticisms of EBP, according to Karen Healy, is that it reinforces a "top down" model, where the practitioner becomes: "the user of knowledge, not the maker of it" (2005, p. 99).

While there is almost universal agreement that practice should become more evidence based and research informed (Healy, 2005), the question of what constitutes good evidence and the most appropriate research methodology remains contested. This has provoked arguments between "champions and critics," and "one of the problems with EBP is that its rational scientific worldview constrains the answers it can supply" (Trinder, 2000, p. 236). One of the crucial lessons this debate has exposed is the realization that all evidence requires careful interpretation (Healy, 2005).

EBP has been further criticized for promoting a: "hidden managerialist agenda" (Pease, 2007, p. 10), as part of the modernizing search for greater efficiency savings. While practitioners accept the need for the efficient use of public resources and good accountability, a preoccupation with the gathering and processing of evidence, if taken to its ultimate conclusion, could lead to the "McDonaldisation of social work" (Harris, 2003).

In such a climate, the moral-political dilemmas of everyday practice can easily become submerged in the technical-rational task of processing evidence. It follows that EBP may offer practitioners false certainties by encouraging an instrumental, depoliticized and competence-based approach that supports managerial priorities (Houston, 2001).

An alternative to EBP is practice-based research (PBR), which has developed in the US (see Dodd and Epstein, 2012). PBR rejects the use of RCTs and employs qualitative methods, such as interviewing, observation and group discussion. PBR is closer to what we have called research-informed and evidence-enriched practice. The social worker is likely to find a more eclectic and epistemologically pluralist approach more flexible and useful, as it can be applied to a broader range of practice scenarios in conditions of uncertainty.

Why is Evidence-Enriched Practice Important?

Research has the capacity to contribute to a process of critical enquiry and emancipation, rather than be used as a Trojan horse for greater cost control and surveillance. This in turn enables us to be true to social work values against a backdrop of managerialism.

Research has the potential to be used as a: "basis for critical review and reflection, including comparison of different ways of providing similar services, an analysis of factors which influence quality and a pointer to unintended or unexpected outcomes" (Cheetham, 1998, p. 26). One way to develop the emancipatory potential of research is to formulate an integrated model of practice evaluation, combining the three perspectives of accountability, critical knowledge production and development. This would achieve a balance between criticality and effectiveness (Stepney and Rostila, 2011).

If social workers are going to work with difference, complexity and ambiguity, as well as provide high-quality services, then the capacity for critical enquiry and reflection should be enhanced (Payne, 2014). Critical enquiry requires practitioners to become more research minded and policy orientated, and be able to integrate these elements into their practice. Developing critically reflective methods of practice (see Schön, 1984), as set out in Part II, is necessary if social work is to combine effectiveness with a commitment to social justice (Stepney, 2006; Thompson and Thompson, 2018).

What are its Limitations?

It should be recognized that the relationship between research and practice can be problematic and create tensions for practitioners. This is illustrated from the field of child protection and safeguarding (Packman and Hall, 1998; Rutter, 2006; Featherstone et al., 2014). Agency policies in this field have become increasingly defensive, prescriptive and procedurally driven, thereby restricting professional initiatives and judgement (Parton, 2011). One of the reasons for this is that, in the UK, exercising professional judgment, informed by research evidence from serious case reviews (DCSF, 2008), to achieve a good balance between protection and prevention went horribly wrong in the Baby Peter case. This had worrying echoes of lessons not learned from the Victoria Climbié case seven years earlier.

The Baby Peter Case

Peter Connelly (known as Baby Peter) was a 17-month-old baby from London who died in 2007. He was the victim of almost unimaginable abuse, resulting in more than 50 injuries over an eight-month period. During this time, Peter was seen a number of times by social workers and various health professionals, including a pediatrician and nursing staff. This was one of the UK's most serious cases of child abuse that caused shock and outrage among both the public and politicians. This was partly due to the horrific nature of Peter's injuries, and partly because he lived under the jurisdiction of the same Children's Services in London that had seriously failed seven years earlier in the case of Victoria Climbié. The resulting public inquiry had led to child protection measures being implemented that were supposed to prevent such cases happening again (see Laming, 2003).

In the post-Baby Peter era, protection and risk management have become the order of the day, rather than family support, even though the research evidence to support this remains contested (Frost and Parton, 2009) – see also Chapters 3 and 17 in this volume. One of the general problems that the Baby Peter case highlighted was the need for practitioners to absorb the key findings from research carried out on an analysis of data from serious case reviews, namely: "that over half the children who suffered serious injuries had been living in families where domestic violence, parental mental ill health and substance misuse co-existed" (DCSF, 2008, p. 7). Clearly, alarm bells should ring where these three problems are found to co-exist.

A number of further limitations can be identified, along with the problem of operating in conditions of uncertainty:

1. Beth Humphries (2000) argues that research should be empowering and treat people as subjects, listening to the voice of the client, rather than as objects listening to the "science" (see also Thompson and Thompson, 2016).
2. There is a danger that practitioners may focus on the generalities supported by research, rather than analyze the specifics in each unique case scenario.
3. It is easy to slip into a medicalized model of practice where research has a positivist basis.
4. There are many aspects of social work that have yet to be researched.
5. Research is often biased – for example, carried out by men without considering gender dynamics.
6. Research findings are sometimes contradictory, so it is important to look for the "best available evidence" (as suggested by Sheldon, 2011), but busy practitioners may not do that, and may use research selectively and therefore misleadingly.

Responding to Uncertainty

Another limitation in promoting evidence-enriched practice is the degree of uncertainty and unpredictability that is a central characteristic of social work. Thompson (2017) and in Chapter 9 in this volume, sets out the key ideas of existentialism in relation to dealing with uncertainty. One of the implications of this is that we should always be prepared for the unexpected and predict the unpredictable. So, can an evidence-enriched practice enhance social work's capacity to operate in situations of uncertainty, especially for its clients, who remain amongst the most marginalized and excluded groups in society? The following practice focus illustrates the challenge.

Practice Focus 2.2

Mary was a frail, sprightly and fiercely independent woman in her late 70s who lived alone, but unfortunately suffered a bad fall while out shopping. She ended up one late Friday afternoon in the Emergency Room of the city hospital. After a preliminary examination, which indicated serious bruising, but no broken bones, the nurse in charge decided that Mary could be discharged, particularly as they had virtually no spare beds available for the weekend.

Ben, a hospital social worker was called to arrange some home care but, following a brief assessment, he discovered that Mary could not walk unaided and had no relatives or friends nearby who could come and look after her. Ben therefore argued that Mary should not be discharged, but admitted for observation over the weekend and a more considered decision made on Monday. Ben pointed out the risks and uncertainty of leaving Mary at home over the weekend, their shared ethical duty of care and the problem of arranging emergency home care, and, importantly, cited research evidence on good practice to meet the needs of frail older people at the margins of care (Challis and Hughes, 2002).

Eventually, after a lively discussion with first, the nurse, and then the senior bed manager, a bed was found and, in the event it proved fortuitous because, on Monday morning, it was discovered that Mary had a large blood clot in her leg and badly torn knee ligaments. She remained in hospital for ten days and was then transferred to a rehabilitation unit before returning home with a substantial care package. Ben, the hospital social worker, was later commended for his intervention, especially the calm and reassuring way he had acted in Mary's best interest – by creating order in a situation of uncertainty, looking for disconfirming evidence highlighting the risks of premature discharge, resisting pressure from nursing colleagues and using appropriate research findings to good effect.

Using Research in Practice

In exploring how research-informed practice might be developed, Martyn Jones (2012) reminds us of three core ideas:

- First, research produces useful knowledge for practice, but the involvement of practitioners can help to ensure that it is in an accessible and transferable form.
- Second, the processes of research and practice are mutually compatible. However, the link is dynamic and needs to be activated and reflected upon by researchers and practitioners through collaboration and dialogue.
- Third, conditions can be created for practitioners to undertake research. When this happens it can become a regular part of the job, as in Practice Focus 2.1, to find out the latest research on child neglect. It can also create opportunities and support for social workers to carry out a modest evaluative research project (Jones, 2012, pp. 276–80).

Using research in practice is not a straightforward exercise or something that can be "tacked on" at the end of a busy day. It requires resources, senior management support and planning, as well as appropriate knowledge and skills. This is something that clearly takes time to develop and would be enhanced by a collaborative partnership between practice agencies and research active staff in the local university social work department. Research will certainly help to promote the crucial balance in practice between criticality and effectiveness. In this way there is a much better chance that building research capacity and incorporating it into practice will be seen as an opportunity for staff development, rather than something that reluctantly has to be done or resisted by those who claim they "just get on with the job" and never have time to draw on theory, let alone research evidence.

Conclusion

For very many years social work practice was based largely on untested assumptions about what was likely to be effective and make a positive difference and what was not. In the wake of the medical profession being caught out for dispensing drugs without an adequate research base to justify their use, "evidence-based practice" became a big issue across the human services, including social work. With it came a shift back to a positivist approach that came to be heavily criticized for not being suitable for making sense of the complexity and fluidity of social life and for encouraging a medicalized approach to social problems and social work concerns. That first wave – what might be called the "strong form" of evidence-based practice – is now steadily being replaced by a "weaker" and more realistic form in the shape of research-informed, evidence-enriched practice that fits much better with human experience in general and social work values in particular.

Whatever theoretical approaches or methods we adopt in our practice, we would do well to make sure that, as far as reasonably possible, our decisions and our actions are informed by the best research evidence currently available, alongside – and not instead of – other important bases of understanding.

In Chapter 1 we noted the importance of "theorizing practice," of drawing on our professional knowledge base in order to make sure that our practice is *informed* practice. What Chapter 2 has highlighted for us is that we also need to include research evidence as part of our "portfolio" of sources of understanding in the context of critically reflective practice. In Chapter 3 we will complete our analysis of the "three pillars" of understanding by exploring how the legal and policy context also needs to be part of the professional knowledge base we draw upon in practice.

References

Becker, S. and Bryman, A. (2004). *Understanding research for social policy and practice: Themes, methods and approaches.* Bristol, UK: Policy Press.

Berger, P. and Luckmann, T. (1971). *The social construction of reality.* Harmondsworth, UK: Penguin.

Bernard, H. R. (2013). *Social research methods: Qualitative and quantitative approaches* (2nd Edn). Thousand Oaks, CA: Sage.

Challis, D. and Hughes, J. (2002). Frail old people at the margins of care: Some recent research findings. *British Journal of Psychiatry*, 180, pp. 126–30.

Cheetham, J. (1998). The evaluation of social work: Priorities, problems and possibilities. In Cheetham, J. and Kazi, M. (eds) *The working of social work.* London: Jessica Kingsley Publishers.

D'Cruz, H. and Jones, M. (2004). *Social work research: Ethical and political contexts.* London: Sage.

Department for Children, Schools and Families (DCSF) (2008). *Analyzing child deaths and serious injury through abuse and neglect: What can we learn? A biennial analysis of serious case reviews 2003–2005*, Research Report DCSF-RR023. London: The Stationery Office.

Dodd, S. J. and Epstein, I. (2012). *Practice-based research in social work*. New York: Routledge.

Featherstone, B., Morris, K., and White, S. (2014). A marriage made in hell: Early intervention meets child protection. *British Journal of Social Work*, 44, pp. 1735–49.

Frost, N. and Parton, N. (2009). *Understanding children's social care*. London: Sage.

Gergen, K. J. (2009). *Invitation to social construction* (2nd Edn). Thousand Oaks, CA: Sage.

Harris, J. (2003). *The social work business*. London: Sage.

Healy, K. (2005). *Social work theories in context*. Basingstoke, UK: Palgrave Macmillan.

Houston, S. (2001). Beyond social constructionism: Critical realism and social work, *British Journal of Social Work*, 31, pp. 845–61.

Hugman, R. (2005). Looking back: The view from here. *British Journal of Social Work*, 35, pp. 609–20.

Humphries, B. (ed.) (2000). *Research in social care and social welfare*. London: Jessica Kingsley Publishers.

Jones, M. (2012). Research minded practice in social work. In Stepney, P. and Ford, D. (eds) *Social work models, methods and theories: A framework for practice* (2nd Edn). Lyme Regis, UK: Russell House Publishing, pp. 272–86.

Joseph Rowntree Foundation (2015). *Developing evidence-enriched practice in health and social care with older people*. www.JRF.org.uk.

Kuhn, T. (1970). *The structure of scientific revolutions* (2nd Edn). Chicago, IL: University of Chicago Press.

Kumar, M. (2009). *Quantum: Einstein, Bohr and the great debate about the nature of reality*. London: Icon Books.

Laming, Lord (2003). *Report of the Inquiry into the death of Victoria Climbié*. London: The Stationery Office.

Newman, T., Moseley, A., Tierney, S., and Ellis, A. (2005). *Evidence-based social work: A guide for the perplexed*. Lyme Regis, UK: Russell House Publishing.

Packman, J. and Hall, C. (1998). *From care to accommodation*. London: HMSO.

Parton, N. (2011). Child protection and safeguarding in England: Changing and competing conceptions of risk and their implications for social work. *British Journal of Social Work*, 41, pp. 854–75.

Payne, M. (2014). *Modern social work theory* (4th Edn). Basingstoke, UK: Palgrave Macmillan.

Pearson, G. (1975). *The deviant imagination*. Basingstoke, UK: Macmillan.

Pease, B. (2007). Critical social work theory meets evidence-based practice in Australia: Towards critical knowledge informed practice in social work. In Yokota, K. (ed) *Empowering people through emancipatory social work*. Kyoto: Sekai Shisou-sya.

Popper, K. (1959). *Objective knowledge*. Oxford: Clarendon Press.

Rorty, R. (1991). *Objectivity, relativism, and truth* (Philosophical Papers, Vol. 1). Cambridge, UK: Cambridge University Press.

Rubin, A. and Babbie, E. (2015). *Essential research methods for social work* (4th Edn). Boston, MA: Cengage Learning.

Rutter, M. (2006). Is Sure Start an effective preventive intervention? *Child and Adolescent Mental Health*, 11(3), pp. 135–41.

Sayer, A. (2000). *Realism and social science*. London: Sage.

Schön, D. (1984). *The reflective practitioner: How professionals think in action*. New York: Basic Books.

Sheldon, B. (2011). *Cognitive-behaviour therapy: Research and practice in health and social care* (2nd Edn). London: Routledge.

Stepney, P. (2006). Mission impossible? Critical practice in social work. *British Journal of Social Work*, 36(8), pp. 1289–307.

Stepney, P. (2009). English social work at the crossroads: A critical view. *Australian Social Work*, 62(1), pp. 10–27.

Stepney, P. (2012). An introduction to social work theory, practice and research. In Stepney, P. and Ford, D. (eds) *Social work models, methods and theories: A framework for practice* (2nd Edn). Lyme Regis, UK: Russell House Publishing, pp. 20–35.

Stepney, P. and Rostila, I. (2011). Towards an integrated model of practice evaluation balancing accountability, critical knowledge and developmental perspectives. *Health Sociology Review*, 20(2), pp. 133–46.

Thompson, N. (2017). *Theorizing practice* (2nd Edn). London: Palgrave.

Thompson, N. and Thompson, S. (2016). *The social work companion* (2nd Edn). London: Palgrave.

Thompson, S. and Thompson, N. (2018). *The critically reflective practitioner* (2nd Edn). London: Palgrave.

Trinder, L. (2000). A critical appraisal of evidence-based practice. In Trinder, L. and Reynolds, S. (eds) *Evidence-based practice: A critical appraisal*. Oxford, UK: Blackwell, pp. 212–41.

Webb, S. (2006). *Social work in a risk society*. Basingstoke, UK: Palgrave Macmillan.

3

THEORY AND METHODS IN A POLICY AND ORGANIZATIONAL CONTEXT

INTERNATIONAL PERSPECTIVES

Paul Stepney

> Social work's continuing legitimacy as a profession rests on its commitment to social justice and community welfare.
>
> (Hardcastle and Powers, 2004, p. v)

Introduction

Discussions about the policy and organizational context of practice have become increasingly important, even if there is a temptation to pass over them quickly because they appear overly theoretical, heavy going and rather boring. This was certainly the initial view of a group of international students I taught at Tampere University in 2016. I am pleased to say that this aversion to social policy soon began to change once we started to explore contemporary social problems, such as poverty, homelessness and exclusion, and noted how consumerism and new technology were affecting the ability of practitioners to address them.

At a time of heightened public expectations and political scrutiny social work finds itself at a "policy to practice crossroads" – caught between modernizing policy reform and demanding practice realities, against a backdrop of widening inequalities and insecurity in the labor market (Stepney, 2012). This clearly presents an extremely challenging context for social work and one that requires a good understanding of policy and organizational issues if practitioners are to develop critically

reflective methods of practice. This is the ambitious task we have set ourselves in this chapter which, along with Chapters 1 and 2, is intended to
lay the foundations for those that follow in Part II of the book.

The study of social policy, as one of the new social sciences, is
informed by concepts and ideas that derive from two broad visions or
utopias. These are particularly significant for understanding how policy and organizational factors shape practice. First, we can identify an
individual utopia where social problems are believed to be caused by
individual failings, so policy should seek to change individual behavior
and encourage people to adapt and conform to existing social arrangements. Second, we can construct a *social utopia* where problems are seen
to derive from wider social conditions and structural inequalities, therefore policy should be concerned with promoting wider social change
(Fitzpatrick, 2011). Social policy frequently tries to do both, although,
as we shall see, recent modernizing policy reform has tended to stress
the need for individuals to change and take greater responsibility for
their own welfare.

In theorizing about policy and organizational issues we can approach
the task of explaining a phenomenon in two general ways: *transcendence* and *immanence* (Fitzpatrick, 2011). The first suggests we need to go
beyond the immediate context of the policy in question and examine it
from the outside. Habermas (1984) was a disciple of this approach, arguing that "critical distance" is necessary if we are to understand what the
policy is about and assess its contribution to social justice and well-being
(Jordan, 2007). The second approach suggests that, rather than transcend
the policy, we should completely immerse ourselves in it and its context.
Thus, we can only fully understand what is going on by studying policy
from within. Foucault (1984) was an exponent of this approach, arguing
that we should immerse ourselves in life's contingencies and contradic-
tions, and look beyond the stated aims of policy to see its unintended
consequences.

As we search for convincing explanations of contemporary policy to
practice conundrums and their implications for theory and methods, the
position adopted here is that we need to embark on both forms of theorizing. The recent modernization of the welfare state is illustrative of
this debate, including the different visions and choices we face as social

workers, and this will be examined before looking at policy and organizational issues in greater depth.

Social Work and the Modernization of the Welfare State

Social work in the United Kingdom is very much in the front line of
welfare reform and has been reshaped by the policies of successive governments to modernize the welfare state. This began in the 1980s under
Margaret Thatcher within parameters of cost containment, efficiency
and effectiveness, and has continued to the present day. The result is the
development of what might be called "the conditional and affordable
welfare state" (Stepney, 2012). By the new millennium the UK welfare
state, under the stewardship of Tony Blair, was characterized by targeted
support for the working poor, United States-style labor market activation for unemployed people (workfare), protection for vulnerable people at high risk, and self-help for pretty much everyone else. The result
has been increasing polarization and social divisions, with inclusion for
hard-working families with children alongside more soup kitchens for
homeless people and food banks for those in poverty.

In other European countries modernization has a different meaning,
reflecting contrasting priorities and culturally specific goals. Overall, policy has sought to combine efficiency with equity in efforts to tackle social
exclusion. However, after the 2008 recession, followed by a dramatic rise
in the number of migrants and asylum seekers entering Europe, governments have been divided about their social priorities. This feeds into a
longer-term debate about how to manage increasingly differentiated and
socially divided populations (Clarke, 2004). Even the Nordic countries of
Denmark, Finland, Norway and Sweden have found it necessary to adapt
to the "global competition state paradigm," strengthen efficiency over
equity and scale down their more emancipatory aims (Kananen, 2014).

In the United States welfare tends to be associated with social security benefits and, in terms of Federal government expenditure, continues
to play a residual role in tackling poverty alongside growing inequality
and divisions (Mullaly, 2010). There are many reasons for this, not least
because "a lack of faith in government in general is a factor" (Heffernan,
2003, p. 164). After the 2008 recession unemployment peaked at around
10% in 2010 but then began to fall. The opposite happened in the Euro

area due largely to harsher austerity measures – see Figure 3.1. This is part of a longer-term trend associated with technological development, outsourcing and loss of manufacturing jobs in what is called "the rust belt states" (Scherer, 2016). However, as the economy recovered and gross domestic product (GDP) grew, median incomes for two thirds of all US households fell. Between 2007 and 2013 incomes have either stagnated or fallen, with the lower middle class and working class hardest hit (Krugman, 2013). Many of these are the "forgotten people" who supported Donald Trump in the 2016 presidential election (Krugman, 2016). Significantly, in public debate the term welfare is attributed to failure and dependency, and this, together with Republican opposition in Congress, undermined President Obama's plan to extend health care insurance.

In both Australia and Canada, a market-based ideology predominates and has led to cutbacks in state welfare and a realignment of provision (Mullaly, 2007). Thus, we can say that, during the past decade, public welfare in Canada, the UK, Australia and the US has experienced a serious legitimation problem and has been restructured in line with the priorities of the global market. The middle class, as a percentage of the population, has fallen in these countries, and it is this group the welfare state has traditionally relied upon for support, both ideologically and financially through their taxes. In the Nordic countries, less

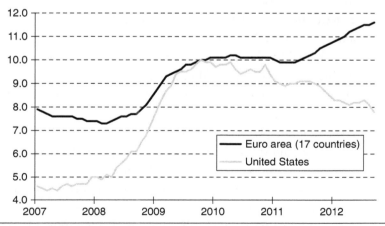

Figure 3.1 Unemployment rates in US and Euro area (from END THIS DEPRESSION NOW! By Paul Krugman. Copyright © 2012 Melrose Road Partners. Used by permission of W.W. Norton & Company, Inc.).

dramatic restructuring measures have occurred, but this has still led to some retrenchment.

The implications for social work have been significant, and therefore two important questions arise. First, to what extent has modernization led to a reshaping of social work practice? Second, what are the implications for theory and methods, in particular, for developing critically reflective methods of practice?

To What Extent Has Modernizing Policy Reshaped Social Work Practice?

Overall, it is clear from the foregoing discussion that modernization has been a highly complex process. None the less, if we create "critical distance" and immerse ourselves in the debate, then it becomes possible to identify five dimensions that, taken together, have had a significant influence on social work practice. The five dimensions are:

1. Practitioners have reduced professional autonomy and are subject to extensive bureaucratic regulation, greater organizational control and now spend a disproportionate amount of time behind a computer screen. Re-establishing greater autonomy and achieving a better balance between direct work and administration are important for developing critically reflective practice.

2. Practitioners continue to draw upon a broad range of theory and methods (as examined in Part II), but operate within a context shaped by the management of risk (Webb, 2006), an acute problem especially in child protection work (Featherstone et al., 2014). There is a need to incorporate strategies of prevention in protection plans (Stepney, 2014).

3. Assessment in practice draws upon a critical social science knowledge base, and this underpins a broad range of skills-based competencies. However, this typically involves completing tick-box checklists. Practitioners need to expand and enrich their assessments with "critical breadth and critical depth" (see Chapter 1).

4. Social work's professional culture locates itself within a humanitarian vision of social solidarity, betterment and the "good society." It is a good time to restate this. However, this vision must be balanced against managing the social casualties of the market and

what may be termed "mopping up the expendable waste prod-
ucts of the 'goods society'" (Pearson, 1975, cited in Stepney, 2014,
p. 306) – an important balance to achieve.

5. Social work internationally remains firmly committed to equal-
    ity, social justice and upholding individual freedom and human
    rights. However, in national policy the change agent and advo-
    cacy role (see Chapter 16) must be balanced against protection of
    the public and effective use of resources.

Clearly, we need to be careful about suggesting that we are standing at
the dawn of a new form of practice emerging. However, the impact of
policy on practice has been quite dramatic, and cutbacks in welfare budgets have made it extremely difficult for practitioners to balance restricted
resources for crisis work, to safeguard children and vulnerable adults, with
preventive work in the community. In Britain, this was a balance that
went horribly wrong in the Baby Peter case, with worrying echoes of
lessons not learned from the Victoria Climbié case seven years earlier.

The Baby Peter Case

As discussed in Chapter 2, Peter Connelly (known as Baby Peter) was a
17-month-old baby from London who died in 2007. He was the victim
of almost unimaginable abuse, resulting in more than 50 injuries over an
eight-month period. During this time, Peter was seen a number of times
by social workers and various health professionals, including a pediatrician and nursing staff. This was one of the UK's most serious cases of
child abuse that caused shock and outrage among both the public and
politicians. This was partly due to the horrific nature of Peter's injuries,
and partly because he lived under the jurisdiction of the same Children's
Services in London that had seriously failed seven years earlier in the
case of Victoria Climbié. The resulting public inquiry had led to child
protection measures being implemented that were supposed to prevent
such cases happening again (see Laming, 2003).

The fallout from these cases damaged social work's professional
reputation (Jones, 2014), and has led to an over emphasis on defensive
protection-dominated practice. Although this is perfectly understandable, in the long term it will do little to either develop critically reflective
practice or improve the reputation of the profession. However, one of

the problems in seeking to enhance professional standing is that social work relies upon wider political and public support. Appropriate recognition, validation and support, not just in Britain but across the globe, has become conditional on further policy reform, organizational improvement, better leadership and more effective management – the principal recommendations in the Baby Peter case (Laming, 2009). Further analysis of policy and organizational factors is therefore required, noting the decisive impact they have had on theory and methods.

Managerialism vs Professionalism

The challenge of ensuring that welfare modernization was delivered in a way that brought markets, partnerships and consumers together was achieved by introducing new "managerial forms of organizational coordination and control" (Clarke et al., 2000, p. 6). The new managerialism propagated a new set of expectations and values associated with efficiency, effectiveness and cost containment that became superimposed upon the expert knowledge and skills of the professional. In other words, social workers were required to adapt their practice to suit organizational requirements and managerial priorities. Professionalism has thus been redefined in terms of organizational criteria where autonomy becomes subordinate to the goals of efficiency and effectiveness, resulting in more bureaucracy and a climate of mistrust (Thompson, 2017).

The new managers, many with private sector backgrounds in information technology or financial management, provided strategic leadership during modernization. This ensured commitment to centrally determined objectives and budget discipline, whilst devolving responsibility for professional decision making to front-line staff. Constraints on professional autonomy have clearly had an impact on practice.

The Impact of Managerialism on Theory and Methods

In a study of community mental health teams in Finland it was found that managerial control, allied to a new audit system, assisted managers to monitor performance more closely and reinforced certain methods, while excluding others (Saario and Stepney, 2009). Practitioners found that the audit system rewarded single contacts and closure of cases, thereby encouraging short-term interventions, such as crisis work and task-centered practice. In contrast, longer-term multiple contacts and ongoing relationships

received little reward, thereby discouraging therapeutic approaches, rehabilitation and social support. Supervision sessions reflected this concentration on outcomes related to case closure, which left little time for
theorizing to find more creative solutions. Similar problems can be found
in the UK (Stepney, 2012) as the following practice focus illustrates.

Practice Focus 3.1

The local municipal council had been forced to make cuts to public
services due to a substantial reduction in their welfare budget. They
had therefore decided to close the local social services office and
transfer services to the civic center three miles away. This would
save money, enable the three social work teams to be reorganized
and allow a new audit system to be introduced. Senior management
insisted that this would create a more streamlined, efficient and
effective service, but staff and clients were not so sure. A meeting
was organized by the three team managers and attended by all staff
affected. There was a lively debate of the policy and organizational
factors behind the proposed reorganization. The consensus was that
the changes were an attempt to regulate the work of the teams more
closely by audit and control, to concentrate resources on protection, especially of high-risk clients, encourage, wherever possible,
case closure and refer low risk-clients to voluntary sector agencies.
An alternative plan was drawn up, supported by all staff, that recognized the need for efficiency savings and reorganization to avoid
duplication, but suggested that this could be achieved by: reducing
the costly "out-of-area" placement of vulnerable children and mental
health clients, training more local people as family support workers,
achieving a better balance between administration and direct work,
and giving greater emphasis to prevention in protection plans. To
this end it was proposed to operate a drop-in service in a health
center with support from family doctors and nursing colleagues. To
the surprise of some staff, the principles underpinning the plan were
broadly accepted by senior management. Hence, a working party
was set up to look at how the new policy could be implemented to
promote good practice, but within the new budgetary framework.

Managerialism has played a decisive role in the fragmentation of provision and subordination of professional discretion to "business priorities," consumerism and a new more strident organizational culture (Harris, 2003).

Consumerism

Modernization of welfare services has been accompanied by the introduction of market principles, particularly in adult services, where clients have been recast as consumers. In the UK, individual budgets and personalized care have been introduced to reinforce the consumerist approach (Stepney, 2014). Underpinning consumerism is the notion of "choice." The new consumers are given the opportunity to exercise choice, from the range of services on offer, just as they would when shopping in a supermarket.

One of the problems is that this rational choice model assumes that clients have the necessary information, together with sufficient skill and resources, to choose the care and support they need. Unfortunately, the market in care does not operate in this way. Further, marketization has taken place during a period when welfare budgets have been contracting. In the UK, consumerism has created tensions among practitioners in local social services teams with increased workloads, limited resources and the introduction of strict eligibility criteria. The views of clients suggest that they see enhanced provision and "choice" as largely illusory (Ferguson and Woodward, 2009).

The Impact of Consumerism on Theory and Methods

Research studies report that consumerism as a central plank of modernization has led to low morale, increased stress, with more practitioners considering leaving the profession (Huxley et al., 2005). In addition, consumerism has contributed to the fragmentation of services. Theorizing is largely confined to high-risk work in child protection and mental health where clients are often involuntary and "choice" not appropriate. Short-term methods are applied to clients assessed as medium risk, and self-help for all low risk work. It is only the very best practitioners that have resisted this trend and engage in theorizing to find the most creative and preventive solutions (Stepney, 2014). Consumerism and managerialism have clearly had an impact on the practitioners' organizational culture.

Organizational Culture

The culture of an organization is an important concept that shapes the experience of its members and yet is something slippery and difficult to define. It refers to the largely informal rules, assumptions, life practices and traditions that become embedded in the everyday working lives of people in organizations. An organizational culture can be very positive, enabling, open and create a sense of solidarity, or it can be negative, defensive, closed and have the opposite effect by reinforcing an "every person for themselves" attitude. I have worked at four universities in Britain and one in Finland and have experienced both ends of the cultural spectrum, as well as something in between.

In social work where the job is emotionally and intellectually demanding and marked by considerable uncertainty, there is an obvious need to create a positive organizational culture that promotes mutual support and learning. The question is whether, under conditions of modernization, consumerism and managerialism, a more individualistic, closed and uncritically passive culture has emerged? This is what Thompson (2017) calls an anti-intellectual "keep your head down and just get on with the job" approach. It is difficult to know how widespread this is, although the impact on theory and methods has surfaced in research.

The Impact of Organizational Culture on Theory and Methods

Research suggests that modernization has produced a more business-like, instrumental and calculative organizational culture in fieldwork teams (Ferguson and Woodward, 2009; Stepney, 2014). There now appears to be less joint working, with practitioners reporting that they have little scope for group work, and care management is increasingly linked to meeting agency performance targets. The following practice focus indicates what might be done.

Practice Focus 3.2

Venus was a social worker in a child protection team who complained that no-one had time to talk and share experiences any more, such that many staff felt unsupported. A new team manager had just been appointed and quickly picked up on this. At the last team meeting she created additional time and asked everyone to carry out a "cultural audit" using such dimensions as: support, openness to change, sharing experiences, creativity and problem solving. The information that emerged got everyone talking, both about current problems and what needed to change. It was agreed to have a regular spot in team meetings to discuss such issues, and another social worker suggested that next week the team could look at peer supervision. Venus went away feeling that the team had taken a positive step forward.

The importance of creating a positive and supportive organizational culture raises two other organizational issues: the need for good supervision and teamwork.

Supervision

As social work becomes more demanding, there is an increasing need for high-quality supervision. This requires appropriate resources, particularly time and space, and managers and supervisors with the necessary knowledge and skills. It also requires commitment and motivation, and during times of increased pressure this may be missing.

There are numerous models of supervision, and, for present purposes, two contrasting approaches can be identified. The first may be called a mechanistic approach where the focus is purely on monitoring performance. This is concerned with checking whether the work is being carried out to a satisfactory standard, progress on cases and any problems preventing early case closure. Although every agency legitimately requires monitoring, it becomes a restricted form of supervision. The second is an organic exploratory model where the focus goes well beyond monitoring to include brainstorming, problem solving, theorizing and sharing of ideas and experiences.

Under conditions of modernization and managerialism there has been a tendency for the more restricted form of supervision to become dominant. The impact on theory and methods has been discouraging, with less time for identifying relevant theory and discussing methods. However, there is evidence that more skilled practitioners have taken the initiative to enrich formal supervision sessions with more theoretical content and develop forms of peer supervision (Stepney, 2014). Peer supervision implies the need for good teamwork.

Teamwork

Organizational culture can have a decisive influence on the way people who work alongside each other in teams interact – for example, how they communicate and whether this is co-operative and collaborative, how conflicts are resolved, whether team members share experiences and support each other, effectiveness at problem solving and so on (Trevithick, 2012). In social work, team roles are likely to be significant, and thus the seminal work of Meredith Belbin remains highly influential and relevant. Belbin (1993) identified nine team roles: plant, resource investigator, co-ordinator, shaper, monitor evaluator, team worker, implementer, completer/finisher and specialist (p. 22).

Unsurprisingly, it has been found that the most effective teams are those where there is a good balance of team roles across members. In other words, good teams need a creative plant and shaper as much as they need completer/finishers and good team members. There is evidence that modernization and the culture surrounding it has contributed to the individualization of all work processes and away from joint working in the community (Stepney and Popple, 2008). This has undermined creative potential and tried to turn everyone into implementers and completer/finishers. Hence there is a need to recognize the problems this can create and take steps to redress the balance as part of staff training and continuous professional development.

The Impact of Teamwork on Theory and Methods

The impact of this move away from team working has been to reduce the level of discussion within teams and sharing of ideas about the need for theorizing. It has also individualized team members who can easily become isolated and unaware of the work of their colleagues. Further, group work has fallen down the pecking order of appropriate methods as practitioners adopt individual one-to-one strategies and have less time to invest in the necessary planning and organization required for group work. So there is an urgent need for good teamwork and to identify opportunities for joint working and developing mutual support.

The reshaping of practice by the policy and organizational factors discussed so far cannot be fully understood without acknowledging the huge impact of globalization. It is therefore time to examine this broader policy debate.

Social Work, Globalization, Neoliberalism and Demographic Change

Social work throughout the developed world now operates against a backdrop of economic globalization where the restructuring of welfare reflects the criteria of the global market. A neoliberal political philosophy has become dominant, stressing the importance of the individual and the pre-eminence of the market. Both these ideas imply a residual role for government. Welfare must therefore underpin the working of the market and not become a drain on public resources. Modernizing policy has led to a growth in standardized and routinized services, despite the claims of consumerism and policies of personalization (Stepney, 2014).

According to Fitzpatrick (2011) globalization refers to: "the increasing worldwide interdependence of individuals, localities, public and private organisations, economies, nations and socio-cultures" (p. 174). This is not to argue that globalization is a distinctive process producing predictable outcomes, but is the cumulative effect of different socio-economic and political processes. Although such processes are associated with borderless frontiers, transnational communication and trade, increasing mobility of capital, the blurring of national identities and so on, the tangible effects of globalization may mask a number of partial, contradictory and highly conflictual tendencies (Clarke, 2000). Further, globalization has affected national economies during a period when the rise of GDP has been slowing down in both European nations (Eurostat, 2016), as well as globally in the US, Canada and Australia (Mullaly, 2007).

Alongside the winds of global economic change, demographic trends are significant. There has been a steady rise in Europe's ageing population, with the percentage of those 65 or over increasing from 16.6% in 2005 to 18.9% in 2015 (Eurostat, 2016). The proportion of working age people has been shrinking while those over 65 is expanding, due to the post war "baby boomers" reaching retirement age. If we look at those over 80, referred to as "the very old", we see similar trends. If we look at Europe's population the proportion of those 80 or over is projected to increase dramatically from 5.3% in 2015 to 12.3% by 2080. Very old people are increasing as a proportion of Europe's retired population, and are projected to rise to 22% of all older people in the EU by the year 2020 (Eurostat, 2016).

While many older people care for themselves, with advancing age comes an increasing likelihood of ill health, disability and mobility problems. In fact, people are known to consume on average a similar amount of health resources in the last year of their life as the rest of their life (Stepney, 2012). These trends suggest that we are going to require substantial additional funds for health and social care in the future, at a time when the number of informal carers, particularly women, is projected to fall. This is due to more women in the labor market, higher divorce rates, geographical mobility, community fragmentation and carers growing older.

The net result of globalization and neoliberalism has been a significant rise in global inequality, so how have governments responded to this global challenge?

Globalization and Four European Social Models

> [T]he challenge is to conceive and implement social reform aimed at greater economic flexibility and better social protection.
>
> (André Sapir, 2013, p. 5)

If citizens face a number of common problems, such as poverty and exclusion, then the response of European governments in terms of social policy has been marked by considerable diversity (Sapir, 2013). The differences are historic and can be traced back to different systems of social protection. The seminal work of Esping-Andersen (1990) has been extremely influential in identifying three welfare state typologies that can be analyzed in terms of commodification and stratification – the extent to which state welfare offers protection against the commodifying effects of the market and reduces class-based outcomes.

The three typologies have established the framework for much subsequent comparative social policy research. First, there are the liberal welfare regimes, characterized by the UK and the US. Liberal regimes have modest levels of social insurance contributions and benefits (pensions, disability, sickness and unemployment benefits), but have more extensive "safety nets" through means tested social security benefits and targeted support for the working poor.

Second, there are the corporatist welfare states epitomized by Germany, which have more generous and non-stigmatizing social insurance benefits, financed by substantial contributions from earnings. The disadvantage is that it perpetuates income inequalities, favoring men over women, and penalizes those outside the labor market. Third, are the social democratic welfare states, exemplified by the Nordic countries, that have extensive welfare services financed by high levels of taxation and social insurance contributions. In Sweden and Finland, the welfare state is viewed as contributing to social solidarity, such that redistribution and universalism receive widespread public support.

The three typologies have been reformulated by Sapir (2013) (see Figure 3.2), comparing welfare states on the basis of equity and efficiency.

The regimes have responded differently to the forces of globalization. The liberal regimes have witnessed greater social deregulation, use of the market and privatization. This has widened incomes and employment opportunities, with a modest minimum wage in the UK and a

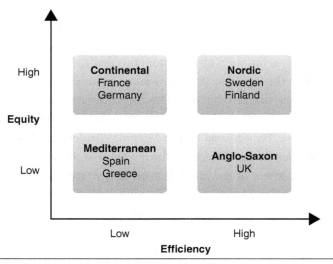

Figure 3.2 Four European social models (cited in Stepney, 2012, p. 9).

substantial number of working households at risk of poverty due to low wages. Unemployment has remained high in many parts of England and across the "rust belt states of the mid-west" in the US (Krugman, 2016). Employment opportunities were confined to a small growth in high-tech companies, and a larger growth in low-status service work stimulated by the market in social care. Many of these jobs are low paid, insecure and taken up by women and new migrants.

In the continental welfare states of France and Germany, unemployment has remained high, but tackling social exclusion, rather than poverty, remains a priority. Social care services can be found in the "third sector," but do not employ large numbers of people. However, according to Sapir (2013), although the continental model is equitable, and 39% of the population benefit from redistribution, reform is required to improve efficiency.

In the Nordic countries, although "the golden age of universalism" may be over (Anttonen and Sipilä, 2012, p. 32), the "Nordic Model of Welfare," despite some retrenchment, retains a strong commitment to equality and social solidarity (Kananen, 2014). The Nordic countries have the highest rates of redistribution, generous rewards for labor market participation and lowest poverty levels in Europe (Sapir, 2013). Older people typically live in service flats and do not expect to be cared for by their children. None the less, public welfare is expensive to administer and, with elements of a more pluralist approach gaining momentum, have been subject to some reform. However, one of the features of the Nordic model is that welfare services are supported by an extensive bureaucracy, staffed largely by women, and this segmentation of female employment is acknowledged as a problem.

In the Mediterranean countries employment protection is a priority alongside support for older people. The family plays an active role in welfare, both for younger people, who leave home later than in other countries, and for older people who need care (Hantrais, 2004). This puts pressure on women to provide informal care. The Mediterranean model has the lowest redistribution of resources rates and highest number of people at risk of poverty, which contributes to it being judged the least equitable and efficient of the four models. Reform is therefore required (Sapir, 2013).

From the foregoing debate, how might we use policy constructively to develop critically reflective methods of practice?

Policy and Critically Reflective Practice

From the previous discussion, it follows that there is a need to achieve a better overall balance, in particular, by recognizing the policy and organizational context of practice, but not being molded into passive compliance with it. This involves using practice skills in a critically reflective, research-enriched (see Chapter 2) and policy-informed way. This would enable practitioners to balance effectiveness, in every aspect of practice, with a wider commitment to social inclusion and justice.

One concrete way of demonstrating this is to move away from a defensive, protection-dominated approach, especially in child protection and work with vulnerable adults, and balance prevention strategies with protection plans (see Chapter 17 in this volume). There is good evidence of the effectiveness of prevention that would allow resources to be redirected away from costly statutory interventions towards integrating services with informal networks of support (Stepney, 2014). This would have gone a long way to overcoming the problems that emerged in the Baby Peter and Climbié cases, as well as improving the image and standing of the profession.

Conclusion

We have covered an enormous amount of ground in this chapter concerning the way policy and organizational factors impinge on social work practice. Social policy is often seen as dry and theoretical, but, while there is an element of truth in this, it can also be stimulating to study. It is vitally important for us to understand what is at stake, how policy and organizational factors shape our professional lives, the problems we face and what might be done about them.

We have focused particularly on the UK and the US, with brief reference to Australia and Canada, while looking in some depth at Europe to illustrate the way various governments have modernized welfare in response to globalization and the problems this creates. We have noted how modernization has reformed welfare by promoting consumerism, managerialism and the extensive use of the market, which has constrained professional autonomy. This has had a decisive impact on the organizational culture of social work agencies and impinged upon the working lives of practitioners.

Practitioners find themselves caught between modernizing policy reform and demanding practice realities, against a backdrop of widening inequalities. This has led to more defensive and protection-dominated practice. However, the Baby Peter case has demonstrated the folly of ignoring prevention. The challenge facing social work, during times of financial austerity, is to demonstrate our understanding of policy and organizational factors so that we may combine effectiveness with a commitment to social justice. This requires recognizing the importance of "theorizing practice" to develop critically reflective methods of practice, and in Part II of the book this will be applied to a range of theories and methods.

References

Anttonen, A. and Sipilä, J. (2012). Universalism in the British and Scandinavian social policy debates. In A. Anttonen, L. Häikiö and K. Stefánsson (Eds) *Welfare state, universalism and diversity*. Northampton, MA: Edward Elgar Publishing, pp. 16–41.

Belbin, M. (1993). *Team roles at work*. Oxford: Butterworth-Heinemann.

Clarke, J. (2000). A world of difference? Globalisation and the study of social policy. In G. Lewis, S. Gewirtz and J. Clarke (Eds) *Rethinking social policy*. London: Sage.

Clarke, J. (2004). *Changing welfare, changing states: New directions in social policy*. London: Sage.

Clarke, J., Gewirtz, S. and McLaughlin, E. (Eds) (2000). *New managerialism new welfare?* London: Sage.

Esping-Andersen, G. (1990). *The three worlds of welfare capitalism*. Cambridge: Polity Press.

Eurostat (2016). *Europe in figures: Eurostat yearbook 2016*. Luxembourg: European Commission (www.europa.eu.int/comm/eurostat).

Featherstone, B., Morris, K. and White, S. (2014). A marriage made in hell: Early intervention meets child protection. *British Journal of Social Work*, 44, pp. 1735–49.

Ferguson, I. and Woodward, R. (2009). *Radical social work in practice: Making a difference*. Bristol: The Policy Press.

Fitzpatrick, T. (2011). *Welfare theory: An introduction to the theoretical debates in social policy* (2nd Edn). Basingstoke, UK: Palgrave Macmillan.

Foucault, M. (1984). *The Foucault reader*, edited by Paul Rabinow. Harmondsworth, UK: Penguin.

Habermas, J. (1984). *Theory of communicative action, Volume one*. Boston, MA: Beacon Press.

Hantrais, L. (2004). *Family policy matters: Responding to family change in Europe*. Bristol, UK: Policy Press.

Hardcastle, D. and Powers, P. (2004). *Community practice: Theories and skills for social workers* (2nd Edn). New York: Oxford University Press.

Harris, J. (2003). *The social work business*. London: Sage.

Heffernan, J. (2003). Care for children and older people in the United States: Laggard or merely different? In A. Anttonen, J. Baldock and J. Siplilä (Eds) *The young, the old and the state*. Northampton, MA: Edward Elgar Publishing, pp. 143–66.

Huxley, P., Evans, S., Gately, C., Webber, M., Mears, A., Pajak, S., Kendall, T., Medina, J. and Katona, C. (2005). Stress and pressures in mental health social work: The worker speaks. *British Journal of Social Work*, 35(7), pp. 1063–79.

Jones, R. (2014). *The story of Baby P: Setting the record straight*. Bristol, UK: Policy Press.

Jordan, B. (2007). *Social work and well-being*. Lyme Regis, UK: Russell House Publishing.

Kananen, J. (2014). *The Nordic welfare state in three eras: From emancipation to discipline*. Farnham, UK: Ashgate.

Krugman, P. (2013). *End this depression now*. New York: W. W. Norton & Company.

Krugman, P. (2016). Seduction and betrayal. *New York Times International Edition*, December 3–4: p. 12.

Laming, Lord (2003). *Report of the inquiry into the death of Victoria Climbié*. London: The Stationery Office.

Laming, Lord (2009). *The protection of children in England: A progress report*. London: The Stationery Office.

Mullaly, B. (2007). *The new structural social work* (3rd Edn). Don Mills, ON: Oxford University Press.

Mullaly, B. (2010). *Challenging oppression and confronting privilege*. Don Mills, ON: Oxford University Press.

Pearson, G. (1975). *The deviant imagination*. London: Macmillan.

Saario, S. and Stepney, P. (2009). Managerial audit and community mental health: A study of rationalising practices in Finnish psychiatric outpatient clinics. *European Journal of Social Work*, 12(1), pp. 41–56.

Sapir, A. (2013). Globalisation and the reform of European social models. *Breugel Policy Brief*, Brussels (www.slideshare.net/bluelucy/globalisation-and-the-reform-of-european-social-models).

Scherer, M. (2016). Donald Trump: The person of the year, *Time*, 88 (25–26): pp. 28–51.

Stepney, P. (2012). An overview of the wider policy context. In P. Stepney and D. Ford (Eds). *Social work models, methods and theories* (2nd Edn). Lyme Regis, UK: Russell House Publishing, pp. 1–19.

Stepney, P. (2014). Prevention in social work: The final frontier? *Critical and Radical Social Work*, 2(3), pp. 305–20.

Stepney, P. and Popple, K. (2008). *Social work and the community: A critical context for practice*. Basingstoke, UK: Palgrave.

Thompson, N. (2017). *Theorizing practice* (2nd Edn). London: Palgrave.

Trevithick, P. (2012). Groupwork theory and practice. In P. Stepney and D. Ford (Eds) *Social work models, methods and theories* (2nd Edn). Lyme Regis, UK: Russell House Publishing, pp. 236–54.

Webb, S. (2006). *Social work in a risk society*. Basingstoke, UK: Palgrave Macmillan.

PART II
SOCIAL WORK THEORIES AND METHODS IN PRACTICE
INTRODUCTION

While Part I set the scene by examining three key aspects of the wider context in which theory and methods are used, Part II now focuses down on specific theoretical approaches that can be helpful, each in their own particular ways, in addressing the practice challenges we face. We have chosen 14 perspectives in total, with one chapter per approach, but we could easily have chosen several more – this is by no means a comprehensive review of social work theory and methods. This brings us back to the book's subtitle, "The Essentials." What we offer here is a gateway to the wider literature and we strongly recommend that you use this book as a stepping stone to fuller accounts of the topics covered here, as well as the approaches not covered here.

Each chapter has been produced by one or more experts in that particular field. They bring their experience and expertise to the subject in a succinct account that gives you "the essentials" of their chosen theoretical area. Reading a particular chapter will not make you an expert in that area or equip you necessarily to put the ideas into practice. But, what each chapter should do is give you a basic foundation of learning that you can build on over time. Each chapter should give you plenty of food for thought and set you thinking. We hope, too, that the respective chapters will enthuse you sufficiently to want to know more, to engage with the wider literature and develop your learning in whatever reasonable ways you can.

A big question raised by the subject matter of Part II, of course is: How do I know which method or approach to use in what circumstances? There is no easy or straightforward answer to this, but we can offer two important pieces of guidance. One is that the ideas underpinning the approach should give you some strong clues as to when it would be applicable (the use of crisis intervention in situations involving crises being an obvious example). The second is to revisit the idea of critically reflective practice, as discussed in Chapter 1. This means that you need to use your thinking skills to weigh up the situation, carefully analyze it, and match up as best you can the circumstances you find yourself in with what our professional knowledge base can tell us about such circumstances. This is the "artistry" of reflective practice that Donald Schön (1984) wrote about. It is not simply a matter of following procedures or using formulas. It is about using our intelligence and knowledge in a context of the underlying skills and values that we need.

So, as you work your way through from chapter to chapter, give some thought to the important question: In what circumstances might I use these insights? The more experienced you become over time, the easier it will become to make those links.

Reference

Schön, D. (1984). *The reflective practitioner*. New York: Basic Books.

4

PSYCHODYNAMIC THEORY

Malcolm Payne

Counseling, Psychotherapy and Social Work

Why would a social worker do counseling and psychotherapy? And should they, because these professions have separate accreditation? Some practitioners gain additional accreditation in one or both fields when their work needs it. Others add some beginning counseling and psychotherapy training to their social work qualification to build up skills that they find useful. There is, therefore, considerable overlap in the practice of each profession. In the USA and some other countries, social work has a much stronger emphasis on counseling and psychotherapy than in the UK and in countries where its role is primarily in public social provision.

Counseling and psychotherapy have many models of practice that are shared with, and have influenced, social work. Knowing about shared ideas is a positive way for caring and helping professions to work together with appreciation of different approaches. Since psychodynamic ideas arise from an important early psychological theory, understanding them helps you appreciate the implications for practice of later developments in psychology.

Psychodynamic ideas are an important source for all three professions. They had their impact on social work before the three professions separated, so it has developed its own. You can, also, often see psychodynamic ideas coming out in other theories. For example, attachment theory, used in work with children with behavior difficulties and in bereavement care, focuses on people's psychological attachments to others who are important to them. This originally emerged from research on behavior problems that came about when children were deprived of contact with their mothers, an important emphasis in psychodynamic theory (Bowlby, 1969, 1973, 1980). Attachment theory, therefore, has psychodynamic origins, even though current elaborations of it are at a considerable distance from its early sources and based on recent research. The same is true of psychodynamic social work theory: relationship-based practice, perhaps the most important developing set of ideas in this tradition (Goldstein et al., 2009; Ruch et al., 2010; Megele, 2015), has a similarly distant connection with its psychodynamic base.

What is Psychodynamic Theory?

Psychodynamic theory is the current general name given to theory that originated in the psychoanalysis of Sigmund Freud. He was a Viennese doctor who made contributions to neurology and created the first internationally influential theory of psychology in the first part of the twentieth century. Psychoanalysis had huge cultural influence, and some of its ideas are part of everyday understanding about how human minds work. Freud popularized, for example, the idea that much of our mental functioning is unconscious. He tried to understand how thinking unknown to our conscious mind nevertheless influenced our behavior and actions.

A well-known example is "Freudian slips," in which we use the wrong word apparently by accident, but in a way that reveals some of our hidden thinking. The American President, Donald Trump, for instance, said in a press conference on 17th March 2017: "The United States has been treated very, very unfairly by many countries over the years and that's going to stop. We're a very powerful company ... country." Internet comment explicitly referred to this as a "Freudian slip," showing how current Freud's cultural ideas are. It showed perhaps that Trump was thinking that his presidential role was like being a company boss (Cohen, 2017).

Freud had many followers who developed his ideas in different directions (Borden, 2009). Melanie Klein and his daughter, Anna Freud, for example, had considerable influence on British psychology and social work in the 1950s and 1960s (Salzberger-Wittenberg, 1970). Some also disputed aspects of his theories, forming related but different psychologies and practices. For example, Carl Gustav Jung (2002), a Swiss psychoanalyst, split from Freud early in the twentieth century, and developed theories that influence Jungian counseling and psychotherapy today. At a greater distance, Carl Rogers (1951), an American psychologist, developed "person-centered therapy" in the 1950s (it was originally called "client-centered"), picking up, but transforming, psychoanalytic ideas into a foundation for humanistic therapies. Many counselors follow developments of his model of practice (Wilkins, 2015). It is named to emphasize the whole person's psychological health, distinguishing it from practice focusing on internal psychological conflicts or individual behaviors. It is therefore unconnected with "person-centered care planning" used in UK adult social care, which develops ideas about clients being at the center of decisions about their care.

Psychodynamic practice is connected to, and built upon, the body of theories and practices that Freud, his followers and detractors created. It is "psychodynamic" in two ways:

- It claims that mental energy and the interplay of forces in our mind (the psyche) provide the impetus and direction for our behavior. The psyche is in this way dynamic – that is, it is active and powerful in deciding and changing how we act.
- More broadly, the inside workings of our minds (intra-psychic) have an impact on our actions and relationships in the social world outside our minds (extra-psychic). This has been important in social work because it emphasizes how our thinking both comes from and affects our social relationships. If we want to influence the social, we must have an impact on the psychological as well. If we want to help with the psychological, we must see how social experiences and relationships explain and develop people's thinking.

Some Basic Psychodynamic Ideas

Connected with these ideas, psychodynamic theory has a theory of child development that emphasizes how, in relationships, the child is parent to the adult: what happens to us in our childhood relationships gives us powerful experiences that form how we react in adult relationships. This leads to the concept of transference: in social work theory, this idea describes how we transfer early experiences of relationships into present behavior. Transference continues with all our life experiences, but early ones are often particularly important. This is because we usually only have a limited circle of relationships with parents, especially our mothers, and with brothers and sisters in early childhood. When we are trying to help people with relationship and behavior problems, if we look at how people behave now, we can often see how present patterns of behavior built up over time from past experiences. Connected with this is counter-transference. This proposes that, if we look at how we react to people we work with, we can often see the relationship falling into patterns of behavior that reflect their early experience. Transference helps us understand how early experiences have produced present behavior. A case example may make these ideas clearer.

Practice Focus 4.1

Jenny was a social work student working with Catherine, a young single parent who had a very disorganized daily life and routine that put her young baby and toddler at risk of neglect. Jenny became protective of Catherine, trying to shield her from critical relatives and officials who wanted her children to be taken away from her. They spent a lot of time together, with Jenny demonstrating economical shopping and cooking skills and more effective child care strategies. Jenny's supervisor pointed out that good time management means that social workers cannot usually take up this kind of role. Thinking this through with her supervisor, Jenny realized that Catherine's mother treated her in a very controlling way and did a lot of things for her throughout her childhood and young adulthood. Her transferred expectations of relationships with an older woman had led them through counter-transference into the same pattern of relationships. An alternative course for Jenny might have been to use her good relationship with Catherine to build up new experiences of successful independent household management and child care. This would also be better time management.

This case example shows how the psychodynamic emphasis on relationships works. By seeing reflections of past relationship experiences in present behavior patterns, we can identify how relationships have shaped the issues we are trying to deal with. We emphasize looking for evidence of patterns in relationships, both then and now: we do not make assumptions from one piece of behavior or one past event. Our practice also needs to build up relationships purposefully with the people we work with, because experiences of new relationships can help to modify the impact of past relationships. New relationship experience helps people to realize how they can manage the limitations of previous experiences and become less reliant on past patterns.

Since the basic idea of psychodynamic practice is that our minds give us impetus in living our lives, two important focuses are where this dynamism comes from, and how we direct and manage it. This gives importance to what Freud originally described as "drives" (our internal dynamism) and the ego, an aspect of our mind that perceives reality (the external environment). You could see our ego as the rational part of our mind helping us to manage the less rational bits of ourselves, so that we can live successfully in the real world. The less rational aspects of ourselves are often expressed through our emotions: affection, aggression, anger, anxiety, depression, despair, hate, hope, hostility, love. This is important for social workers, because they often deal with people whose situation means that they are powerfully affected by such emotions.

Social workers have valued this way of thinking about people, first, because it respects the reality that we human beings are always a mixture of factors that we sometimes think of as positive and negative. Second, it is also useful, that psychodynamic theory values both the emotional, feeling aspects of our humanity as well as the rational, thinking parts of our make-up. Both are important in helping people.

The third worthwhile feature of this theory for social work is that it sees every individual as part of a wider set of relationships. The social work formulation of this idea started out as "the person-in-situation," but more recently is "the person-in-environment" (Karls and Wandrei, 1994). These concepts led psychodynamic social work to be referred to as "psychosocial" theory (Woods and Hollis, 1999). Following these ideas, we never think of anyone in our assessments and interventions as defined by their behavior alone. We must always see them as created within and by their relationships in the wider family, community and society that they are part of. On the other hand, we can never see the situation or environment as the only factor in determining how someone lives their life, because they are always a "person," partly formed by how their ego manages their drives.

Differentiating Problem Behavior: Psychodynamic Ideas

Psychodynamic practice often focuses on "object relations." This psychoanalytic jargon refers to how we deal with people and things outside ourselves, relationships with other people or with social institutions and their requirements of us. Difficulties in dealing with the matters outside ourselves can lead to problems with our behavior and other people's perceptions of it, and to mental health or psychological problems involving feelings and attitudes. Psychodynamic theory is good for tackling such issues.

Since much of our mental processing of the world around us is unconscious, we sometimes react without rationally thinking things through. Much of the mental energy that impels us in our relationships and behavior is also unconscious. Psychological and behavior difficulties, therefore, are often a mystery to us, even though they develop in response to our earlier relationships and life experience. The unconscious mental processing of these relationships is not instantly available to us. It is not that we are thinking about something else, or have just forgotten it; it is deeply buried. Thus, the mental processes that generate current reactions to life seep in, or sometimes burst out, in unexpected and irrational ways. So our ego, our mind's managing agent in dealing with object relations, develops ways of controlling how we respond to external pressures and difficulties and internal thinking processes that may not help us with other people. These forms of control are called "defense mechanisms."

An important defense mechanism that often causes difficulties and underlies other defenses is repression; this is where something that is happening to us or that we are thinking about is so unpleasant or causes us so many difficulties that our mind buries it deep in our unconscious and does not permit it to emerge. Other defense mechanisms include displacement, where we take out our anger or anxiety about one part of our lives, say difficulties at work, in another part of our lives – for example in our family relationships. Inexplicable reactions to children or our partner can sometimes be explained by difficulties that we cannot express elsewhere in our life. Denial is a process of burying feelings about a life problem because we feel it is socially unacceptable to express them. For example, if someone gets angry about something their spouse does, while at the same time believing that they should always be loving, they may hide away their anger. Projection arises when we attack other people for their behavior or beliefs unduly strongly, because we ourselves fear that we may give in to such behavior or beliefs, too. Often defense mechanisms reflect concerns about moral issues. For example, a father who is over-controlling of a teenage daughter's relationships with boyfriends, may reflect his own fear of being unable to control his feelings of sexual desire.

One of the difficulties with defense mechanisms is that, although they help us manage difficulties in relationships around us, we may take them to extremes. Repressed and otherwise unconscious behavior also leaks out and affects how we behave towards others in unexpected ways. This may prove problematic if it leads to inappropriate expression of emotions, such as anger and aggression, or excessive anxiety, despair and depression.

Resistance is another common problem behavior. It has a special meaning in psychodynamic work: it is not refusing to do something or obstructing normal progress. It occurs when someone wants to make a change in their life, perfectly rational, and seems motivated, but somehow all their efforts come to nothing. A social worker might be helping them with something practical or clearly useful, such as improving child care skills, or managing their anger in their marriage. But, however sensible the programs of improvement we agree on, the people we are working with never seem to be able to carry them out. Once this happens several times, we may realize that some important hidden emotion is preventing them doing what they most want to achieve.

I once worked with a young man in his teens, for example, who often got into trouble taking powerful motor vehicles without the owner's consent, being caught driving them at speed. He agreed several times to avoid social situations that often led up to this behavior, such as going out with friends and drinking. Even so, he often took and drove fast vehicles on his own, not in the social situation we were worried about. By talking at some length about what he felt when he was doing this, it became clear that social pressures and events were not the major factor. Exploring his feelings of excitement and control revealed a motivation concerned with repressing his feelings about his macho father who was contemptuous of his small stature and lack of interest in sport. He was unable to confront his father's attitudes directly, appearing rather apathetic to his parents, and had displaced his anger and frustration into this behavior, trying to demonstrate his masculinity through fast driving. Here it is not just that he wanted to demonstrate his masculinity, but also that he is moved to do this because of his relationships; problem behavior often goes back to relationship.

Psychodynamic Ideas about Intervention

The starting point of psychodynamic intervention is also your relationship with the people you are involved with. You pay close attention to what they are saying and observe carefully patterns of behavior and difficulties, spotting uncertainties and inconsistencies between what is said and done. In talking, you stay neutral in your attitude, because that enables you to be open to the people you are working with so that they can project onto you their feelings about themselves and others. They can express anger about their spouse's behavior, for example, by saying what they would say, but feel they cannot, to the spouse. This acceptance of feelings helps people open up to you, because you are clearly secure about allowing difficulty and emotion to be expressed. It also helps people feel that you really are listening to what they say; your neutrality makes it clear that you are not judging either way, but accepting how they think and feel. Focusing rationally on service delivery is sometimes unhelpful when important emotions are in play.

You look for links and consistencies, too. For example, are they expressing the same feelings about their child's behavior that they feel about their parent, even if this is inappropriate? I once watched a man cajoling his tearful three-year-old daughter to be extraordinarily neat in his tidy house, after previously he had told me how disorganized his mother, who had mental health problems, was in his childhood. His well-kept house was his reaction against his mother's chaos, and his attitude to his daughter expressed a perhaps inexpressible fear of his mother's problems recurring in the next generation.

"Working through" is an important way of dealing with the issues you have identified. As emotions or difficulties come to the surface, the respectful way of dealing with them is to engage with them. Following up the previous example:

> It seems very important to you to keep your house neat and tidy, do you think that's more important for you than other people you know ... why do you think you're unusual in that respect ... what's the most important thing to keep neat ... are there other things that might be a bit less important ... could you emphasize neatness at the end of the day rather than all the time ...?

Detailed exploration may help to give dignity to important feelings and past relationships. Then you can go on to how his daughter feels about it, how she may compare herself with what goes on in friends' houses, whether some things may be more important than others, doing tidiness together and so on. Clarify, summarize, confirm as you come to the point of deciding what to do.

An important point about "working through" is connecting the emotions with the past and how they affect the present. We avoid encouraging people to repeat the same conversation continually about their fears and anxieties: that gets them stuck in a cycle of problems, rather than looking for solutions. It is important to focus on emotions that have been expressed (and clarified: was it anger, frustration or ...?) and events that were observed and you can agree about, so there is a clear focus for intervention.

This account suggests that psychodynamic practice is often concerned with long-term personal change that affects people's social relations. It is best pursued where your responsibilities are long term, and enable you to build relationships with someone and their family and friends. Examples include children in foster or residential care, preventive work with parents, disabled people, people with mental health problems, people with addictions, and older people and caregivers. These are situations where your agency is providing care and support over a period and where their emotions and responses to the social situations that affect them are crucial elements of what you need to tackle together. Such agency responsibilities form an important distinction between social work and counseling and psychotherapy practice.

Consequently, important psychodynamic social work theories use psychological and emotional work as part of a "problem-solving" practice (Perlman, 1957). This involves differentiating among the problems in the social life of the people they help, identifying social issues that need resolving alongside the personal and psychological. The counselor and psychotherapist concentrate on improving psychological functioning as broadly as possible, the social worker does so as part of resolving specific social issues in people's lives. For that, careful analysis of the problems and their social causes is a crucial part of social work, in a way that is not true of counseling and psychotherapy. Functional psychodynamic theory identifies the importance of structuring your interventions according to agency function and to time phases. People come, or are sent, to particular agencies because the purposes of that agency seem relevant to the problems they are facing. Focusing on meeting that function, therefore, is essential to everything else you do and connects directly with the relevant emotional and psychological issues. If your task is child safeguarding, focus on that; if it is adult care assessments, do that first as part of building a long-term relationship. It is also important to manage your work in planned phases, so that things do not drag on. Even though psychodynamic practice may be most suitable for situations where you are dealing with the long term, that does not mean that you can be undisciplined about the issues you are dealing with. You can also build on one achievement to make progress with others, and return to issues only partly resolved.

Conclusion: Critique and Evaluation of Psychodynamic Theory

Psychodynamic theory has been criticized in three important ways. Attack on its influence in social work came, first, from learning theory and what has become cognitive-behavioral therapy. These theoretical positions emphasize clarifying and modifying specific problem behaviors and adaptations to thinking about our perceptions of the external world (see Chapter 5 in this volume). They criticize the metaphorical elements of psychodynamic theory – mental structures, such as the ego or the unconscious do not exist, and responses like defense mechanisms cannot be easily tied down in an experiment or other quantitative research. It was not easy to identify clear results from research on psychodynamic practice in the mid-twentieth century (Fischer, 1976; Sheldon, 1987).

The second area of criticism has been that psychodynamic theory originated in psychiatry, it reflects the cultural milieu of its sources: a largely male, authoritarian, middle-European medical profession which has a limited conception of normal behavior. Early psychoanalytic interpretations of homosexuality, for example, saw it as connected with damaged relationships between mothers and sons, and women are assumed to have mainly domestic and maternal social roles. These are simply wrong in modern conceptions of gender and sexuality.

The third area of criticism has come from critical or radical social work. It is that by emphasizing internal psychological reactions and interpersonal relationships, it leads social work to neglect the social causes of many of the problems that are referred to social work agencies, poverty and inequality among them. It implies an acceptance that social problems arise from people's psychological inadequacies, rather than reacting to clear evidence of social determinants of difficulties, such as the recent work on the social determinants of health, which show that poor people live for longer in ill-health and die younger than rich people (Marmot Review Team, 2010).

There are some answers to these points. One advantage of psychodynamic theory is that it sees people as complex mixtures of drives, resistances and rational management. To be human is to be complex, and many people have valued the rich metaphorical set of ideas offered by psychodynamic theories for understanding and intervening in people's personal reactions to social issues. Briggs's (2005) summary of later research suggests that psychodynamic interventions have empirically demonstrated effectiveness, and developing flexible methods of research have identified positive achievements. Because of its complex conceptual world, psychoanalysis has made contributions to feminist thinking and research, for example in the work of Juliet Mitchell (1975) and

Janet Sayers (1992), and social thinking more broadly. And it is important not to deny the role of psychological and emotional issues in many of the problems that social workers face, and the way that greater resilience to social pressures may be generated by psychodynamic work.

On the positive side, because it helps people "make sense" of what happened to them in the past and how this is affecting current feelings and thoughts that are otherwise inexplicable, many people value a practice that explores and helps them learn from their life experience. Psychodynamic theory also emphasizes the importance of careful observation of behavior to identify patterns, so that we can explore and test out how these have emerged from life experiences and past relationships. Connected with this, psychodynamic theory proposes that we must be precise about differentiating between and clarifying the problems that are presented to social work agencies, and focusing on the responsibilities that our agencies are faced with. Finally, the psychodynamic focus on emotions and relationships offers us a practice model that develops engagement with people and their troubles that stands any social work practice in good stead.

Points to Ponder

1. Thinking about a mainly practical assessment or intervention you have worked on, what emotional and relationships issues were also raised?

2. Reflect on a difficult issue in your own or someone else's life and build up a series of questions that would help in working through the difficulties.

3. Look at a listing of the responsibilities or a social work agency you are involved with: what emotional and relationships issues might arise around each responsibility.

Key Texts

Goldstein, E., Miehls, D. and Ringel, S. (2009). *Advanced clinical social work practice: Relational principles and techniques.* New York: Columbia University Press.

Megele, C. (2015). *Psychosocial and relationship-based practice.* Northwich, UK: Critical Publishing.

Ruch, G., Turney, D. and Ward, A. (Eds.) (2010). *Relationship-based social work: Getting to the heart of practice.* London: Jessica Kingsley Publishers.

References

Borden, B. (2009). *Contemporary psychodynamic theory and practice*. Chicago: Lyceum.

Bowlby, J. (1969, 1973, 1980). *Attachment and loss*. (Vols. 1–3) London: Hogarth Press.

Briggs, S. (2005). Psychoanalytic research in the era of evidence-based practice. In: M. Bower (Ed.) *Psychoanalytic theory for social work practice: Thinking under fire*. London: Routledge, pp. 15–30.

Cohen, B. T. (2017). Trump just made a Freudian slip that reveals how he REALLY feels about America. Retrieved 4th April 2017 from: http://occupydemocrats. com/2017/03/17/trump-just-made-freudian-slip-reveals-really-feels-america/.

Fischer, J. (1976). *The effectiveness of social casework*. Springfield, IL: Charles C. Thomas.

Goldstein, E., Miehls, D. and Ringel, S. (2009). *Advanced clinical social work practice: Relational principles and techniques*. New York: Columbia University Press.

Jung, C. G. (2002). *The undiscovered self*. London: Routledge.

Karl, J. M. and Wandrei, K. E. (Eds.) (1994). *Person-in-environment system: The PIE classification system for social functioning problems*. Washington DC: NASW Press.

Marmot Review Team (2010). *Fair society, healthy lives: A strategic review of health inequalities in England post-2010* (The Marmot Review). London: Marmot Review.

Megele, C. (2015). *Psychosocial and relationship-based practice*. Northwich, UK: Critical Publishing.

Mitchell, J. (1975). *Psychoanalysis and feminism*. Harmondsworth, UK: Penguin.

Perlman, H. H. (1957). *Social casework: A problem-solving process*. Chicago: University of Chicago Press.

Rogers, C. R. (1951). *Client-centered therapy: Its current practice, implications and theory*. London: Constable.

Ruch, G., Turney, D. and Ward, A. (Eds.) (2010). *Relationship-based social work: Getting to the heart of practice*. London: Jessica Kingsley Publishers.

Salzberger-Wittenberg, I. (1970). *Psychoanalytic insights and relationships: A Kleinian approach*. London: Routledge & Kegan Paul.

Sayers, J. (1992). *Mothering psychoanalysis*. Harmondsworth, UK: Penguin.

Sheldon, B. (1987). Implementing findings from social work effectiveness research. *British Journal of Social Work* 17(6), pp. 573–86.

Wilkins, P. (2015). *Person-centred therapy*. London: Routledge.

Woods, M. E. and Hollis, F. (1999). *Casework: A psychosocial therapy* (5th Edn.). New York: McGraw-Hill.

5

COGNITIVE-BEHAVIORAL THERAPY

Paul Stepney and Paul Davis

Introduction

First there were behavioral approaches that developed from the work of Pavlov (1927), Skinner (1953) and later Bandura (1977), whose social learning theory recognized that behavior is influenced by interpretation (see Sheldon, 2012). As Bandura (1977) famously noted: "humans do not simply respond to stimuli, they actively interpret them" (p. 59). Cognitive theory was also a significant "second wave" influence derived from the work of Ellis (1962) and Beck (1989), who were working with clients experiencing anxiety and depression. Finally, cognitive-behavioral therapy (CBT) emerged as a rational and structured way of first understanding, and then responding to, problematic behaviors drawing on the crucial link across observable behavior/thought processes/emotions and feelings.

CBT was developed in clinical settings by psychologists (Payne, 2014) and, following the influential Layard (2004) report into the United Kingdom's mental health services, has become more widely used by social workers and other professionals (Ronen and Freeman, 2007). Its popularity is in part due to its strong evidential base (Sheldon, 2011), especially in the short term, development of later "third wave" holistic models and the contrast between CBT and traditional longer-term methods. The latter can be criticized for being less effective and resource heavy. Both the traditional and later holistic models of CBT focus on changes that can be brought about relatively quickly (Wills with Sanders, 2013).

The Core Ideas of CBT

Social work often involves attempts to change behavior that is proving problematic in some way to the individual concerned or to others. Much can therefore be gained from a fuller and broader understanding of behavioral change. Behavior is based on beliefs (cognitions) that shape our responses to situations. To change behavior is likely to involve changing the relevant thoughts and feelings and managing physical reactions as well. This is set out in Figure 5.1

This figure can be used when working with clients to understand their cognitive-behavioral reactions to an event. CBT recognizes that there is a conscious thought between an external event and a particular emotional response (Beck, 1989). It draws upon basic elements of operant conditioning, as in working with children where, for example, a child screams and gets a candy to shut her/him up – this behavior is now more likely because it has been reinforced by the reward. On this basis, it is possible to conceptualize this in terms of an ABC chart:

- "A" stands for Antecedent or what triggered the event;
- "B" for Beliefs or interpretation of behavior associated with the event; and
- "C" for the behavioral consequences concerning what follows the event.

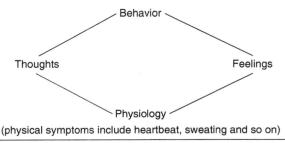

Figure 5.1 The four modalities of CBT.

There are particular beliefs about specific issues, but also "core beliefs" and central cognitions that are very influential. For example, low self-esteem causes us to believe we are not worthy. Work may involve helping people to revise their beliefs so that they do not create negative consequences (cognitive element). It is likely to involve identifying the core beliefs and seeking to change them through gently challenging, questioning their logic, and then replacing them with more constructive beliefs. Alongside this it is important to reinforce positive elements of behavior as well as "extinguishing" negative behaviors. As Skinner (1953) argued, behavior is a function of its consequences. Hence, the role of reinforcement becomes critical in shaping behavior and modeling new responses, but this should be seen within a wider social context of interacting with others.

The following practice focus illustrates a behavioral problem from the field of mental health.

Practice Focus 5.1

Glen was a 50-year-old man who became socially isolated after a succession of negative experiences with neighbors, family and authority figures that go back to his school days. He became ill, lost his warehouse job due to alcohol abuse and became a recluse. He was referred to the drug and alcohol team by his doctor, but intervention could not begin until Glen was able to leave his home. The social worker felt that CBT, combined with exercise and social activities, could help.

Brief Discussion of Practice Focus 5.1

At first, Glen was reluctant to engage with any professionals, but grudgingly agreed to CBT. Central to Glen's core beliefs was that people made him feel inadequate and were out to get him. This was how he felt he had been treated at work, at school and when something went wrong he became the "fall guy." He now avoided social contact and withdrew at any sign of conflict. During CBT, potentially conflictual situations were identified and Glen's negative beliefs were challenged and he was encouraged to think more positively. He had reasonable communication skills, so role play was used to demonstrate that interactions could be rewarding. His interest in gardening and walking was also encouraged. Slowly progress was made, through a process of gradual exposure and exercise, with Glen going out and eventually visiting the drop-in center where, importantly, social activities and support were available.

It follows that CBT should avoid adopting a narrow and individualistic focus, and consider additional psychological and social factors. It is important to recognize how experiences of discrimination can have an adverse effect on self-esteem and other mental health problems. Further, the frustration involved can lead to social isolation, as in the case of Glen, or fuel anger management problems – hence, the need to develop a more holistic, sociologically informed model.

"Third Wave" Holistic Models of CBT

According to Wills with Sanders (2013) traditional CBT models, centered upon the four modalities from Figure 5.1, were based upon three elements – establishing a therapeutic relationship, using scientific and measurable techniques, and concentrating at the level of "symptoms." However, they report that, later, "third wave" holistic models of CBT have emerged that attempt to move beyond this and incorporate additional elements and contextual factors. Holistic models begin (similar to traditional CBT) with the client's presenting problems (for example, "I feel like shit when I wake up in the morning, I try hard but then I find I fail at everything and just give up"), but then seek to understand behavior/ emotion/ thought/physiological processes by incorporating three additional core elements:

1. Acknowledging the significance of external events that have provoked feelings of loss, threat or despair.
2. Examining the client's interpersonal relationships and beliefs, including emotions and imagery, which may have been shaped by earlier childhood experiences (attachment theory).
3. Considering meta-cognitions and undertaking an analysis of how "underlying schemata" of thinking may reinforce a client's problems. For example, a client who says that worrying about

their worries will protect them from nasty surprises, not only reinforces the initial worries, but also creates thought processes that incubates fresh worries (Wills with Sanders, 2013). Ruminating and overthinking will invariably make many problems worse.

More recently "third wave" models have emerged, influenced by two further factors:

4. The growth of acceptance and commitment therapy (ACT), which aims to achieve a balance between acceptance of problems, commitment to values and change (Hayes with Smith, 2005).
5. Allied to ACT has been an increasing recognition of the existential need for mindfulness to help clients live in the present, rather than have their thoughts submerged by past problems and future worries.

Acceptance and Commitment Therapy (ACT)

ACT derives from the work of Steven Hayes and colleagues at the University of Nevada. Hayes was brought up in California, became a clinical psychologist and began practicing CBT. In the 1970s he experienced panic attacks as a young clinician and found that conventional methods did not help. However, when he became an academic and researched what happened during therapy, he recognized that traditional CBT gave insufficient recognition to two important factors:

*   First, the context in which thinking and language takes place. He recognized that our thinking connects up with many environmental and social issues. There is a strong connection between events that cause us suffering and the social context in which they occur.
*   Second, the role of emotions and how traditional CBT teaches people to detect and change negative thoughts, with the danger that they become suppressed. Hayes suggests that acceptance of negative thoughts may be a better way to begin the process of managing problems and healing ourselves.

The implication of this is that a strong focus on the language of "distorted thoughts" can easily lead to clients becoming further entangled in a fusion of negative thoughts. Instead, ACT encourages clients to address acceptance and commitment issues, and the values consistent with the kind of lives they want to lead, before focusing on problem solving and change. ACT has been found to be especially helpful in tackling problems of addiction, anxiety, discrimination and stigma (Hayes with Smith, 2005).

These ideas are at the heart of approaches to mindfulness and how this concept might be incorporated within CBT, to help manage the tension between how life is and how we want it to be – see the "Big Think" interview with Steven Hayes at: http://bigthink.com/stevenhayes.

The following brief practice example illustrates how ACT might work:

> A first-year student, Sara, feels she is a failure and thinks about giving up her course (see Figure 5.2).
> Initial trigger: experiencing difficulty with a particular task, like writing an essay.

Instead of focusing on negative thoughts associated with "failure," the therapist will ask Sara to try and accept that writing essays is something many first-year students find difficult. The therapist said: "It's okay to feel like this, so just let these thoughts float around in your head and be more compassionate with yourself." Once the acute pain becomes accepted and subsides, problem solving with the educational counselor to help with essay writing can begin.

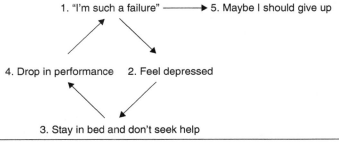

Figure 5.2 Sara, a first-year student, feels she is a failure and thinks about giving up her course.

One of the advantages of holistic models influenced by ACT is that they offer us a way of acknowledging wider contextual factors – in particular, to address issues of stigma and discrimination. For example, one client, Terry (not his real name), told us about the route he took to get from his bedsit to the drop-in center. Terry went back along the seafront and then cut down an alley, across a car park and then along a footpath that ran alongside the center. When we asked him why he took this roundabout route at least a mile longer than was necessary, Terry said: "Because I don't want to go near the shops or be seen by anyone ... I don't want people knowing I come down here." The stigma and discrimination people with mental health problems experience in the community are clearly very real issues.

Using CBT in Practice

CBT has very wide potential applications:

- A broad range of mental health problems, including anxiety, depression, phobias and addictions;
- Parenting issues;
- Anger management in relation to abuse, as well as identity issues; and
- Conflict management.

A number of writers have written usefully about CBT in practice, as well as chapters in theory and methods texts – for example, Payne (2014) and Coulshed and Orme (2012). Using CBT in practice typically involves a structured set of sessions to provide focus and encourage engagement. If handled skillfully and sensitively, and as part of a holistic approach, it can be a very empowering social work method.

According to Coulshed and Orme (2012), CBT can be broken into eight stages:

1. Engagement;
2. Problem focus on particular event or problem;
3. Problem assessment (use ABC chart, also identify feelings/ thoughts/behavior/physiology) and establish as precisely as

possible "in what way would the client like to feel/think/behave differently;"

4. Teach cognitive principles: monitor thoughts, modify negative with positive thoughts ... "should," rather than "should not," "can," rather than "cannot;"

5. Dispute and challenge negative assumptions ... also those who claim they did not think before they acted in an event are declining consciously or unconsciously to remember what was in their mind;

6. Encourage self-disputing – through use of questions, such as: Is there another way of looking at this? Are you expecting yourself to be perfect, are you jumping to the wrong conclusions? (See Palmer and Dryden, 1995, for a more elaborate list of self-dispute questions that can be used.);

7. Set behavioral homework to carry on reinforcing work done in the session using everyday situations and natural reinforcers, such as praise. Also ask the client to keep a record or diary of what happens and review this in the next session; and

8. Ending: self-therapy and building in support to maintain improvement.

(adapted from Coulshed and Orme, 2012, pp. 181–182)

According to Palmer and Dryden, when using CBT the practitioner:

assists clients to become aware of internal automatic thoughts (often negative), cognitive distortions, and underlying schemata or unspoken rules and ... helps them to challenge these stress-inducing beliefs by using a number of cognitive and behavioural strategies.

(1995, p. 303)

Traditional methods of CBT have the following characteristics:

1. Concentrating on the short term "here and now," beginning with "symptoms."

2. Focus on problems defined by the client and factors that maintain and reinforce the problem.

3. Goal directed, mutually agreed with client (similar to task-centered practice).
4. Emphasis on sound empirical evaluation of intervention from baseline data at the outset.
5. Emphasis on "doing" and strategies to practice alternative thoughts/feelings and behavior. The practitioner may be directive. Such strategies can be transferred to tackle other problems, thus empowering the client without further professional help.

Holistic models build upon these features by incorporating five additional components:

*   Acknowledging that external events may create feelings of loss and despair.
*   Examining past and present interpersonal relationships as appropriate.
*   Considering whether underlying schemata concerning the way the client "thinks about thinking" is contributing to the problem.
*   Addressing acceptance, commitment and mindfulness issues before focusing on change.
*   Assessing the impact of social factors, such as stigma and discrimination.

Three Practical Points to Remember when Using Holistic CBT Methods

1. Help clients to recognize that they can think and put their thinking skills to good effect. According to Payne, giving exercises as homework is a good way of reinforcing the concept of "learning by doing" (2014, p. 181). You do not need sophisticated formats – be creative! (worksheets can be accessed from websites or devised to help the client make progress).
2. Consider whether negative thinking should be accepted, as in ACT, or restructured (see Wills with Sanders, 2013, p. 160).
3. Explore alternative strategies for valued action. Use straightforward terminology, chosen by the client.

The following practice focus brings out some of these issues:

Practice Focus 5.2

Asha was a 46-year-old quiet, unassuming woman with long-standing mental health issues who was referred by her doctor. She lived alone and was agitated and anxious when she came to the drop-in center. Her previous work was in retail, including a convenience store. Recently she became worried about the health of a close friend who was supportive during her divorce. In the past she had attended various activity groups, been a volunteer and said CBT helped with her depression. Asha's aim was to make new friends and lead a normal life with fewer worries.

Discussion of Practice Focus 5.2

At the center it was agreed that further CBT could help Asha become more assertive and confident. Further, a work preparation course could assist job searches. CBT concentrated on improving her self-image, positive thinking and being assertive with those around her. This enabled her to be more realistic about what support she could give her friend without feeling guilty. Adult education courses and volunteering opportunities enabled Asha to regain her confidence and become more optimistic about the future. Staff were available throughout to talk through different options and this provided Asha with structure and security.

Using CBT to Tackle Addictions

Cognitive-behavioral methods are applicable to working with clients with addictive forms of behavior, particularly drugs, alcohol and gambling, as well as body dysmorphia, eating disorders, phobias and offending behaviors. The following practice focus highlights the catastrophic effect that drinking can have.

Practice Focus 5.3

Ruth had recently retired and suffered from alcohol addiction following the loss of her husband. She had lost contact with her family and the bank had just repossessed her home. At this point she came to the center for advice, and presented as a capable and intelligent person who needed to talk. After general discussion, the interview progressed as follows:

Social worker: Look, Ruth, what do you see at present as your most serious problem?

Ruth: (Initial silence ...) Well, I don't know where to start, but suppose it's finding somewhere to live.

Social worker: Yeah, that's certainly a serious issue, but what about the drinking? How much are you drinking at present?

Ruth: Oh I don't know ... it varies from day to day. Look, I know what you're getting at ... I've just remembered, I've got to go and pick up a prescription ... I'll come back next week.

Social worker: Okay, Ruth, that's fine, come back when you're ready.

Predictably, a month went by before Ruth came back. However, this time she said she desperately needed help finding somewhere to live but, importantly, she had been thinking and wanted to do something about her drinking. The social worker then drew a circle, calling it "Ruth's cycle of change" and wrote six words around it:

1. Pre-contemplation;
2. Contemplation;
3. Determination;
4. Action;
5. Maintenance; and
6. Exit if successful, but, if relapse, then return to stage 2 or 3.
   (adapted from Prochaska and DiClemente, 1984)

When Ruth first made contact she was at the *Pre-contemplation stage* and ambivalent about addressing her drinking. However, after a month, when the situation deteriorated, Ruth moved from *Contemplation* to *Determination*, as she acknowledged that action was needed. This represented a turning point in favor of change and a good time to consider the range of cognitive and behavioral strategies available. Ruth had a history of good intentions, setting unrealistic goals and then turning to drink when things went wrong. Her self-talk reflected this and needed to be changed.

CBT in the *Action stage* involved drawing up a plan to rebuild her life without drink supported by cognitive and practical strategies, such as positive thinking, assertive self-talk and non-alcoholic rewards to counteract her belief that "something always goes wrong." This was supplemented by moving into sheltered accommodation, where she could make new friends and develop new interests. During the *Maintenance stage* the challenge is to sustain the action plan and monitor progress. However, for some clients, maintenance becomes a major challenge and the possibility of *Relapse* is ever present.

Unfortunately, within two months, Ruth relapsed. She returned to the surreptitious consumption of vodka which undermined her well-being. When an attempt was made to address this, she became instantly hostile and denied consuming any drink. She was not only in denial, but also projected her fear and insecurity onto others for what had happened.

It emerged that Ruth's underlying schema of core beliefs was so profound that this undermined her recovery, unsettled her and provoked a relapse. The issue of loss remains to be addressed. When Ruth is ready, a holistic approach combining the cycle of change, with acceptance and commitment, will be needed. Also transactional analysis may offer insights, as Ruth has a tendency to regress to child-like behavior and seek parenting figures to rescue her (see Payne, 2014, pp. 279–280).

Research Evidence on the Effectiveness of CBT

Sheldon points out that there is a large body of empirical research on the efficacy of CBT (Sheldon, 2012). Bradshaw (1998, 2003) reports on the effectiveness of CBT in working with clients with schizophrenia in the US, and Gould et al. (2001) in the UK. CBT has proved effective in relation to alcohol addiction (Morgenstern and Longabaugh, 2000), although identifying the precise mechanisms at work remains elusive. Earlier, research by Mason and Norris (1990) led to the setting up of Aquarius, an alcohol counseling service in the UK, and more recently a skills manual for workers (Aquarius, 2016). Research evidence on the effectiveness of ACT is still emerging (see Wills with Sanders, 2013).

Long-term Effectiveness of CBT

In a random controlled trial of people with depression carried out by five UK universities, published in *The Lancet* in 2016, it was found that 43% of patients who received CBT maintained improvement over a period of 40 months (www.psych.ox.ac.uk/news/study-finds-cbt-offers-long-term-benefits-for-people-with-depression). In another longitudinal study with people suffering from anxiety disorders, it was found that improvements were maintained over 12 months (DiMauro et al., 2013). This suggests that CBT is effective at least over the short to medium term, although long-term effectiveness is more difficult to establish.

Critiques of Cognitive-behavioral Approaches

A certain amount of controversy and criticism has always surrounded CBT. First, the strength of CBT is that it is an empirically tested method with a good record of effectiveness (Sheldon, 2012). However, as Payne (2014) notes, accepting the efficacy of traditional models of CBT requires acceptance of positivist scientific methods. These have been criticized for being preoccupied with observable and measurable "facts" or hard data. Further, behaviorist claims about objectivity, political neutrality, and mistrust of qualitative methods, have unfortunately aligned CBT with more conservative traditions. Traditional CBT is popular with medical practitioners, clinical psychologists and nursing staff who have been trained in scientific methods of practice.

Significantly, family doctors in the UK are now being recommended to refer patients with mental health problems to CBT practitioners, rather than prescribing anti-depressant drugs. However, as the influential Layard report (2004) noted, there are not enough CBT practitioners available, and this requires considerable investment of funds for training. Now, more than a decade has passed and access to CBT remains limited, with long waiting lists in many areas. In such situations other talking therapies may be appropriate. There is now a golden opportunity in the UK for social workers with CBT training to work in partnership with Health staff, while in the US this is an issue about how to make

CBT available to groups routinely excluded from private market provision. In Europe the availability of CBT is typically through third sector organizations.

Another obstacle is the technical jargon and the perceived formality of the processes involved. While some clients welcome formal structures, others find this off putting. This has led to criticism that CBT is controlling and vests too much power in the practitioner. It is important, therefore, that informed consent is negotiated at the outset, notwithstanding where CBT is a mandatory requirement of a court order for drug-related offences. The potential for manipulation or control is present in all social work methods, consequently, the need for appropriate ethical safeguards.

Conclusion

CBT has come a long way during the past 50 years, and more holistic and "third wave" models now complement those with a traditional problem-orientated focus. Holistic models, such as ACT, where the focus is on acceptance and commitment before change, and the integration of mindfulness, all create a dynamic framework for extending the practice of CBT. Such models, as we noted, are generally supported by good research evidence.

A longer-term perspective is always needed, especially in the mental health field where recovery is more realistic than cure. Further, behavioral activation through social activity and "doing" can be highly therapeutic. It follows that tackling problems of social isolation and creating a positive identity, attached to longer-term social roles, are as important as individual methods. Holistic models of CBT are consistent with developing critically reflective practice, and, importantly, represent an evidence-based way of integrating CBT with other approaches to achieve high-quality practice.

Points to Ponder

1. Is it possible to combine acceptance, as in ACT, with restructuring negative thoughts, as in traditional CBT? Take a practice example, such as a client with anxiety, and explore how this might work.

2. How might holistic models of CBT, such as ACT, be integrated with other methods? What methods lend themselves to this?

3. How might CBT assist practitioners to develop partnership working with colleagues in health and education?

Key Texts

Wills, F. with Sanders, D. (2013). *Cognitive behaviour therapy: Foundations for practice,* (3rd Edn.). London: Sage.

Ronen, T. and Freeman, A. (Eds) (2007). *Cognitive behavior therapy in clinical social work practice.* New York: Springer.

Sheldon, B. (2012). Cognitive-behavioural methods in social care: A look at the evidence. In P. Stepney and D. Ford (Eds) (2012). *Social work models, methods and theories.* Lyme Regis, UK: Russell House Publishing, pp. 123–151.

References

Aquarius (2016). Focus on recovery. www.recoveryfocus.org.uk/join-in/talking.

Bandura, A. (1977). *Social learning theory.* Englewood Cliffs, NJ: Prentice Hall.

Beck, A. (1989). *Cognitive therapy and the emotional disorders.* Harmondsworth, UK: Penguin.

Big Think web portal. http://bigthink.com/stevenhayes.

Bradshaw, W. (1998). Cognitive-behavioural treatment of schizophrenia: A case study, *Journal of Cognitive Psychotherapy,* 12(1), pp. 13–26.

Bradshaw, W. (2003). Use of single-system research to evaluate the effectiveness of cognitive-behaviour treatment of schizophrenia. *British Journal of Social Work,* 33(7), pp. 885–899.

Coulshed, V. and Orme, J. (2012). *Social work practice* (5th Edn.). Basingstoke, UK: Palgrave Macmillan.

DiMauro, J., Domingues, J., Fernandez, G. and Tolin, D. (2013). Long-term effectiveness of CBT for anxiety disorders in an adult outpatient clinic sample: A follow-up study, *Behaviour Research and Therapy,* 51(2), pp. 82–86.

Ellis, A. (1962). *Reason and emotion in psychotherapy.* Secaucus, NJ: Lyle Stewart.

Gould, R. A., Mueser, K. T., Bolton, E., Mays, V. and Goff, D. (2001). Cognitive therapy for psychosis in schizophrenia: An effect size analysis. *Schizophrenia Research,* 48, pp. 335–342.

Hayes, S. C. with Smith, S. (2005). *Get out of your mind and into your life: The new acceptance and commitment therapy.* Oakland, CA: New Harbinger.

Layard, R. (2004). *Mental health: Britain's biggest social problem?* London: The Cabinet Office.

Mason, P. and Norris, H. (1990). *Personal skills training for problem drinkers: A counsellor's guide* (2nd Edn.). Birmingham, UK: Aquarius.

Morgenstern, J. and Longabaugh, R. (2000). Cognitive-behaviour treatment for alcohol dependence: A review of evidence for its hypothesized mechanisms of action. *Addiction,* 95(10), pp. 1475–1490.

Palmer, S. and Dryden, W. (1995). *Counselling for stress problems.* London: Sage.

Payne, M. (2014). *Modern social work theory* (4th Edn.). Basingstoke, UK: Palgrave Macmillan.

Pavlov, I. P. (1927). *Conditioned reflexes: An investigation of the physiological activity of the cerebral cortex.* Oxford: Oxford University Press.

Prochaska, J. and DiClemente, C. (1984). *The transtheoretical approach: Crossing the traditional boundaries of therapy.* Homewood, IL: Dow Jones Irwin.

Ronen, T. and Freeman, A. (Eds.) (2007). *Cognitive behavior therapy in clinical social work practice.* New York: Springer.

Sheldon, B. (2011). *Cognitive-behavioural therapy: Research and practice in health and social care.* (2nd Edn.). London: Routledge.

Sheldon, B. (2012). Cognitive-behavioural methods in social care: A look at the evidence. In P. Stepney and D. Ford (Eds.) *(2012). Social work models, methods and theories.* Lyme Regis, UK: Russell House Publishing, pp. 123–151.

Skinner, B. F. (1953). *Science and human behaviour.* London: Collier Macmillan.

Wills, F., with Sanders, D. (2013). *Cognitive therapy: Foundations for practice* (3rd Edn.). London: Sage. www.psych.ox.ac.uk/news/study-finds-cbt-offers-long-term-benefits-for-people-with-depression.

6

TASK-CENTERED PRACTICE

Ronald Rooney

Ms. Jones, a prospective client, seeks assistance from a social worker. She has special abilities and a limited work history. Ms. Jones wants to get a job utilizing her skills and yet is worried about losing access to her disability payments. How do the social worker and client decide to work together? What influences their decisions? Such decisions are influenced by a variety of factors, such as the helper's beliefs, skills and theories about change and the mission of the setting in which contact takes place (Hepworth et al., 2016).

The task-centered approach can inform such decisions by guiding the social worker and client to come to agreement on specific concerns which can be addressed feasibly in the time available. This recommendation comes from research that suggests that clients often receive five to eight sessions whatever the planned length of intervention (Hoyt, 2000; Reid and Shyne, 1969). A distinguishing feature of this approach is then making good use of available time by establishing a contract to focus on one to three key concerns or target problems to address within eight to twelve sessions.

For example, Ms. Jones might come to an agreement with the social worker that her primary concern is expressed as: "I do not have a job that fits my skills and interests." An assessment period is included to determine whether the problem can be addressed and to consider the surrounding context for addressing those concerns. For example, the context of Ms. Jones' concerns include the fact that Ms. Jones can work only a limited number of hours or she risks losing her support benefits. Hence part of her context is her indecision about the pros and cons of a full-time job and losing benefits. Would this be a wise or foolish decision? Ms. Jones might then agree to undertake a contract with the social worker to meet for eight to twelve sessions. The plan for these sessions might be to assess together her job prospects, including her skills and resources. Together, the social worker and client would develop tasks such as developing a resumé, preparing for job interviews through rehearsal or role plays. Other potential tasks might include consultation with benefit advisers about the risks should she lose benefits and not acquire a satisfactory permanent job. Before and after carrying out tasks, such as job interviews, the social worker and client would examine potential obstacles that might get in the way of progress.

The task-centered approach does not prioritize the social worker's beliefs about what would be appropriate for the client, assuming the problem which he or she wishes to address is not illegal or dangerous. It is the social worker's role to examine with the client whether the concern can be feasibly addressed in the time available.

In this chapter I present a brief history of the approach, outline its key elements, describe how it has been used, suggest contributions and challenges stimulated by the approach and, finally, point to the future.

Origins of the Task-Centered Approach

The task-centered approach emerged from an experimental study of the relative effects of planned short-term service (PSTS) and extended service to family service clients. Contrary to conventional wisdom, clients receiving PSTS received as much long-lasting assistance as those receiving extended service (Reid and Shyne, 1969). In addition, clients were less likely to drop out in PSTS, and those receiving extended service had relatively few additional sessions with more unilateral terminations. This social work study was consistent with later results from other helping professions supporting the efficacy of time-limited intervention (Hoyt, 2000; Wells and Gianetti, 1990).

William Reid concluded that, if clients receiving PSTS could do as well as those receiving continued service, without having a specific model of intervention prescribing more than length of service, intervention might be better with a model to guide it that was designed to produce results in a brief time period. Subsequently, William Reid collaborated with Laura Epstein to develop a model to explicitly guide social workers in time-limited practice (Reid and Epstein, 1972). The model was based on two principles:

1. Work was to be aimed at assisting clients in resolving target problems of their own choosing, and work should be guided where possible by empirical research. Integral to the model was an ongoing testing of the method: continual, public assessment of progress was owed to clients as much as to agencies and funders. Spiritually akin to the problem-solving model (Perlman, 1957), the task-centered approach focused on very specific problems in living. The central theme was the mutual design of tasks to alleviate problems in the environment. Problems were to be described in measurable terms, such that the success or lack thereof could be accessible to client and worker.

2. The model was to be a collaborative one in which the social worker was expert in helping clients reduce problems, not in prescribing or dictating what the problem was or how it should be approached. The approach was therefore an early example of practice being underpinned by the social work value of working in partnership.

Theory and the Task-Centered Approach

The task-centered approach was influenced by several practice models, such as the problem-solving model (Perlman, 1957) and the psychosocial approach (Hollis, 1964). Practice models guide the social worker in deciding what to do, what to assess, and how to intervene. Theories provide a rationale for explaining why to perform an intervention. The task-centered approach is eclectic in its approach to theory. As the approach is focused on how to resolve particular problems, theories are accessed to assist in understanding particular problems. It is in this sense that task-centered practice plays a part in theorizing practice, as discussed in Chapter 1 of this volume.

Among theories influencing the approach are systems theory, communication theory, role theory, psychoanalytic theory and learning theories (Reid and Epstein, 1972, p. 29). They are selected based on their empirical evidence to support theoretical assertions (Reid, 2000). Hence a social worker is free to draw on a range of theories relevant to specific problems. This again exemplifies well the process of theorizing practice, rather than the conventional idea of beginning with theory and then attempting to "apply" it to practice.

Outline of the Approach[1]

The task-centered practitioner is guided to be alert to the priorities of a referral source, yet clear about the model's aim to pursue problems as perceived by clients, as together they explore potential target problems. Target problems are problems in living acknowledged by the client and feasible for reduction or resolution in a limited time period. The task-centered practitioner then works with the client to prioritize identified target problems and specifically describe them in such a way that the success of efforts to improve will be measurable. Specific goals are then set that include measurable indicators of progress. Finally, an explicit contract for a set number of sessions is developed.

After establishing the basic contract, the social worker and client identify general tasks or strategies that they plan to use to address the problem. The tasks are a blueprint to guide efforts. Such strategies should draw on available empirical data about effective methods, but are decided upon conjointly with the client, again reflecting the use of partnership as part of the social work value base. General tasks are then elaborated into specific tasks for the client and social worker to complete between sessions. A key aspect of the approach is the anticipation of obstacles that might prevent success in achieving the task. Finally, task plans are summarized.

The middle phase includes a review of how the target problems are changing and of details of task-completion attempts. The task-centered practitioner praises efforts and returns with the client to explore obstacles that may have blocked achievement. In support of task development efforts, role plays or guided practice are often constructed to practice tasks in a safe environment. In addition, incentives may be constructed to enhance task efforts.

The social worker and client prepare for termination from the beginning session, as they regularly review the number of remaining sessions and tailor efforts toward the time remaining. The final session then includes a mutual assessment of progress and a review of learning about the steps in problem solving. As problems are seldom fully resolved, this stage often includes planning for further work with other formal and informal resources. In some cases, services may be extended or new contracts enacted if the client wishes it and there is reason to believe that the efforts will be successful.

Evidence Base for the Task-Centered Approach

The task-centered approach was an early exemplar of evidence-based practice (Kelly, 2013; see also Chapter 2 in this volume). There are over 200 published works on the approach including applications in ten countries – Fortune et al., 2010; Marsh, 2008). Research on the task-centered approach has included eight controlled studies that generally supported its efficacy (Colvin et al., 2008a; Gibbons et al., 1978, 1985; Larsen and Mitchell, 1980; Newcome, 1985; Reid, 1975, 1978, 1997; Reid and Bailey-Dempsey, 1995; Reid et al., 1980). Studies have been conducted with psychiatric outpatients and with children experiencing school-related problems, with reports of changes persisting over time in two studies (Reid, 1997).

One of the signal contributions of the task-centered approach has been its flexibility. It has been found useful in a range of public and private settings with varied populations: case management with frail elderly people (Naleppa and Reid, 2000), child welfare (Rooney, 1988; Rzepnicki, 1985), clients with serious and persistent mental health problems (Gibbons et al., 1985), students in elementary and high schools (Bailey-Dempsey and Reid, 1996; Colvin et al., 2008a, 2008b; Reid et al., 1980), and sibling aggression (Caspi, 2008), as well as in supervision (Caspi and Reid, 2002). Although most applications have been with voluntary clients in a variety of settings, the approach has also been integrated into approaches for work with clients who are involuntary or do not seek service (Magnano, 2009; Rooney and Mirick, 2017; Trotter, 2015).

Contributions

The task-centered approach has made at least five signal contributions to social work practice. First, Reid and Epstein described a metamodel for how social work models or approaches could be constructed (Reid and Epstein, 1972). Social work has long struggled with how to utilize approaches developed outside the field. Reid and Epstein suggested that the criteria by which information should be selected include the value base of social work, emphasizing collaboration and partnership, empirical evidence and applicability to social work settings and issues. Those criteria remain pertinent, as social work strives to incorporate evidence-based practice appropriately (see Chapter 2 in this volume).

Second, the task-centered approach has consistently modeled an empirical orientation to practice, seeking the best available knowledge as sources of information to assist clients in making informed decisions (Kelly, 2013). The creators consistently modeled this value through continual testing and revision of the approach. In addition, the model incorporated ongoing evaluation for the benefit of client and practitioner, as well as agency. Other contributions have included developing empirically derived practice guidelines (Caspi, 2008) and continued revision based on data of the Partnership in Prevention Program (Colvin et al., 2008a, 2008b).

Third, the task-centered approach has embodied the social work value of self-determination and supported client empowerment and facilitated strengths (Gutierrez et al., 1998; Saleebey, 2012). The approach has been used to teach practical problem-solving skills to clients through developing goals, assessing possible task strategies, anticipating obstacles and then reviewing what might have gotten in the way of task completion.

Fourth, the approach has proven quite flexible in adapting to varied settings and circumstances, ranging from resource provision to counseling. Most competing approaches focus on one area, generally aimed at psychological assistance or therapy (Kelly, 2013).

Finally, that flexibility has extended to recognizing the circumstances of clients who are not voluntary. Reid and Epstein were among the first social work theorists to address involuntary intervention circumstances (Epstein and Brown, 2002; Reid, 1978). The task-centered approach has played a prominent role in two leading approaches to work with involuntary clients (Trotter, 2015; Rooney and Mirick, 2017).

Limitations

One of the challenges facing the approach is also a strength: brief intervention is not the approach of choice for all situations, and the task-centered approach is not an all-purpose model (Gambrill, 1994). Indeed, one of the strengths of the task-centered approach has been its acknowledgment of limitations (Reid and Epstein, 1972). For example, clients who are grieving or have primarily expressive needs are guided to Rogerian techniques, such as reflective listening. Advocates of strengths-oriented and solution-focused approaches have suggested that the task-centered approach, and problem-solving approaches in general, may neglect client capacities and resources and focus on pathology (De Jong and Berg, 2002). While some problem-solving approaches may indeed focus on pathology and ignore resources, the task-centered approach has consistently focused on enhancing client resources and building on strengths. Gambrill suggested that it has borrowed some behavioral techniques without accurately applying them (Gambrill, 1994). It might be argued that borrowing some empirically based techniques and applying them in a new structure of practice is a hallmark of model development (Rothman and Thomas, 1994). Much of the initial research on the approach was conducted by proponents. However, that initial development has led to more than 200 books, articles and dissertations, most contributed by people who were not the original developers (Kelly, 2013).

Future Directions

William J. Reid and Laura Epstein did not become invested in struggles between problem-oriented approaches and strengths-oriented approaches or between empirically based approaches and all others, choosing to focus on areas of common interest, rather than areas of disagreement (McMillen et al., 2004; Shaw, 2004). Indeed, one of the major contributions of task-centered practice in the future may capitalize on the sturdy, flexible technology that adapts to so many social work practice contexts (Kelly, 2013). The future may include more productive exploration of how such approaches can contribute to, and be appropriately blended with, one another. For example, certain solution-focused techniques, such as asking coping questions, scaling questions and forms of the miracle question (see Chapter 10 in this volume) may be integrated as useful adjuncts to task-centered techniques (De Jong and Berg, 2002). However, the solution-focused approach appears to lack a technology for assessing what happens when well-planned goals go awry. Further, while the solution-focused approach is generally admirable in its exploration and facilitation of client resources, proponents might better guide practitioners in situations that are beyond some clients' experience, and outside information can contribute to informed decision making. Rather than focusing on shortcomings of other models, however, exploration of appropriate blending may draw on the strengths of both approaches. For example, the motivational interviewing approach offers considerable promise and an evidence base for assisting clients who do not currently acknowledge problems of concern to others (Miller and Rollnick, 2012). There has been a promising integration of the task-centered approach with motivational interviewing (Fassler, 2007). Integrating techniques designed to assist clients in pre-contemplation, in which they do not see a problem, or in contemplation, in which they have not made a decision to act on a concern, could be a useful adjunct to the problem search phase for task-centered clients who do not initially perceive a concern recognized by others. Such blending with other approaches can augment them as well by incorporating the task-centered approach's valuing of client-perceived concerns and focus on modifying the environment, rather than the more narrowly psychological focus of many other therapeutic approaches.

The context for social work practice, including managed care and concerns for effectiveness in public service, continues to support the relevance of the task-centered approach to helping clients address problems or goals of concern to them and doing so in a timely fashion.

Social work students now and in the future may assume that focusing on developing discreet, measurable and feasible goals with clients around their own expressed concerns is, and always has been, simply good social work practice. They may not know that this conventional wisdom is in large part a contribution of the task-centered approach (Kelly, 2013).

Points to Ponder

1. How much social work practice in your experience is brief and/ or time limited?
2. What is the value in engaging the client as a collaborator in planning and assessing strategies for resolving their concerns?
3. What is the value of an approach that draws on theory eclectically according to the fit and empirical evidence regarding resolution of the particular concerns clients bring?

Key Texts

Reid, W. J. and Epstein, L. (1972). *Task-centered casework*. New York: Columbia University Press.
Reid, W. J. (2000). *The task planner: An intervention resource for human service professionals.* New York: Columbia University Press.
Epstein, L. and Brown, L. (2002). *Brief treatment and a new look at the task-centered approach* (4th Edn) New York: Macmillan.

Note

1. The following section draws largely from Rooney (2010), Reid (2000) and Epstein and Brown (2002).

References

Bailey-Dempsey, C. and Reid, W. J. (1996). Intervention design and development: A case study. *Research on Social Work Practice* 6, pp. 208–28.
Caspi, J. (2008). Building a sibling aggression treatment model: Design and development research in action. *Research on Social Work Practice* 18, pp. 575–85.
Caspi, J. and Reid, W. J. (2002). *Educational supervision in social work*. New York: Columbia University Press.
Colvin, J., Lee, M., Magnano, J., and Smith, V. (2008a). The Partners in Prevention Program: The evaluation and evolution of the task-centered case management model. *Research on Social Work Practice* 18, pp. 607–15.
——. (2008b). The Partners in Prevention Program: Further development of the task-centered case management model. *Research on Social Work Practice* 18, pp. 586–95.
De Jong, P. and Berg, I. K. (2002). *Interviewing for solutions*. Pacific Grove, CA: Wadsworth.
Epstein, L. and Brown, L. (2002). *Brief treatment and a new look at the task-centered approach* (4th Edn.). New York: Macmillan.
Fassler, A. (2007). Merging task-centered social work and motivational interviewing in outpatient medication assisted substance abuse treatment: Model development for social work practice. Doctoral dissertation, Richmond, VA: Virginia Commonwealth University.
Fortune, A., McCallion, P., and Briar-Lawson, K. (Eds.) (2010). *Social work practice research for the 21st century*. New York: Columbia University Press.
Gambrill, E. (1994). What's in a name? Task-centered, empirical, and behavioral practice. *Social Service Review* 68(4), pp. 578–99.

Gibbons, J. S., Butler, J., Urwin, P., and Gibbons, J. L. (1978). Evaluation of a social work service for self-poisoning parents. *British Journal of Psychiatry* 133, pp. 111–18.

Gibbons, J., Bow, I., and Butler, J. (1985). Task-centered social work after parasuicide. In E. M. Goldberg, J. Gibbons, and I. Sinclair (Eds.). *Problems, tasks and outcomes: The evaluation of task-centered casework in three settings.* Boston: George Allen and Unwin, pp. 169–257.

Gutierrez, L. M., Parsons, R. J., and Cox, E. O. (1998). *Empowerment in social work practice: A source book.* Pacific Grove, CA: Brooks-Cole.

Hepworth, D., Rooney, R., Dewberry-Rooney, G., Strom-Gottfried, K., and Larson, J. A. (2016). *Direct social work practice* (10th Edn.). Pacific Grove, CA: Brooks-Cole.

Hollis, F. (1964). *Casework: A psychosocial therapy.* New York: Random House.

Hoyt, M. F. (2000). *Some stories are better than others: Doing what works in brief therapy and managed care.* Philadelphia: Brunner/Mazel.

Kelly, M. (2013). Task-centered practice. In T. Mizrahi and L. E. Davis (Eds.). *Encyclopedia of social work* (20th Edn). Oxford and New York: Oxford University Press, pp. 197–9.

Larsen, J. and Mitchell, C. (1980). Task-centered strength-oriented group work with delinquents. *Social Casework* 61, pp. 154–63.

Magnano, J. (2009). *Partners in success: An evaluation of an intervention for children with severe emotional disturbances.* Albany: State University of New York Press.

McMillen, J., Morris, L., and Sherraden, M. (2004). Ending social work's grudge match: Problems versus strengths. *Families in Society* 85(3), pp. 317–25.

Marsh, P. (2008). Task-centred work. In M. Davies (Ed.) *The Blackwell companion to social work* (3rd Edn.). Oxford: Blackwell, pp. 121–28.

Miller, W. R. and Rollnick, S. (2012). *Motivational interviewing: Preparing people to change addictive behavior* (3rd Edn). New York: Guilford.

Naleppa, M. J. and Reid, W. J. (2000). Integrating case management and brief-treatment strategies: A hospital-based geriatric program. *Social Work in Health Care* 31(4), pp. 1–23.

Newcome, K. (1985). Task-centered group work with the chronically mentally ill in day treatment. In A. E. Fortune (Ed.) *Task-centered practice with families and groups.* New York: Springer, pp. 78–91.

Perlman, H. (1957). *Social casework: A problem-solving process.* Chicago: University of Chicago Press.

Reid, W. J. (1975). An experimental test of a task-centered approach. *Social Work* 20, pp. 3–9.

——. (1978). *The task-centered system.* New York: Columbia University Press.

——. (1997). Research on task-centered practice. *Social Work Research* 21(3), pp. 132–7.

——. (2000). *The task planner: An intervention resource for human service professionals.* New York: Columbia University Press.

Reid, W. J. and Bailey-Dempsey, C. (1995). The effects of monetary incentives on school performance. *Families in Society* 76, pp. 331–40.

Reid, W. J. and Epstein, L. (1972). *Task-centered casework.* New York: Columbia University Press.

Reid, W. J. and Shyne, A. W. (1969). *Brief and extended casework.* New York: Columbia University Press.

Reid, W. J., Epstein, L., Brown, L. B., Tolson, E. R., and Rooney, R. H. (1980). Task-centered school social work. *Social Work in Education* 2, pp. 7–24.

Rooney, R. H. (1988). Measuring task-centered training effects on practice: Results of an audiotape study in a public agency. *Journal of Continuing Social Work Education* 4, pp. 2–7.

——. (2010). Task-centered practice in the United States. In A. Fortune, P. McCallion and K. Briar-Lawson (Eds.) *Social work practice research for the 21st century*. New York: Columbia University Press, pp. 195–202.

Rooney, R. H. and Mirick, R. (Eds.) (2017). *Strategies for work with involuntary clients* (3rd Edn). New York: Columbia University Press.

Rothman, J. and Thomas, E. (Eds.) (1994). *Intervention research design and development for human service*. New York: Haworth.

Rzepnicki, T. L. (1985). Task-centered intervention in foster care services: Working with families who have children in placement. In A. E. Fortune (Ed.) *Task-centered practice with families and groups*, New York: Springer, pp. 172–84.

Saleebey, D. (Ed.) (2012). *The strengths perspective in social work practice* (6th Edn.). Needham Heights, MA: Allyn-Bacon.

Shaw, I. (2004). William J. Reid: An appreciation. *Qualitative Social Work* 3, pp. 109–15.

Trotter, C. (2015). *Working with involuntary clients: A guide to practice* (3rd Edn.). London: Routledge.

Wells, R. and Gianetti, V. J. (1990). *Handbook of the brief psychotherapies*. New York: Plenum.

7
CRISIS INTERVENTION
Neil Thompson

Introduction

Originating in the field of preventive psychiatry in the 1960s, crisis intervention is a long-standing social work method that has waxed and waned in its popularity over time. It has also been widely misunderstood at times. What this chapter seeks to do, therefore, is to establish the key ideas underpinning the approach, demonstrate how useful they can be in a variety of practice situations and, in the process, clear up some common misunderstandings.

Crisis Theory

The theory underpinning crisis intervention is, unsurprisingly, known as crisis theory. It encompasses a number of key concepts and it is the main ones of these that I shall be focusing on here.

What is a Crisis?

A crisis, in the sense in which it is used in crisis intervention, is a turning point in someone's life – that is, they have reached a point where the situation cannot remain the same; it will either get better or it will get worse, but it cannot stay the same. This introduces the first misunderstanding. Some people say things like: "The family have been in crisis for months now." That family may have been in turmoil or wrestling with instability and insecurity for some time, but, if the situation is persisting, then, by definition, it is not a crisis. This is not simply playing with words. As we shall see below, the difference can be crucial, as a crisis intervention approach will not work if it is not actually a crisis in this sense of a turning point that we are dealing with.

An important concept in crisis theory is "homeostasis." This refers to psychological self-regulation. Just as a thermostat regulates a heating system, homeostasis describes how we regulate ourselves psychologically. What this means is that, on any given day, we may feel a bit better than usual or a bit worse, more relaxed or less, more confident or less, and so on, but we will generally be within a certain range (just as a heating system will keep the temperature within a certain predefined range).

The reason that this concept is so important is that a crisis can be defined as a breakdown in homeostasis. Something happens (generally referred to as the "precipitating event") that overwhelms our coping resources, and so we cannot continue as we normally do – we are pushed into a situation where we are challenged to find new ways of coping. For example, someone who is made homeless. They cannot simply do what they normally do to manage their lives – homeostasis has broken down. They now have to find new strategies, ways of addressing the new challenges they now face.

What are the Consequences of a Crisis?
It is not difficult to understand that a crisis situation can generate considerable distress, anxiety and nervous tension. That nervous tension is particularly important. This is because it can result in either: (i) a vicious circle of anxiety in which tension begets tension, potentially producing a panic reaction (see the discussion below of a "crisis spiral"); or (ii) that tension being used constructively to develop new coping methods.

This echoes the point above that a genuine crisis is a situation that will either get better or it will get worse, but it cannot stay the same. This is where crisis intervention comes into the picture. The aim of crisis intervention is to influence the crisis situation in a positive direction, to try and harness the nervous tension generated so that it can bring about learning and growth, new approaches and new strategies. It involves capitalizing on the motivation generated by the crisis. That is, it can be used to open the door to opportunities to not only "survive" the crisis, but also to benefit from it. It is interesting to note that the two Chinese characters for crisis are *Wei Chi* meaning danger and opportunity (Chui and Ford, 2012). People can come out of crises stronger, better equipped for the next crisis and more resilient (in the sense that a crisis can produce growth and enhancement) especially if they have the support and guidance of someone who understands crises, is suitably responsive and supportive and has the skills to make a positive difference. In many cases that person can and will be a social worker.

However, it can also be the case that a crisis produces a highly negative set of outcomes. What can occur is a "crisis spiral," a vicious circle in which a crisis reduces a person's ability to cope. That reduced level of coping may well then leave them ill-equipped to deal with the next crisis (and, indeed, may actually be part of the reason as to why that crisis arose). The next crisis may then reduce coping abilities (and confidence) further, making it more likely that the next challenge could amount to a crisis. What is happening in such crisis spiral situations is that coping methods and confidence are being reduced at each turn, while the likelihood of challenges arising is increasing. This "double whammy" effect can be highly detrimental and wreak havoc in a person's life.

In my experience of social work I have found that many of the people I was called upon to help had experienced one or more crisis spirals. Consider the following basic case scenarios:

- Jeff's wife left him because she met another man at work. Jeff went to pieces because this loss hit him so hard. He started neglecting himself and constantly looked as though his mind was elsewhere. As a result of this he lost his job as a customer service manager, as the way he was presenting himself was just not consistent with an ethos of customer care. This meant that he was unable to pay the mortgage and faced eviction. The last straw was that, in his distracted state, he caused a road accident in which a young child was seriously injured. The net result was that Jeff had a mental health crisis and was admitted to a psychiatric unit. He never fully recovered, despite years of social work support.

- Sharon had been on the receiving end of Justin's verbal and emotional abuse for some time, but when he came home drunk one night and physically assaulted her quite severely, she decided to leave and take her two children with her. They went to a refuge for women experiencing domestic violence. Justin had control of the family finances, so she found herself without any income. Her efforts to get an emergency payment from the local welfare benefits office did not produce immediate results, and so she started to panic. As a result of this, she tried to steal some groceries from a local store, as she had no food for her children. She was arrested and, in her panic, lashed out at the police officer. She would not normally have done this, but she was so worked up in her current circumstances that she was behaving quite out of character. Because of the assault, she was kept in custody overnight and her children were placed in temporary foster care. Sharon was mildly claustrophobic and found the experience of being in a cell extremely distressing. In fact, she found the whole experience quite traumatizing. The distressing and disempowering effects of that traumatic experience stayed with her for many, many years.

- Cindy had been sexually abused by her stepfather when she was 11-years old. She disclosed to her mother, but she was not believed. Her distress manifested itself in the form of challenging behavior, and this soon led to her being excluded from school. That, in turn, led to her getting into trouble with the police. Her life had been turned upside down, but this was only the beginning. As soon as she turned 16, she left home, despite her mother's protestations. She headed for the nearest big city and, perhaps predictably, she soon found herself homeless, and before long, she was drawn into drug use and eventually prostitution.

In each of these cases, one crisis led to another and to another – a crisis spiral had occurred. Whether or not social work intervention at any stage could have prevented these spirals is not clear, as we do not know enough about the precise circumstances, but it is fair to say that the potential for high-quality social work practice, drawing on crisis theory, to "nip crisis spirals in the bud" is immense, and so the investment of time and effort in developing crisis intervention skills should be a very worthwhile one.

If you think carefully about the two possible sets of consequences I have outlined (positive growth and development vs. a destructive crisis spiral), what you should be able to recognize is that there is a very positive role for highly skilled intervention at the point of crisis to bring about highly beneficial changes, while also avoiding the development of highly destructive crisis spirals. Consider just how harmful a crisis spiral can be and compare that with how positive and empowering the promotion of growth and development can be. Once you have that clear in your mind you should be able to see the value of crisis intervention as a social work method. You should also be able to understand why, as a method that dates back many decades, it has stood the test of time and continues to be a widely used approach (although, as we shall see below, also widely misused).

How does Crisis Relate to Loss and Trauma?

It is interesting (but sad) to note that theoretical and research work around crisis intervention has tended to develop separately from the theoretical and research developments in relation to loss and grief on the one hand and psychosocial trauma on the other. We are now seeing links across these fields of interest, but they have largely operated as separate "silos," each exploring their areas of interest without placing a major emphasis on the interconnections. It is therefore worth exploring, albeit briefly, how issues relating to crisis dovetail with issues of loss and trauma.

In terms of loss, it can be helpful to acknowledge that there is a two-way relationship between crisis and loss, in the sense that: (i) a crisis can produce a grief reaction (people mourn for the stability and security they have lost and possibly for other things they have lost in the process – a relationship, for example); and (ii) loss situations can provoke a crisis (a major bereavement, becoming homeless, getting divorced and so on). In undertaking crisis intervention work, therefore, we need to make sure that we do not lose sight of the grief issues involved, as a failure to address them may well prevent us from making progress.

There are also links with trauma. A traumatic experience is one that leaves us wounded in a psychological and social sense. It describes a situation that profoundly destabilizes us in a number of ways. Examples of trauma would include being the victim of a serious crime; being present in a terrorist attack; being abused; witnessing a death, particularly a violent one; and multiple bereavements (such as in a disaster situation). Clearly, a trauma is also likely to be a crisis – a turning point that challenges us to develop ways of coping with our new, highly demanding situation. There will also be losses involved – again, the loss of stability and security and quite probably many other losses besides. The relationship is again a two-way one, in the sense that losses arise from trauma, but trauma can also be triggered by significant losses. In my book *Grief and its challenges* (Thompson, 2012), I make the point that grief challenges our coping abilities, crisis overwhelms them and trauma devastates them.

It should be clear, then, that there are significant links across the three areas of crisis, loss and trauma, and so we would do well to bear this in mind when engaging in crisis work.

What also binds the three together is the idea of the positive potential arising from suffering (Davies, 2011). Tedeschi and Calhoun (1995) write of the potential for "post-traumatic growth," by which they mean how someone can grow and develop, become stronger, as a result of experiencing a trauma. For example, that person may be more appreciative of life, more willing to take advantage of opportunities that were previously passing them by. Similarly, Schneider (2012) writes of "transformational grief," which refers to how loss can bring positive changes to a person's life. Although grief may be extremely painful, exhausting and frightening, it can also bring positive changes – consider how many people's lives have been enriched by, for example, becoming hospice volunteers following the death of a loved one in that hospice, and thereby gaining great meaning and satisfaction from doing so.

There is a very clear theme strongly emerging here: challenging situations and the suffering associated with them bring many negatives, but they also bring great potential for making positive changes too – and that is what is at the heart of crisis theory and its associated practices.

Crisis Theory in Action: Crisis Intervention

Having clarified some of the key elements of crisis theory, we now turn our attention to how these ideas can be used in practice. Perhaps the first point to emphasize is that it is essential to be able to identify what is and what is not a crisis. Unfortunately, the term "crisis" is often used loosely to refer to either an emergency or a situation characterized by a high degree of nervous tension, but where there is no actual "turning point," no "make or break" moment. It is important that we do not allow this usage to confuse and mislead us. As I have argued in an earlier work, crises and emergencies can overlap at times, but they are actually different entities:

> A crisis is a turning point in someone's life, a situation where existing coping methods are no longer adequate and new ways of coping have to be found. This is often mistakenly equated with an emergency – that is, a situation that has to be dealt with urgently. The truth of the matter is that crisis and emergency often overlap but they often do not. Consider the following examples:
>
> 1. A 15-year-old girl finds that she is pregnant and her parents throw her out of the house, saying that they are disowning her.
> 2. A single mother with two young children arrives in a social services office late on a Friday afternoon because her benefits [payment] has not arrived and the Social Security Office is closed. The matter is easily resolved by a loan from an emergency fund that the duty social worker has access to. The mother copes quite calmly with the whole situation, confident that the Department would not let her children go without food over the weekend.
> 3. A 16-year-old boy who has spent the past three years in residential care moves into an outreach facility as part of a plan that had been agreed more than a year previously.
>
> In the first case we are encountering a situation that is both a crisis and an emergency. That is, it is a turning point in the young girl's life, but it is also a situation that has to be dealt with

urgently. The second case scenario represents an 'emergency' in so far as it needs an urgent response – the situation cannot safely be left, but it is not actually a crisis in so far as it does not represent a turning point. The third scenario, by contrast, describes a turning point and therefore a crisis situation, but it is not an emergency – it does not require an urgent response.

(Thompson, 2002, p. 21)

So, if we want to make use of crisis theory to inform our practice, we need to make sure that it is actually a crisis that we are dealing with and not confuse this with an emergency. Similarly, we may often encounter situations characterized by high levels of nervous tension, and thus seem very similar to a crisis situation, but the person concerned is succeeding in coping with the situation, however fraught and anxiety ridden that situation may be.

I am certainly not saying that we should not intervene in non-crisis emergencies or high-tension situations, but what I am saying is that, if we treat them as crisis situations, our efforts to draw on the insights of crisis theory will mislead us and ultimately fail. For example, one of the consequences of a crisis is that people are more likely to be willing to try new coping methods, to learn new ways of tackling their problems and challenges, whereas someone who is settled firmly within home-ostasis will be much more resistant to change if there is no crisis to impel them.

So, the first conclusion we can draw about using crisis theory is that we have to be quite sure that it is indeed a crisis we are dealing with, that the person concerned has reached a turning point.

On a similar note, we also need to distinguish between crisis interven-tion and what, in an earlier work I described as "crisis survival" (Thomp-son, 2011). This is how they differ:

Crisis intervention: steps taken to maximize the positive potential of the crisis; assistance, guidance and support geared towards devel-oping new and better coping skills. The focus is on empowerment and growth and reaching a higher level of coping once homeostasis is re-established. In this way resilience is promoted.

Crisis survival: steps taken to help someone cope with the stress and challenges of the turning point they have reached; assistance, guidance and support geared to making the situation manageable and less distressing. The focus is on getting through the difficulties unharmed and re-establishing homeostasis as quickly as possible. No contribution is made towards promoting resilience.

Careful consideration of these two accounts will show that, while they may look similar and may have certain things in common, they are actually very different – indeed, fundamentally so. So, our second practice conclusion is that we have to focus on crisis *intervention*, rather than crisis *survival*.

We also need to give some consideration to the importance of timing. Crises, by their very nature are time limited. Because a crisis is a turning point (things will either get better or they will get worse, but they cannot stay the same – otherwise it is not a crisis), time is of the essence. One of the principles of crisis intervention is that *intensive* short-term intervention is likely to prove far more effective in bringing about positive change than longer-term *extensive* intervention. This means that, if we are tardy in getting involved, we can easily "miss the boat," in so far as the situation may have resolved itself and the opportunities for growth, development and empowerment disappeared with it.

A key implication of this is that we need to be time sensitive in our response to crisis situations, and that, in turn, has implications for: (i) our time management skills and effectiveness; and (ii) our organizational systems. In terms of (i), when a crisis arises, we may need to reschedule certain activities and create the space to intervene intensively in the short term. For example, if someone contacts you in crisis on a Thursday and you arrange to see them the following Tuesday, treating the matter as if it were a routine situation, you may have missed the opportunity – the "crisis window" may have closed by then. In terms of (ii), this may be something you will need to discuss in a team meeting or raise with your manager. For example, I have come across social services agencies that normally take up to two weeks or even longer to allocate a new referral. In such settings the opportunity to do crisis intervention is likely to be limited, unless the crisis is also an emergency and therefore goes to the top of the priority list and results in a more rapid allocation.

In my experience, crisis intervention works best where: (i) there is good team support that enables team members to help each other create space, where necessary, to respond promptly and intensively to a crisis situation (where people are prepared to offer cover for routine matters to free up time for a crisis response); (ii) individual staff have good organizational skills that enable them to juggle their commitments and create the opportunity for a rapid response where needed; and (iii) the organizational systems are suitably flexible, responsive and supportive to enable a crisis intervention approach.

What is also important in making the best of the opportunities for positive change that crisis intervention brings is to recognize two things: (i) well-developed interpersonal skills are crucial – people in crisis are likely to feel vulnerable and will be reluctant to trust anyone who does not come across well; and (ii) crisis intervention is not exclusive; you can use other methods alongside it (for example, a solution-focused approach, task-centered practice or family therapy) in the right circumstances. Effective crisis intervention therefore requires a good level of skills, but also offers considerable flexibility and promise in return.

Conclusion

In the technical, theoretical sense, a crisis is a turning point in somebody's life, a situation in which the increase in nervous tension and the sense of threat motivates the individual(s) concerned to explore new ways of coping and managing their challenges that they may not have been prepared to countenance while in a settled, non-threatened state (homeostasis). Crisis intervention (as opposed to crisis survival) involves seeking to capitalize on the crisis and the motivation it generates by helping people to grow, develop and be empowered by their experience. In this respect, it has much in common with the notions of post-traumatic growth and transformational grief.

It is not to be confused with the common-sense, everyday sense of crisis which tends to be used loosely and informally to mean either an emergency or a highly tense situation. These are common enough in social work, but if they are not actually crises, in the formal sense, then adopting crisis intervention methods will not be an appropriate response. It is therefore important that we are clear about what we mean by crisis and are able to distinguish between genuine crises and situations that may be very challenging for all concerned, but are not actually turning points (and thus the motivation to make changes may not be present).

Using crisis intervention can be very demanding, but also very rewarding, in terms of both the positive results that can be achieved for clients and the job satisfaction and personal growth that can be gained from making such a positive difference.

So, all in all, crisis intervention is not a panacea; it does not guarantee success, but when used appropriately by a skilled practitioner, it can produce highly significant positive changes that can not only be highly beneficial in their own right, but also help develop resilience to prevent future problems and to better equip the individual to respond to any problems that do arise.

Points to Ponder

1. How would you know whether a situation you encounter is a crisis or not?
2. What are the loss and grief implications of a crisis?
3. How could you avoid limiting yourself to a "crisis survival" approach?

Key Texts

Thompson, N. (2011). *Crisis intervention* (2nd Edn.). Lyme Regis, UK: Russell House Publishing.
Everstine, D. S. and Everstine, L. (2013). *Strategic interventions for people in crisis, trauma and disaster* (2nd Edn.). New York: Routledge.
Yeager, K. and Roberts, A. R. (2015). *Crisis intervention handbook* (4th Edn.). New York: Oxford University Press.

References

Chui, W. H. and Ford, D. (2012). Crisis intervention as common practice. In P. Stepney and D. Ford (Eds.) *Social work models, methods and theories.* Lyme Regis, UK: Russell House Publishing, pp. 80–101.
Davies, J. (2011). *The importance of suffering: The value and meaning of emotional discontent.* London: Routledge.
Schneider, J. M. (2012). *Finding my way: Healing and transformation through loss and grief.* Traverse City, MI: Seasons Press.

Tedeschi, R. G. and Calhoun, L. G. (1995). *Trauma and transformation: Growing in the aftermath of suffering.* Thousand Oaks, CA: Sage.

Thompson, N. (2002). *Building the future: Social work with children, young people and their families.* Lyme Regis, UK: Russell House Publishing.

Thompson, N. (2011). *Crisis intervention.* (2nd Edn.) Lyme Regis, UK: Russell House.

Thompson, N. (2012). *Grief and its challenges.* Basingstoke, UK: Palgrave Macmillan.

8

NARRATIVE APPROACHES

Louise Harms

Introduction

In many ways, narrative ideas are at the heart of all social work practice. In different practice contexts, we work with people's unique stories to support change and promote well-being for individuals, families, groups and communities. What I aim to do in this chapter is introduce you to some of the key ideas that underpin narrative approaches and look at how you can incorporate these ideas and their related skills into your social work practice.

The Role of Personal Narratives

In using narrative approaches, we are focusing specifically on the stories people live by. Each one of us has many stories that we carry within ourselves, whether we are conscious or not of those internal stories. For example, think about your story of deciding to become a social worker: what have been the reasons for this choice of career, and what story do you tell yourself, and others, for why you are pursuing this area of work? This is an example of a story that we carry about our professional self, and one, no doubt, that changes over our professional career as different events come to shape our experience. It can be thought of as our personal narrative as a social worker, and it has been shaped by our own experiences, and our beliefs in our interests and abilities.

Narrative approaches recognize, however, that this personal narrative has not emerged in isolation, but comes about as a result of our experiences within our families, various groups and culture, across our own lifespan and is indeed often intergenerational. Therefore, narrative approaches emphasize that we always live in the context of broader social and cultural stories. Our stories are shared with and shaped by others, and in turn, our stories shape the broader social and cultural contexts in which we live. So, your decision to become a social worker might be regarded as a very positive career step or perhaps as a controversial and problematic one, depending upon all of these factors. Whether it is our career, or other areas of our lives, such as our relationships, our self-esteem or particular experiences of loss and trauma, for example, as human beings we will innately engage in creating stories about these experiences.

Our personal and sociocultural stories all have different qualities and impacts. Stories of blame, fault or anger may haunt and distress us. Stories of poverty, colonization or lack of opportunity may oppress and limit our lives, or motivate us. Stories of "if only" or "what if," for example, may color experiences after grief or trauma. Stories about our personalities, needs and abilities will shape how we relate to each other. Positive stories can uplift us and give us confidence. For example, the sharing of intergenerational cultural stories is seen by many to be about building and maintaining strength (Wingard and Lester, 2001) in many Australian Aboriginal and Torres Strait Islander communities, despite a history of colonization and dispossession, and is an important means of building cultural voice (see, for example, Bacon, 2013). In creating these stories, we are able to build a particular sense of meaning, continuity, predictability and understanding relating to the world around us and our part in it.

As social workers using narrative approaches, we work with a belief that these stories shape experience and actions, and, most importantly, can and do change in positive ways. If we are using narrative approaches in our practice, we are focused therefore on understanding "the primacy of personal meaning, the construction of identity in a social field, and the revision of life narratives that are incoherent or restrictive"

(Neimeyer, 2009, p. xvi). We are aiming to encourage personal stories that contribute to well-being and resilience in people's lives.

Theoretical Influences

There are many different ways of listening and working with the stories of the people we work with, influenced by different theoretical perspectives. Two dominant ones are social constructionist theories, and the more radical post-structural and anti-oppressive theories.

Social constructionism has helped us think about the relativism of our social contexts and experience, and the role and power of language in shaping experience and meaning (Crotty, 1998). Narrative approaches based in this theoretical space emphasize the importance of helping people find constructive and coherent beliefs in order to function well. So, this is often seen as a shift to focusing in on understanding a person's subjective truths, rather than any objective truth or reality (Neimeyer, 2009, p. 17). You can hear some links here with cognitive behavioral or psychodynamic approaches, in that they also seek to release a person from unhelpful internal narratives about themselves and their circumstances. These approaches have emerged from disciplines such as psychology and sociology, and are often used in practice settings where people are dealing with life experiences such as illness, loss or grief (Neimeyer and Stewart, 1996; Neimeyer et al., 2014).

Other narrative approaches are built on more radical theoretical traditions, including anti-oppressive or anti-discriminatory (Thompson, 2016) and post-structural (such as Foucauldian, see Gordon, 1980) ones. While placing as central an understanding of a person's subjective, individual narrative, these theories encourage us to seek to transform the broader social and cultural contexts as well as an individual's lived experience. That is, a person's narrative is seen as emergent from their context, but also in the reality of those contexts, such as poverty, colonization, unemployment or violence. These lived experiences are just as important to challenge as the internal narratives people live with.

Therefore, these theoretical underpinnings mean that people's strengths are emphasized and that socially just processes and outcomes are sought. It is to be hoped that you can hear the resonance with core social work principles. These approaches have emerged from social work, and related sociological, feminist and political theories.

Putting Narrative Ideas into Practice

So, how can you put these ideas into practice? As I have flagged above, it is important to note that there are different theoretical influences on narrative approaches, which in turn will influence your practice in specific ways. However, there are a number of common areas of focus and skills that you can use in a variety of practice settings, which include listening to a person's narrative and then de-constructing and re-authoring that narrative in a variety of ways, particularly by listening for preferred stories and by externalizing problem-saturated ones.

Listening to Personal Narratives

Common to all of the narrative approaches is an emphasis on listening to the person's story. This may sound like a self-evident emphasis in any social work practice approach. However, as you have probably noticed, in many contexts, deep listening to, and the witnessing of, the specific details of people's stories, as they have constructed them, does not always occur. To illustrate this point, reflect on this situation, in which I have de-identified many of the details:

Practice Focus 8.1

When I was a social worker in a pediatric hospital intensive care unit, I worked with a mother who was distraught. She had accidentally run over her child as she reversed her car in the driveway of their home. It was a horrific accident, and many of the hospital staff were deeply distressed for this mother also, as the child died not long after arriving at the hospital. This mother repeatedly said at that time that she had "killed" her child. Everyone around her in the hospital kept saying to her that she had not killed her child. This was clearly an understandable effort to try to make her feel better. At one level this was true, of course, in that it was a horrific accident, and there had been no intent to kill. But, the new dreadful reality this mother had to come to terms with was that she had in fact caused the death of their child, albeit accidentally. The mother realized very early on how intolerable this was as a social story, as well as her own parental story. It was as if no-one around her would allow her to carry that story, as it was so overwhelming to contemplate. They did not want this mother to have to live with this narrative. No-one wanted her to feel so responsible for such an accident. Yet the challenge of this situation was that this mother needed to give these words to her experience, as to her they fitted what had happened. These words rang true to her, and, in longer-term contact, they were the words that gave her a coherence and meaning that she had to come to terms with.

So, this example highlights the importance of finding the right words to experience and of forming a sense of coherence through those words. This is what Robert Neimeyer, a psychologist who has written extensively about narrative approaches to loss, would see as focusing on "the situated, interpretive activity of individuals and groups" (Neimeyer, 2009, p. 24). You can hear in the practice example above how hard it was for this mother to engage in this interpretive activity. She felt others were not allowing her to express what she saw as her truth. At this point, you might like to reflect on your reaction to this story and what it evokes for you.

There are arguably many stories that are not able to be tolerated by others, given their nature. This has been identified in other situations – such as for survivors of the Holocaust (Reiter, 2000), or of sexual assault – which may evoke difficulties in really deeply listening to such interpersonal atrocities. Or, the listening to, and interpretive work with, stories that may be difficult when these stories challenge our own ethical stances or go against cultural ways.

Narrative approaches also recognize that other stories may not be heard because the storyteller does not have a dominant voice – their experiences are rendered silent, or are stigmatized or assumed. This may be because of particular experiences. Many going through illness and hospitalization experiences, for example, have noted this (Frank, 2010); but so too have parents who have been involved in child protection interventions or those who have perpetrated crimes. Many who experience poverty or violence have emphasized how marginal or ignored their stories are. Narrative approaches emphasize the importance of finding ways of telling stories (whether in verbal, written or creative arts form) in empowered ways, so that ultimately a new coherence and control can be brought to the narrative and the ownership of that story.

Using narrative approaches to listen to people has the purpose of encouraging them:

> to identify the private stories and the cultural knowledges that they live by; these stories and knowledges that guide their lives and that speak to them of their identity.
>
> (White, 2016, p. 28)

So, the first step in using a narrative approach in your social work practice is that of supporting people to give voice to these private stories that are unhelpful or oppressive in order to begin transformative processes.

A Focus on De-constructing and Re-authoring

The aim of narrative approaches is more than listening to a person's story. That is the first step. In becoming aware of private stories and the broader social and cultural knowledges that influence them, narrative approaches then focus on the deconstruction of these private, personal problems. Therefore, the second critical step is that of de-constructing and moving to a re-authoring of these stories. After you have read this next practice example, we will look more closely at some de-constructing and re-authoring techniques.

Practice Focus 8.2

A woman was working late at her workplace, when all other employees had gone home. Her employer came into her office, locked the door behind him, and then physically and sexually assaulted her.

> She told no-one of this experience, and, for financial and face-saving reasons, kept on working in this agency. Since that time, she has experienced ongoing feelings of self-blame and shame, as well as sleeplessness and weight loss. She is very distressed about the loss of intimacy with her husband – she finds she cannot be with him alone, and feels terrible guilt that she is unable to explain to him what had happened. She believes that she should have been able to avoid it, and that she should not be feeling how she is about what happened.

In de-constructing this story with this woman, questions might first focus on understanding a problem-saturated story in detail: understanding the plot, timelines, the various people involved, and the meaning that has been given to the experience. There are also, however, two specific strategies of: (i) connecting with a preferred story (other than a problem-saturated one); and (ii) externalizing the problem.

Connecting with a Preferred Story

In this practice example above, you can hear that there were a lot of "shoulds" that this woman lives with. By focusing on these "shoulds," it could place her as the problem: she should have behaved or thought differently. The strength of a narrative approach these "shoulds" highlight what is of value to her and open up the conversation about these values. This can be referred to as the "absent but implicit" (White, 2016) aspect of a person's story – that is, values or experiences that are not being explicitly spoken about, but are implicit in what is being problematized. In asking these sorts of questions, it is possible to start to understand what a person holds as a core value or what is of worth to them. That is, it starts to give a sense of what her preferred story of herself is about. These ideas are often particularly important in relation to people's experiences of trauma and loss (Harms, 2015), where things that have been of worth and value may have been shattered by these experiences.

This enables a focus to be built around a person's preferred story of themselves: how would someone like to be living differently with an issue or problem, for example? Particular questions, referred to as "landscape of consciousness questions," can be asked that tap into what a person sees as of ultimate worth. As White suggests, these questions:

> Encourage the articulation and the performance of these alternative preferences, desires, personal and relationship qualities, and intentional states and beliefs, and this culminates in a "re-vision" of personal commitment in life.
>
> (2016, p. 33)

Externalizing the Problem

De-constructing a personal narrative can also occur through a process of externalizing the problem. This is one of the central ideas in many narrative approaches that evolved from family therapy – that the "person is not the problem. The problem is the problem." This is a critical objectification process whereby a person, family or group is encouraged to externalize, rather than internalize, a problem. This objectification can be achieved by asking specific types of questions – referred to as "relative influencing" questions (White and Epston, 1990). As the name suggests, such questions seek to understand the relationship and layers of influence that exist between a problem story and a person's life. So, in the practice example above, it might be that the woman is feeling the problem is her failure to protect herself from the assault she experienced, or her failure to leave on time, or her inability to relate to her partner. Externalizing the problem might focus instead on seeing violence or the perpetrator's behavior as the problems that she is having to live with, and enquiry might focus on how these problems of violence or this perpetrator's behavior are experienced in her life (what is the relative influence).

You can hear the strong connection for social work here: when a person is experiencing difficulties, it is not because of some internal psychopathology, but a result of the ways in which people have come to internalize broader aspects of a particular relational, social and/or cultural situation. This process of objectifying the problem brings to light very different issues of power and control for a person in thinking about their particular circumstances.

These questions might include asking "landscape of action questions" (White, 2016, p. 30), whereby a person is asked about the past, present and future of unique outcomes relating to their problem. So, in relation to the earlier practice example, questions might focus on when the violence is not influencing her and what she is doing to resist violence taking over her life, for example. These are ways of shifting the focus to an objectification of the problem. You can hear that this enables a particular emphasis on people's strengths – encouraging listening for when the problem has not been experienced as a problem, where there may have been a moment of resistance to the problem and acting or thinking in different ways about the problem. By exploring what was different about these circumstances, it becomes possible to start to explore how that can be capitalized on in the future, shifting a problem-saturated story to a strengths-based one. This discussion may also encourage her to connect with support groups and social action against gendered violence, for example, by placing the problem she encountered in a wider social discourse of violence.

Forming Testimony

Linked with the idea of social action arising from personal encounters with problems, some narrative approaches also privilege a variety of ways of witnessing and/or documenting a person or group's experiences. This enables engagement in some of the more socially transformative work that is the intention of some narrative approaches. While it is transformative and healing for someone to establish a new meaning construction or identity, some narrative approaches would see this as missing the opportunity to engage in the transformation of broader social and cultural meanings and practices.

Working in the context of communities affected by trauma and loss in many different international contexts, for example, collective narrative practice aims to bring narrative approaches into group or community level interventions. The aim of these interventions is to address this key question:

> How can we respond to stories of social suffering in ways that not only alleviate individual sorrow, but also enable and sustain local social action to address the broader injustices, violence and abuses in our varying contexts?

(Denborough, 2012, p. 53)

One way of responding is through forming a documented record of testimony, whether in a written or creative expression form. These testimonies, formed from community consultations and processes, become powerful records of individual and social stories. Social workers in many contexts can engage in or encourage these practices.

De-centering our Role as Social Workers

Given the strengths-based and social justice commitments of narrative approaches, they naturally translate into thinking about our own role very actively. The intention is to participate in de-centered ways as the social worker (White, 2016). This has been one of the areas that has been critiqued with narrative therapy – given that the questions are very specific in their form and their focus, this necessarily raises the question as to whether a narrative practitioner can be interacting in neutral ways, without unduly influencing or controlling the direction of an interview or an intervention. This requires a constant reflection on, and acknowledgement of, power in relationships. It also requires reflexivity as a social worker, recognizing our own past and present experiences and how these come to shape our interactions with others.

Research Evidence for the Effectiveness of Narrative Approaches

Like many other areas of social work practice, building an evidence base for the effectiveness of narrative approaches is challenging (Connolly and Harms, 2015). Narrative practice is also a relatively new practice approach when compared to many others. In recent years, however, researchers have been studying the impact of narrative approaches in some particular settings. A study comparing narrative therapy to cognitive behavioral therapy for depression, for example, found that both interventions were successful when compared to a non-intervention group in reducing depression scores (Lopes et al., 2014). Another has looked at the effectiveness of narrative therapy with children's social and emotional skill development, and showed over two years that there was significant improvement in "self-awareness, self-management, social awareness/ empathy and responsible decision making" compared to those in a control group (Beaudoin et al., 2016). These recent studies are providing important insights into the effectiveness of narrative approaches, and an encouraging evidence base is emerging.

However, other ways in which the "evidence" of narrative approaches can be established include providing testimony, through written or creative documentation of narrative work, and tangible evidence of social and cultural change. There are many ways in which social workers can gather together stories with individuals and communities. Documented stories of resilience and hope provide strong affirmation of narrative approaches, so we can and should be creative in how we approach this question of evidence and efficacy.

Conclusion

In this chapter, I have introduced some key narrative ideas for you to think about in relation to your social work practice. Narrative approaches provide very specific ways of working with people's stories to influence well-being and change at individual and sociocultural levels. Their appeal is that they integrate political thought and action into therapeutic interventions in ways that are congruent with core social work beliefs about the importance of strengths-based approaches and social justice in all that we do.

Points to Ponder

1. What do you see as some of the core narratives that influence your life, and where do you think they emerged from?
2. In what ways do you think you could incorporate narrative approaches into your practice?
3. Narrative approaches provide a way of addressing social and cultural change as much as individual change. In what ways do you think this could happen in your practice?

Key Texts

Denborough, D. (2012). A storyline of collective narrative practice: A history of ideas, social projects and partnerships. *International Journal of Narrative Therapy and Community Work*, 1, pp. 40–65.
Neimeyer, R. (2009). *Constructivist psychotherapy*. Hove: Routledge.
White, M. (2011). *Narrative practice: Continuing the conversations*. New York: W. W. Norton & Co.

References

Bacon, V. (2013). Yarning and listening: Yarning and learning through stories. In B. Bennett, S. Green, S. Gilbert, and D. Bessarab (Eds.). *Our voices: Aboriginal and Torres Strait Islander social work*. South Yarra: Palgrave Macmillan, pp. 136–65.

Beaudoin, M., Moersch, M., and Evare, B. (2016). The effectiveness of narrative therapy with children's social and emotional skill development: An empirical study of 813 problem-solving stories. *Journal of Systemic Therapies*, 35(3), pp. 42–59.

Connolly, M., and Harms, L. (2015). *Social work: From theory to practice* (2nd Edn.). Port Melbourne: Cambridge University Press.

Crotty, M. (1998). *The foundations of social research: Meaning and perspective in the research process*. St Leonards: Allen & Unwin.

Denborough, D. (2012). A storyline of collective narrative practice: A history of ideas, social projects and partnerships. *International Journal of Narrative Therapy and Community Work*, 1, pp. 40–65.

Frank, A. W. (2010). *Letting stories breathe: A socio-narratology*. Chicago: University of Chicago Press.

Gordon, C. (Ed.) (1980). *Power/knowledge: Selected interviews and other writings, 1972–1977 Michel Foucault*. Brighton: Harvester Press.

Harms, L. (2015). *Understanding trauma and resilience: A multidimensional approach*. London: Palgrave.

Lopes, R. T., Gonçalves, M. M., Machado, P. P., Sinai, D., Bento, T., and Salgado, J. (2014). Narrative therapy vs. cognitive-behavioral therapy for moderate depression: Empirical evidence from a controlled clinical trial. *Psychotherapy Research*, 24(6), pp. 662–74.

Neimeyer, R. (2009). *Constructivist psychotherapy*. Hove: Routledge.

Neimeyer, R., and Stewart, A. (1996). Trauma, healing and the narrative emplotment of loss. *Families in Society: The Journal of Contemporary Human Services*, 77(6), pp. 360–75.

Neimeyer, R., Klass, D., and Dennis, M. (2014). A social constructionist account of grief: Loss and the narration of meaning. *Death Studies*, 38(8), pp. 485–98.

Reiter, A. (2000). *Narrating the Holocaust*. London: Continuum.

Thompson, N. (2016). *Anti-discriminatory practice: Equality, diversity and social justice*. (6th Edn.). London: Palgrave.

White, M. (2016). *Narrative therapy classics*. Adelaide: Dulwich Centre Publications.

White, M., and Epston, D. (1990). *Narrative means to therapeutic ends*. New York: Norton.

Wingard, B., and Lester, J. (2001). *Telling our stories in ways that make us stronger*. Adelaide: Dulwich Centre Publications.

9
EXISTENTIALISM
Neil Thompson

Introduction

Existentialism is a long-standing philosophy that has proven influential in many ways, although its impact on social work has mainly been indirect – for example, through the counseling literature (May, 1995; van Deurzen and Arnold-Baker, 2005; Yalom, 1981). However, it is none the less an important theoretical perspective that can cast light on various aspects of social work. It can tell us a great deal about the problems and challenges clients encounter that bring them to our attention, the problems and challenges we encounter in carrying out our social work duties and the relationship between the two.

One of the things that makes existentialism such a potentially useful theoretical underpinning for social work is that it is a philosophy of everyday life – not an abstract philosophy concerned with eternal truths or metaphysical principles, but a pragmatic framework of understanding rooted in what Sartre called "lived experience" (*le vécu*, to use the technical term – Sartre, 2003).

What is also of benefit is that it is a holistic theory – that is, it seeks to make sense of human experience in general and not just a particular aspect (unlike, for example, family therapy's specific focus on family dynamics and related matters). This gives it considerable explanatory power.

The Beginnings

An examination of the key concepts that give it that explanatory power forms the next part of the chapter and this leads in to a discussion of how such ideas can be helpfully drawn upon in practice. However, before exploring these ideas I will give a brief overview of some of the theory's historical roots, mainly in the ideas of nineteenth-century thinkers, Søren Kierkegaard (1813–1855) and Friedrich Nietzsche (1844–1900), and Jean-Paul Sartre (1905–1980) in the twentieth century.

Kierkegaard was a staunch Christian, but he was critical of conventional understandings associated with Christian doctrine. His view was that to be a good Christian was not a matter of unthinkingly following established dogma, but, rather, finding your own way in the world – making your own decisions and finding your own path to honor God. As Watts puts it:

> Kierkegaard emphasised above all the need to become a 'true individual', passionately committed to a path that has been *personally* chosen. He observed that the majority of people merely exist as part of an anonymous 'public', simply conforming to the dominant way of living and thinking.
>
> (2003, p. 5)

This introduces the notion of "authenticity," an important point, to which we shall return below. But for now we should note that Kierkegaard was arguing that we should be seeing our own way forward – taking responsibility for living our own life.

Nietzsche's work was highly incompatible with Kierkegaard's in many ways, but there were also significant overlaps. Nietzsche rejected Christianity and denied that there was an absolute source of values in life, thereby differing from Kierkegaard, but sharing with him the idea that we must find our own way forward. He saw humanity as ranging from the herd mentality at an animal level at one extreme and the "Übermensch" at the other. Übermensch is generally translated as "superman" or "overman" (although Mensch is not gender specific and does not therefore relate only to men). Despite a common misunderstanding, this was not intended to refer to any sort of racially superior being. What Nietzsche was basically saying was that very many people do not rise much, if at all, above their animal nature and largely follow the crowd ("the herd" – and here he is echoing strongly Kierkegaard's view), while some will go to the opposite extreme by fulfilling their potential, taking hold of their lives and being in charge of themselves, as far as possible – what he referred to as "self-overcoming" (Nietzsche, 1995).

Building on the Foundations

The ideas of these two thinkers in the nineteenth century proved influential in shaping existentialist thought in the twentieth century and beyond. The most notable thinker was Jean-Paul Sartre. Sartre (2003) emphasized that we are "condemned to be free." What he meant by this is that we are constantly faced with choices, and those choices always have consequences. Even in the most restricted circumstances, we still have to make choices (and face their consequences). There is no escape, although people will often try by adopting an attitude of what Sartre called "bad faith" – that is, by trying to deny our freedom via such routes as: "I can't help it; it's my nature;" "It's the way I was brought up;" and/or "I had to do it that way; I had no choice."

On this basis, existentialism can be understood as a philosophy that involves exploring what it means to be free, to have choices and to face the responsibility of having to manage those choices and their consequences. Having established some sense of its roots, let's now explore some of the key ideas and their implications for social work practice.

The Key Ideas

Existentialism is a highly complex, multidimensional school of thought, and so it would be entirely unrealistic to cover it comprehensively in one chapter. What follows is therefore necessarily selective, but should, I hope, be enough to show clearly how much it has to offer as a basis for understanding so much of what happens in the social work world.

As its name implies, existentialism is a philosophy of existence. It is concerned with the fundamental questions of what it means to exist – what does it mean to be a human being? To explore the basis of the philosophy, I will summarize some of existentialism's ways of answering that very question.

Before we begin, please do note that I will be using some technical philosophical terms, but do not be concerned by this, as I shall explain each one – no knowledge of philosophy or its jargon is needed to benefit from the lessons that this chapter has to offer.

The Existential Project

Here we are using "project" in a technical sense, not its everyday one. Each day we "pro-ject" ourselves forward – that is, we throw ourselves into the future. We have hopes, aspirations and plans that influence our actions. In this sense, our expected future is shaping our present, just as our present actions are shaping our future. We shall return to this point below when we discuss the "progressive–regressive method."

In everyday terms what that means is that we are not fixed entities (the "real me") going on a journey through life. We *are* that journey. Our sense of self comes from our constant interaction with our day-to-day realities, the choices we make, the obstacles we encounter and so on. As Bakewell puts it:

> But as a human being, I have no predefined nature at all. I create that nature through what I choose to do. Of course, I may be influenced by my biology, or by aspects of my culture and personal background, but none of this adds up to a complete blueprint for producing me. I am always one step ahead of myself, making myself up as I go along.
>
> (2016, p. 6)

The existential project, then, is a way of describing the nature of human existence. One of its characteristics is the idea of constant change – an understanding of our existence as fluid and constantly evolving, which brings us to two further closely related concepts.

Contingency and Flux

These two ideas both follow on from the idea of the existential project. "Contingency" refers to the idea that there are few certainties in life.

While much of life is familiar and predictable, there is always the potential for change – and, at times, quite radical change (for example, a major bereavement or other life-changing event). Indeed, social work intervention is often called for at times when such a radical change has occurred (see Chapter 6 in this volume on crisis intervention).

The significance of the notion of "contingency," then, is that there is always the possibility for change – our lives are fluid and not set in stone. However, the more prevalent notion of a fixed personality can lead people to assume that change is not possible, and can therefore contribute to a sense of "stuckness," of not being able to move forward positively.

This is where the idea of "flux" comes in. Flux refers to the fact that change is the basis of reality. If things stay the same it is because we are making it that way, we are "reconstructing" them through the choices we make and the habits we form. For example, if a positive relationship persists, it is because we are actively sustaining it, we are constantly reaffirming the status quo in one or more ways. Another example would be what are seen as personality characteristics. If we stopped behaving in accordance with those traits, they would cease to exist. They persist only because we renew them. The technical term for this is "negentropy." Entropy refers to the natural tendency towards decay and deterioration, so negentropy is the process of constantly counteracting entropy through renewing and rebuilding (in the same way that we would maintain a wooden fence by repainting it every so often to counteract the natural tendency towards decay).

To a certain extent, the idea that we do not have fixed personalities is counterintuitive – that is, it goes against common sense, but that is because such "common sense" is based on the dubious premise that life is basically stable and largely unchanging (even though the Earth is rotating on its axis at anything up to 1,000 miles per hour and is travelling through space at speeds approaching 70,000 miles per hour). Each day we get older, each day we change a little, but the fact that the change is generally slow does not mean that it is not happening. To be human means having to face uncertainty (contingency) and constant change (flux). It also means to be mortal, to recognize that our lifespan is finite. These can be quite challenging realizations, but they put us in a stronger position to address the challenges we face in life – they make us more authentic, an important point to consider in more detail.

In Search of Authenticity

Earlier I mentioned Sartre's notion of bad faith, the common tendency to pretend that we are not free, to evade responsibility for ourselves and our choices. The opposite of bad faith is "authenticity," and this means being true to our nature as constantly evolving beings, people who are every day making choices and living with the consequences of those choices. This takes us back to Nietzsche's idea of "self-overcoming" and Kierkegaard's idea of choosing our own path.

To be authentic means being prepared to face up to our own freedom and the choices we make as part of it, to take ownership of our lives and the direction we are taking it in. Without authenticity, existentialism proposes, we hold ourselves back, we distort our reality and, in effect, disempower ourselves. This clearly has implications for social work practice at two levels: (i) the need for our own authenticity (for example, in relation to professional accountability); and (ii) the value of supporting, encouraging and nurturing authenticity in clients and caregivers (Thompson, 1992).

A careful consideration of the range of problems and circumstances that we commonly encounter in social work will soon reveal that a process of (inauthentic) self-disempowerment is a recurring theme, especially where people assume that they are not capable (due to low self-esteem perhaps) or are held back by problems associated with anxiety and/or depression.

In this regard, then, being human means wrestling with the challenge of avoiding bad faith and embracing authenticity – an authenticity that may be obstructed by the various tentacles of bad faith and the deeply ingrained self-defeating attitudes that are so often part of people's upbringing ("essentialism," to use the technical term) and therefore of their self-image. Sadly, many groups of people in our society receive strong messages as part of their upbringing ("socialization" to use the technical term) that certain possibilities are not available to them – "That's not for people like me." That can include aspects of education, employment and social activities.

The Dialectic of Subjectivity and Objectivity

A key element of existentialist thought is the recognition that there is a subjective dimension to everything we do. There is an objective world "out there," but we have to interpret it, to make sense of it – and that is where the subjective element comes in. The dialectic of subjectivity and objectivity therefore relates to how the objective world and each person's interpretation of it interact with one another constantly.

Consider it in this way:

1. My perception and understanding of the world (subjectivity) are largely shaped by the culture I was brought up in, the cultural context I am living in now, the media and so on (objectivity).
2. The social world (objectivity) is shaped by how people behave in relation to it (the actions they take) based on people's desires, wishes, feelings, intentions and so on (subjectivity).
3. A to-ing and fro-ing interaction (dialectic) between subjectivity and objectivity therefore continues on an ongoing basis. This becomes the basis of human experience at an individual, micro-level and of history at a societal, macro-level.

The significance of this dialectic is that it helps us to understand the role of authenticity and the need for us to take ownership of our actions. What happens in the social (objective) world owes much to the actions taken by people, individually and collectively, which, in turn, are based on our (subjective) understandings – our worldview. It brings us back to the core concept that there are always choices, and choices always have consequences.

Meaning and Spirituality

In an earlier work, I asked: "How do we make sense of our lives? How does social work play a part in shaping the meanings of people's lives? To what extent can social work itself be seen as a process of meaning making?" (Thompson, 2016b, p. 114). This links well with the idea of the dialectic of subjectivity and objectivity. The meanings we attribute to our lives are subjective, but they are, of course, rooted in our external (objective) reality – they are not free floating, unconnected with the material and social world.

Human beings are, in a very real sense, meaning-making creatures. Wherever we go, whatever we do, we create meanings, we tell stories about ourselves, our circumstances and experiences – in technical terms, we develop "narratives" (see Chapter 8 in this volume).

Meaning is also fundamental to spirituality, our sense of who we are and how we fit into the wider world – our worldview (Moss, 2005). There is now a growing and significant literature on the need to include a spiritual dimension in social work (see, for example, Holloway and Moss, 2010). Existentialism, with its emphasis on meaning, can play an important role in doing this (see Thompson, 2017).

Existentialism in Practice

Existentialism is a complex philosophy, and not a simple or straightforward "method." However, this does not mean that it does not have practical applications. It can cast significant light on situations involving loss and grief; crisis and trauma; interpersonal conflict; self-defeating behaviors; change and turmoil; and so on. In this section we examine some of the main ways in which the key ideas can be drawn upon in a range of practice situations.

Exploring Choices

An "essentialist" attitude – that is, one that is based on an assumption that each individual is a fixed entity and cannot change – seriously limits our range of options. In this way, people who adopt such an attitude reflect Nietzsche's view that we should aim for "self-overcoming." In social work terms, this means moving away from processes of self-limitation and self-disempowerment.

The prevalence of essentialist attitudes often means that people are unaware of the choices available to them – the idea that we cannot change forecloses a range of options and thereby blocks progress. Consequently, one social work technique rooted in existentialist thought is the exploration of choices, the gentle and constructive challenging of self-defeating attitudes. This can include building confidence and addressing anxiety and/or depression.

In my study of leadership (Thompson, 2016a), I emphasized the importance of the concepts of "facticity" and "transcendence," and these can also be seen to apply to social work practice (and, indeed, to human existence in general). "Facticity" refers to the fact that there will always be things that we have no control over, things that will happen that we just have to accept (losing our job, being the victim of a crime or abuse and so on). However, this is where "transcendence" comes in. To "transcend" means "to go beyond." The key point is this: whenever we encounter facticity, we also face transcendence – that is, while there will be things we cannot prevent or eradicate, we will always be able to choose how we react to them, how we "go beyond" them.

This reflects the existentialist understanding of control, namely that: (i) we never have *complete* control over our lives and circumstances (facticity); and (ii) we never have *no* control; we can always choose how to react – indeed, we have to choose how to react (transcendence). A skilled social worker can therefore help clients explore how they react in terms of what options they have. An essentialist attitude focuses on the facticity (the lack of control), while an existentialist approach focuses on what can be controlled, the options available (transcendence).

Facing Challenges

In an earlier work I highlighted the significance of "challenges":

Human existence presents us with a series of challenges to meet or problems to solve. These can be classified under three broad headings:

- *Life course challenges* These are the changes we encounter as we move through the life course: growing up, establishing independence and so on, right through to facing up to death.
- *Challenges of circumstance* These are the challenges and problems that arise for specific individuals in specific circumstances – that is, the challenges we face as a result of the particular goals we are trying to achieve or lifestyle we are trying to live.
- *Sociopolitical challenges* These are the problems that can arise as a result of our position in society, our 'social location'. These include poverty, racism, sexism and other forms of exploitation.

(Thompson, 2015, p. 23)

One social work technique that can usefully be drawn upon, therefore, is to work closely with clients to help them: (i) make sense of the challenges they face; and (ii) develop strategies for addressing those challenges. Being clear and explicit about what the challenges are can pave the way for creative problem-solving approaches that then serve as the platform for strategy building.

Promoting Authenticity

Maintaining our own authenticity is the first step, after which we need to explore how we can help others to achieve and sustain authenticity, to "own" their lives more. This can involve drawing on other methods – for example, narrative therapy (see Chapter 8) to help develop more empowering narratives; or cognitive behavioral therapy (see Chapter 5) by identifying self-limiting beliefs as "core" beliefs to be reviewed.

But, whichever method or approach is adopted, it can be enhanced by an understanding that authenticity is an important goal – people will struggle to make progress with the challenges they face if they are allowing bad faith (self-defeating attitudes) to prevent them from embracing new ideas, new strategies and thus new potential solutions.

The Progressive–Regressive Method

Earlier I mentioned the concept of the "existential project," the way in which our lives can be characterized as "pushing ourselves" forward in time. Our future plans, expectations and so on play a part in shaping our present actions, and, of course, those actions in the present play a part in shaping the future. The progressive–regressive method takes this a step further.

The basic principle is that, if we want to understand the present circumstances (which, as social workers, we certainly do), we need to consider the influences of the future, as described above (the progressive element), plus the influences of past life experiences and circumstances, upbringing and so on (the regressive element). These "temporal elements" (past, present and future) are constantly interacting and influencing one another in powerful ways. To put it another way, to understand today, we need an appreciation of the influence of both tomorrow (in terms of plans, aspirations and so on) and the influences of yesterday (in terms of how our experiences have shaped our identity and worldview).

This method can be used to inform our assessment as we make efforts to make sense of the situation we are dealing with. In this sense, it could be seen as a form of assessment tool. However, it can also be used as a tool of intervention – for example, by talking explicitly to the person(s) concerned about how future and past elements are influencing the present situation and how changes could be made to improve that situation. Of course, as with any method, it would be important to choose the right circumstances to put this into practice; it would not be a case of simply applying it across the board to all scenarios.

Conclusion

"There are no guarantees" is a sentiment closely associated with existentialism. It is also something that applies very well to the social work world. However, there are steps that we can take to maximize our chances of making a positive difference. Drawing on the insights of existentialist thought can be one of those steps. This is because existentialism is concerned with what it means to be human, including the existential challenges of maintaining a positive identity in turbulent circumstances; managing positive relationships with others; responding to the demands of loss, grief and trauma; and so on. Social work, is of course, about helping people address their life challenges, whatever their nature and source. Existentialism is about making sense of those challenges and the broader human context in which they arise.

Important Note

I made the point earlier that existentialism is a complex philosophy. It relies on a number of concepts that can be quite difficult to understand if you are not familiar with them. So, if you have found this chapter difficult to understand, there is no cause for concern. It *is* complex and difficult material. It is therefore recommended that you come back to this chapter at some point and read it again. It should make more sense on second reading – especially if you bear in mind that the material is, by its very nature difficult to assimilate (but worth the effort because of the important insights it brings).

Points to Ponder

1. How can an emphasis on choices and consequences help to empower people?
2. Why and in what ways is authenticity an important social work concept and value?
3. In what circumstances might you be able to put the progressive–regressive method to good use?

Key Texts

Thompson, N. (2017). *Theorizing practice* (2nd Edn.). London: Palgrave Macmillan, especially Part 3.
Bakewell, S. (2016). *At the existentialist café: Freedom, being and apricot cocktails.* London: Chatto & Windus.
van Deurzen, E. and Arnold-Baker, C. (2005). *Existential perspectives on human issues: A handbook for therapeutic practice.* Basingstoke, UK: Palgrave Macmillan.

References

Bakewell, S. (2016). *At the existentialist café: Freedom, being and apricot cocktails.* London: Chatto & Windus.
Holloway, M. and Moss, B. (2010). *Social work and spirituality.* Basingstoke, UK: Palgrave Macmillan.
May, R. (1995). *The discovery of being: Writings in existential psychology* (2nd Edn.). New York: W. W. Norton & Co.
Moss, B. (2005). *Religion and spirituality.* Lyme Regis, UK: Russell House Publishing.
Nietzsche, F. (1995). *Thus spoke Zarathustra.* New York: Random House.
Sartre, J-P. (2003). *Being and nothingness: An essay on phenomenological ontology.* (2nd Edn.). New York: Routledge.
Thompson, N. (1992). *Existentialism and social work.* Aldershot, UK: Ashgate.
Thompson, N. (2015). *Understanding social work: Preparing for practice* (4th Edn.). London: Palgrave.
Thompson, N. (2016a). *The authentic leader.* London: Palgrave.
Thompson, N. (2016b). *The professional social worker: Meeting the challenge* (2nd Edn.). London: Palgrave.
Thompson, N. (2017). *Theorizing practice* (2nd Edn.). London: Palgrave.
van Deurzen, E. and Arnold-Baker, C. (2005). *Existential perspectives on human issues: A handbook for therapeutic practice.* Basingstoke, UK: Palgrave Macmillan.
Watts, M. (2003). *Kierkegaard.* Oxford, UK: Oneworld.
Yalom, I. D. (1981). *Existential psychotherapy.* New York: Basic Books.

10

SOLUTION-FOCUSED PRACTICE

Suki Desai

Introduction

This chapter is organized around one particular case scenario in which Bharti, a social worker, examines how she can engage in critical social work practice with a client, Janice, who has been diagnosed as having a mental health condition. Traditionally, social work practice has adopted a range of interventions with clients that place the social worker in the role of the "expert" and the people that they are working with as recipients of this expertise, adopting what is commonly known as a medical approach (or model) to their intervention. Solution-focused practice is different, in that it essentially begins with the solution. In other words, the client starts from a premise of a problem-free future.

The concepts of solution-focused therapy and solution-focused brief therapy were originally developed by de Shazer (1985, 1988, 1994) and Berg (de Jong and Berg, 2013) and used by them in the context of family therapy intervention. Both Berg and de Shazer were heavily influenced by the works of Milton Erikson, a psychotherapist. Erikson believed that a person has the strength, capacity, and resources to solve their own problems and that the role of the practitioner should be to enable the individual to unlock this potential. Berg and Miller (1992) suggest that the approach is "atheoretical," primarily because it is pragmatic. This is not to suggest that solution-focused practice is devoid of an ideological or philosophical basis. Indeed the increasing popularity of this intervention is its intrinsic affinity to anti-discriminatory practice, especially in the modern-day context of social work, which places an emphasis on working from a strength-based approach and in partnership with clients. By shifting the focus of "expertise" from the social work practitioner to the person that they are working with, solution-focused practice undermines the historical relationship between social work and its clients. This relationship is based on Derrida's notion of "différance," which claims that traditional relationships between social workers and their clients are based on power, position, and conditions where the client occupies the position of the "other," and is perceived as being different from the collective norm. This has led to the pathologization of social work clients as problematic, uncooperative, and deviant in the past.

People experiencing mental distress have felt similar disassociation from society. Their marginalization within society is supported by how governmental agencies respond to them – for example, through extreme interventions, such as loss of their liberty through detention under mental health legislation, or by the marginalization of well-meaning professionals who see them as a "problem" to be solved. This can be a real challenge for any practitioner who wants to intervene with clients in ways that make them feel empowered. This is often because mental health systems are designed to respond to clients in medicalized ways where professionals claim expertise over the client's mental distress. Solution-focused practice enables service users to visualize how they would like their life to be, and, in this respect, they identify their own goals and future.

This case study is not a definitive use of this approach. It is simply one example. A more comprehensive account of the approach can be found in MacDonald (2011).

Assessment and Goal Setting

Case Background

Bharti is a social worker based in a Community Mental Health Team who has been allocated the case of Janice, a 66-year-old African–Caribbean woman who has been experiencing severe anxiety and has a diagnosis of depression. During the allocation meeting Janice's consultant psychiatrist has said that Janice's anxiety and depression are linked to her worry about the future of her two adult children who live with her in the family home. Both children have a mental health diagnosis. Joseph has a diagnosis of schizophrenia and Alicia has a mild learning disability. The psychiatrist has said that Janice's anxiety has been getting worse and that she is unsure why this is the case. She has increased her medication dosage and believes that Janice's problems are to do with her home circumstances.

Social work encounters begin with an assessment. An assessment is a tool that the social worker uses in order to enable them to plan future work with their client. It is also a tool that can work very well with solution-focused practice. Both social work assessments and solution-focused practice promote the concept of empowerment. Empowerment is also an essential value base linked to recovery approaches in mental health which are based on the notion that recovery from mental health conditions is not linked to the cure of the individual, and is instead based on "individualised meaning that is not necessarily about being symptom-less" (Ryan *et al.*, 2012). These aspects work together and promote the concept that any *problem* that is linked to Janice's situation does not lie with her as an individual or her children, but with the *situation* in which she and they find themselves (see Thompson, 2015, for further reading on social work assessments and empowerment). In this respect, de Shazer (1985) claims that the assessment interview that Bharti carries out with Janice should be "text focused," meaning that it is Janice who provides a view of her situation. As a social work professional Bharti feels comfortable with this, as it forms the core value base of social work.

While a detailed history is not an essential element of solution-focused practice, in her first meeting with Janice, Bharti has noted that she is very keen to talk about what is happening and to tell her story. Mental health clients are often marginalized in society. They are often perceived as being irrational, dysfunctional, and sometimes dangerous. Thus, Bharti recognizes that allowing Janice the time and space to tell her story is also part of a healing process that enables her to feel a sense of control. While social work practitioners recognize the importance of this intervention, they can minimize its effectiveness through a range of actions. For example, this can be through poor planning where they have not allowed enough time for the visit and, rather than arranging another appointment, they intervene by making statements, such as: "I don't need to know all this detail," or: "I've come across this sort of problem before." Such statements can have a negative impact. It can make the client feel that their story is not unique, and this results in their closing down their interaction. It also changes the nature of the interaction to what de Shazer (1985) identifies as: "reader focus," in this respect, such statements demonstrate to the client that it is the social worker (as the expert practitioner) who has the specialist knowledge about what is going on. Other aspects that interfere with effective interaction can be very basic lack of attention to details, such as not explaining to a client why note taking is important, remembering to turn off mobile telephones, not constantly looking at the time, and so on. Paying attention to these issues demonstrates respect and shows empathy and a concern for the client.

In order to demonstrate to Janice that she is listening Bharti uses Janice's own words and phrases to build a relationship with her. De Shazer (1985) suggests that using the client's own words, or "language matching," allows the social worker to build up a relationship with them more quickly. In addition, when working with people who experience mental distress, talking about emotions is a common occurrence. How someone feels and what they feel about other people, or their situation, are common responses in mental health interventions. Solution-focused practice does not endorse talking about emotions. This is based on the assumption that talk about emotions is less behavioral, and hence less open to change. However, when working with clients who experience mental distress, there may be reasons to talk about how someone might be feeling, in order to assess whether they might be feeling suicidal, or have a desire to hurt someone else. The use of scaling questions endorsed by solution-focused practice can enable the social worker to gauge how intense the feelings are that the client is experiencing. For example, in assessing the severity of her anxiety Bharti might ask Janice to tell her how anxious she is feeling on a scale of one to ten, where ten is extremely anxious. This allows Bharti to move Janice away from emotional talk, while at the same time recognizing that the situation that she finds herself in is emotive.

It also enables Bharti to slow down the interview, assess any potential risk factors, and track progress.

As part of goal setting and identifying what Janice wants to achieve, Bharti might also ask Janice what it is that she would like to get out of the intervention. While to a social work practitioner this might seem an obvious question, for clients this is likely to be a difficult question to answer. Thompson (2015) suggests that not addressing this aspect properly can undermine the role of the social worker as a professional problem solver. In order to enable Janice to address this important question Bharti helps her to unravel it by enabling her to focus on what it was about her situation that has resulted in her visit. She does this by asking her questions such as:

- Let us focus on your feelings of anxiety. How intense are your feelings of anxiety (using the scaling technique)?
- How many times in the day and night do the feelings of anxiety become intense?
- How do you deal with the feelings of anxiety?

These questions also enable Janice to understand the context of Bharti's involvement with her, as well as allowing Bharti not to feel overwhelmed. Thompson (2016) highlights the importance of recognizing the need for the social worker to balance out positive and negative emotions that social work encounters can induce and warns that it is the client who misses out when social workers feel overwhelmed. For example, by not enabling Janice to establish what it is that she wants from their encounter, Bharti risks the possibility that Janice might say what she wants is for Alicia to be placed in residential care. This is because Joseph is threatening to move out of the family home and Janice is worried that Alicia will be left alone and vulnerable without her brother's support (in the event of her death), and this is the source of her increased anxiety and depression. Indeed, this may be Janice's expectation. Berg and de Shazer (1993, p. 9) claim that problems cannot be solved "with the same kind of thinking that has created the problem." When a person is experiencing a heightened anxiety state it is often difficult for them to think of solutions; this does not mean that they are not capable of doing so. In addition to *how* questions, Bharti also uses *what* questions:

- What happens immediately before you experience extreme anxiety?
- What happens next?
- What is said and by whom?
- Who notices that you are experiencing extreme anxiety?

These questions that specifically focus on behavior enables Bharti to establish a working hypothesis of the situation. This situation informs her that:

1. Joseph is wanting to assert his independence and leave the family home to pursue his own life.
2. Janice's anxiety and depression have likely arisen as a result of this announcement.
3. Alicia's behavior has become difficult for Janice to manage, possibly because Alicia is picking up on the fact that she is the cause for the arguments between her mother and brother.
4. Alicia does not want to move out of the family home.
5. Janice believes that, as her older brother, Joseph has responsibility to look after his sister and he cannot do this if he is not living in the family home.

Time for Reflection

Often social work supervision has a tendency to focus on what is happening with the client, and Thompson (2016) reminds us that it is just as important for the social work practitioner to acknowledge their own feelings. The pressure from managers to resolve issues quickly and close cases, expectations held by clients, and the bureaucracy that surrounds social work practice all place a heavy demand on the social worker. These pressures have to be managed alongside thinking creatively, working anti-oppressively, and empowering clients. Thompson (2016) suggests that the social worker needs to be resourceful, robust and resilient in order to work in partnership with clients and in order to promote empowerment. This is particularly important when working with people who experience mental distress. Empathizing with people who experience such distress can be challenging. The negative feelings generated by mental distress are likely to be overpowering for clients. The social worker has to not only absorb and hear the client's negative emotions, but also actively to think about how to emotionally manage what they are hearing, as well as what to say next. It is therefore important not to try and address all of a client's issues in one assessment interview. While established and experienced social work practitioners might be able to skillfully accomplish a great deal in one interview with a client, newly qualified practitioners, or those practitioners who are new to the methodology, may need more time to make sense of what is happening in the encounter.

Reflective learning is one way to manage the social work encounter. Trevithick (2012, p. 96) draws on Kolb's work to claim that reflection involves "active engagement." She suggests that reflection enables the social work practitioner to also acknowledge that they too are "being changed by the experience" that they are seeking to understand. This is important for several reasons. First, social work discipline is not determined by any one particular model or type of intervention. It has a long history of using theories, concepts, and ideas from other fields. Solution-focused practice is one example. While this chapter refers to solution-focused practice, de Shazer (1985) locates the practice in brief therapies, and refers to it as solution-focused brief therapy. What is important is that the basic tenet of the approach shares fundamental ideas and practices. This can be liberating for the social work practitioner, as intervention is not based on a formulaic interpretation of the model.

Second, there is a lot of emphasis placed on creative practice or thinking more creatively when undertaking practice, and it is not always easy to recognize what this means in reality. Social workers who engage proactively in critically reflective learning recognize that nothing is static and that everything is open to interpretation. As Thompson states: "If theory is to develop over time, then it needs to remain attuned to the needs of actual practice, while also adopting a critical perspective on the practice world" (2017, p. 252). The creativity is linked to how the theories, models, and methods that practitioners use in practice can be molded, manipulated, and adapted so that they still retain their basic tenets, but allow the social work practitioner to use them in ways that are relevant in the real world. Bharti has to engage in reading, learning, understanding, and connecting with the essential traits of solution-focused approaches so that when she uses this approach in practice she appreciates how it functions in a way that enables her to get to the heart of the problem situation. However, the manipulation of any theory, model, or method is not just limited to this. The influence of the real world or the practice world also influences how certain tenets of any theory are no longer applicable and have to be changed. In order to engage with this, Bharti has to have the confidence to discuss openly and share her ideas with other practitioners, including those from a range of multidisciplinary settings. She has to have confidence in her own self and be prepared to be challenged, and, if necessary, change her direction. Not engaging in critical reflection of this nature leads to the third point, namely that social workers can be in danger of becoming mechanistic and uncritical practitioners. In this scenario, for example, Bharti could have uncritically accepted that the future care of Alicia is the main problem, and hence start a process that leads to the institutionalization of the most vulnerable member of the family.

The Miracle Question

Bharti has decided to engage with Janice using solution-focused practice because she believes that, despite her current negative outlook on life, Janice is an extremely resourceful woman. She wants Janice to be able to return to being this resourceful person again. An aspect of solution-focused practice involves a technique that de Shazer (1988) developed in aiding practitioners to set goals with clients. De Shazer (1988) describes this as the *miracle question*. The miracle question involves exploring with the client the answer to the following question:

> Now I want to ask you a strange question. Suppose that while you are sleeping tonight and the entire house is quiet, a miracle happens. The miracle is that the problem which brought you here is solved. However, because you are sleeping, you don't know that the miracle has happened. So when you wake up tomorrow morning, what will be different that will tell you that a miracle has happened and the problem which brought you here is solved?
>
> (de Shazer, 1988 p. 5)

The open-endedness of the miracle question enables clients to engage in limitless possibilities to engage in solutions. However, asking such a question can also elicit reactions that the social worker may not have anticipated – for example, hilarity, silence, or an acknowledgement by the client that they have no idea. Janice found the question amusing and told Bharti she was not sure what she wanted her to say. Bharti acknowledged that the question was strange and repeated it again to Janice by talking slowly and deliberately so that Janice was aware that Bharti was being serious. Bharti allowed a long silence at the end so that Janice had some time to think about her response. In order to help Janice engage Bharti also asked her some supplementary questions:

- Will you know at once that a miracle has happened? How do you think you will know this?
- Who else do you think will notice?
- How will they be able to tell?

Unravelling the miracle question in this way allows Janice to recognize a range of potential scenarios. Janice would know, for example, that a miracle had happened because the atmosphere in the house would be much calmer. She would be able to recognize the calmness because she would feel less stressed and she would wake up in the morning and there would be no headache and no knot in her stomach. Janice believed that the first person to recognize this would be Alicia, because she feels that Alicia picks up on her stress. Janice also believed that Joseph would also notice, because they would stop arguing. By slowly working through these responses and using scaling questions to gauge how Janice is feeling, Bharti is able to engage Janice in problem solutions. Each time that Janice reverts back to problem talk Bharti interrupts by asking her additional questions that refocus Janice back to solution talk. For example, Janice feels threatened by Joseph's decision to move out of the family home, mainly because she recognizes that she has no control over this decision. Her reaction has been to convince him otherwise. Rather than exploring this in detail, Bharti asks questions that move Janice away from negative descriptions about her relationship with Joseph. For example, she asks her to describe her relationship with Joseph at those times when they are not arguing about his moving out. Bharti again uses scaling questions to enable Janice to connect with her emotions and her feelings about Joseph. In subsequent meetings with Janice Bharti helps her to change her interactions with Joseph so that their conversations are not about moving out but other things that they share in common. Bharti also enables Janice to explore her emotions in the context of what would happen if Joseph were to leave and how the atmosphere at home could still be calm. Bharti uses her social work skills of "questioning," "confirming what has been said," and "sticking to the point and probing further" (Trevithick, 2012, p. 72). Bharti's challenges allow Janice to understand that her problems are not insurmountable and neither do they need to adversely affect her mental health.

While the miracle question provides a useful tool for exploring solutions its appeal can lead inexperienced practitioners to leap into using this question without a real understanding, analysis, and assessment of what is happening in the client's lived world. It is useful therefore that any practitioner wanting to use this approach utilizes a range of skills and support networks that are available to them, such as using reflective learning to analyze for themselves what they believe is happening, and using other colleagues, such as community psychiatric nurses or psychologists who are sympathetic to the approach. Goal setting in this approach also enables social workers to demonstrate accountability, not only to their line managers, but also their client. For example, once Janice is able to interact more positively with Joseph, Bharti can also involve Alicia and Joseph in how they, as a family, manage their short-term and long-term situation. Bharti can adopt a role as an advocate in ensuring that Alicia's views are also heard. When emotions become heightened or unrealistic solutions are suggested (such as, Alicia should move into residential care, or, Joseph should not leave the family home) Bharti can use a combination of the responses of the miracle question and scaling questions to manage the situation until a resolution that is acceptable to them all as a family is achieved.

A further cautionary note regarding the miracle question is that, for some people, who practice a range of faiths and religion, the presumption that human beings possess the ability to create a miracle may be perceived as offensive. In order for the client to not misinterpret the miracle question its use must be considered alongside a clear assessment of the client's cultural and religious interpretation of the word in order for it to be anti-oppressive.

Conclusion

Solution-focused practice shares similarities to narrative approaches in social work. Both approaches are deemed to be critical approaches because they move away from perceiving clients as people who are defined solely by their mental health condition or distress, their physical impairment, their age, gender, and sexual orientation. Solution-focused practice challenges the perception of how it is that we (as society) have come to "know" how people with mental health conditions or distress should be treated or managed. Gomm and Davies (2000) claim that knowledge is socially constructed, and, in this respect, the predominant medical approach fails to recognize what Foucault (1972) refers to as the power/ knowledge coupling. This interconnection of knowledge and power challenges the notion that power is one sided. Foucault claims that power does not belong to any one person or group and that it can be exercised by anyone. In this respect it is possible to see that Janice is not powerless or a victim of her mental distress. She too has the capability and capacity to exercise power in managing and changing her destiny.

Points to Ponder

1. How could failing to adopt a strengths-based approach cause harm?
2. In what circumstances might you be able to use the miracle question?
3. In what ways is resilience important?

Key Texts

Kent, M., Davis, M. C. and Reich, J. W. (Eds.) (2013). *The resilience handbook: Approaches to stress and trauma*. New York: Routledge.
MacDonald, A. J. (2011). *Solution-focused therapy: Theory, research and practice* (2nd Edn.). London: Sage.
Saleebey, D. (2012). *The strengths perspective in social work* (6th Edn.). London: Pearson.

References

Berg, I. K. and de Shazer, S. (1993). Making numbers talk: Language in therapy. In S. Friedman (Ed.). *The new language of change: Constructive collaboration in psychotherapy*. New York: Guilford Press, pp. 5–24.

Berg, I. K. and Miller, S. D. (1992). *Working with the problem drinker: A solution-oriented approach*. New York: Norton.

de Jong, P. and Berg, I. K. (2013). *Interviewing for solutions* (4th Edn.). Pacific Grove, CA: Brooks/Cole.

de Shazer, S. (1985). *Keys to solution in brief therapy*. New York: Norton.

de Shazer, S. (1988). *Clues: Investigating solutions in brief therapy*. New York: Norton.

de Shazer, S. (1994). *Words were originally magic*. New York: Norton.

Foucault, M. (1972). *The archaeology of knowledge*. London: Tavistock.

Gomm, R. and Davies, C. (Eds.) (2000). *Using evidence in health and social care*. Maidenhead, UK: The Open University Press.

MacDonald, A. J. (2011). *Solution-focused therapy: Theory, research and practice* (2nd Edn.). London: Sage.

Ryan, P., Ramon, S. and Greacen, T. (2012). *Empowerment, lifelong learning and recovery in mental health*. Basingstoke, UK: Palgrave Macmillan.

Thompson, N. (2015). *Understanding social work: Preparing for practice* (4th Edn.). London: Palgrave.

Thompson, N. (2016). *The professional social worker: Meeting the challenge* (2nd Edn.). London: Palgrave.

Thompson, N. (2017). *Theorizing practice* (2nd Edn.). London: Palgrave.

Trevithick, P. (2012). *Social work skills and knowledge: A practice handbook* (3rd Edn.). Buckingham, UK: Open University Press.

11

MEDIATION

Wing Hong Chui

Introduction

This chapter discusses the relevance and use of mediation in social work practice. Mediation is widely perceived as one of the best non-confrontational methods to use for resolving conflicts between individuals, groups, organizations, communities and, at times, nations (Liebmann, 2000; Griffiths, 2013). It has become very popular for managing conflicts in a variety of contexts, ranging from our daily life to major international arenas (Jeong, 2010). This chapter is structured into three parts. The first part briefly defines what mediation is and then traces its historical development. The second part examines the role of mediators in various mediation approaches. By using illustrative examples from different fields of practice, the third part discusses how social workers can skillfully use mediation to promote the transformation of clients and yield the best outcomes by resolving the disputes.

What is Mediation?

Mediation is not a novel term because it: "occurs when we have a difference of opinion with someone with whom we are interacting," no matter whether the difference is a trivial or major issue (Turner and Rowe, 2013, p. 271). Conflict is inevitable in daily life, yet responses toward conflict and the resultant consequences can vary significantly. People often interpret conflict negatively to mean aggression, hostility, violence, or abuse. It is not difficult to imagine that minor conflicts or conflicts of a trivial nature can escalate into violence and abuse. However, this is only the case when conflict is not resolved and managed properly. It is important to note that conflict is not necessarily destructive and "indeed, it can present us with an opportunity to strengthen relationships and achieve personal growth" (Kruk, 1997, p. 1). Conflict does not always have to lead to family breakdowns or domestic violence; rather, conflict can also help strengthen family bonding through accommodating and compromising differences between family members. Therefore, learning how to respond to it effectively and skillfully would be essential toward living a harmonious life. Social workers have a key role to play in this regard. One important role that social workers have to play is to facilitate conflict resolution between service users, colleagues, supervisors and other community members.

Mediation is regarded as one of the key techniques to use in conflict resolution, which is a core competency for social workers and helping professionals (Barsky, 2007; Mizrahi and Davis, 2008). In the social work profession, apart from promoting the social functioning of our clients, promoting harmonious relationships among people in the community is another key mission. In line with the concepts of empowerment and the principle of self-determination, the focal concern of social workers revolves around understanding the client and their underlying beliefs and values. Similarly, in dealing with a dispute between two parties, the social worker must listen to the conflict narratives in order to help them arrive at a resolution or settlement. Mediation offers a specific approach for conflicting parties to resolve their dispute through developing a conflict competence. According to Bishop et al., resolving conflict competence refers to "the measure of a person's ability to successfully respond to and resolve interpersonal conflict" (2015, p. 21). In a mediation program, the social worker would assume the role of a facilitator, promoting dialogue and understanding between the conflicting parties and working toward a win–win solution. Therefore, social workers must have a solid grounding in the principles, techniques and best practices of mediation.

Mediation has been used in a wide range of contexts and is rapidly growing in social work and other areas of the human services, such as marriage and family disputes, divorce, post-divorce parenting, child protection and criminal justice (Kruk, 1997). Liebmann (2000) comments that several mediation initiatives have been introduced in the United Kingdom since the 1970s, and some of these examples were industrial or employment mediation, family mediation, school conflict resolution and mediation, victim-offender mediation, community mediation, commercial mediation, medical mediation, environmental mediation, elder mediation and organizational and workplace mediation.

Based upon my experience of social work, I was aware that many of my clients had experienced one or more disputes or conflicts, such as the following:

- The marriage between Elizabeth and her husband had not been going very well. While both agreed to apply for a joint application for a divorce, each of them wanted to fight over the rights to obtain custody over their three children. They also refused to reach an agreement in relation to the arrangements for maintenance and for the three properties they owned.
- Simon had been disturbed by the noise made by his next-door neighbors. They played loud music after midnight and early in the morning. Despite numerous attempts to discuss the situation with the neighbors face to face, the situation had remained the same. Simon was very emotionally and physically disturbed under such circumstances.
- Jason was a student in a nationally top-ranked primary school and had lately become very aggressive, both verbally and physically toward his best classmate, Tony. Jason had been angry with Tony since he was excluded from joining Tony's team in the recent inter-class basketball competition. Then, Jason called Tony a "faggot" and a "moron" when they came across each other, and even stole his stationery before an examination.

In relation to the case scenarios, what are the reasons for the conflict and how would you like to deal with these if you were a social worker? While acknowledging various ways of resolving conflict, mediation offers one solution to handle such conflicts by facilitating interaction and promoting collaborative problem-solving skills between individuals and groups. It is a preferred option for resolving conflicts of different kinds, because it focuses on the future, rather than on past behavior and provides the disputed parties with a forum to facilitate understanding and to restore broken relationships. Kruk defines the term mediation precisely and concisely in the following terms:

> Mediation is a collaborative conflict resolution process in which two or more parties in dispute are assisted in their negotiation by a neutral and impartial third party and empowered to voluntarily reach their own mutually acceptable settlement of the issues in dispute.
>
> (1997, p. 4)

In the early days, mediation was simply seen as a straightforward, non-confrontational process that involved discussions, suggestions, looking for alternatives and choosing the best option of dealing with the difference. Notably, the mediation process has become more sophisticated because of better conceptualization and refinement by a number of professionals in social work, business and legal settings in the past few decades. Kruk (1997, pp. 4–6) is the pioneer that has highlighted the seven core components of mediation which are in many ways consistent with the social work values of dignity and worth of person, importance of human relationships, self-determination and collaboration:

- Mediation is a distinct process or practice model that consists of several well-defined stages.
- Mediation is used when there is a dispute, conflict or disagreement between two or more parties.
- Collaboration that includes assertiveness and co-operation is the preferred mode of bringing those involved together into resolving their own conflicts.
- Areas such as communication, problem solving, exploring and evaluating options and reaching a mutually acceptable agreement should be the focus.
- The mediator needs to be neutral and impartial throughout the whole process.

- Empowering the parties to be responsible for making decisions and determining the outcome is essential.
- The process of reaching the agreement is free of coercion or control.

In sum, the ultimate goal of mediation is to help the parties involved find a win–win situation by facilitating the participation of all parties, usually within a limited timeframe. It is intended that no one should be left out or feels that he or she is being manipulated or betrayed by another party. This is to be achieved with the assistance of a third, neutral party who is often professionally trained and, ideally, accredited. To be an accredited mediator, qualified social workers will be required to undertake further specialized training and meet the requirements of an appropriate accreditation body in the country in which they are practicing. In recent years, there is evidence to suggest that national organizations or professional bodies have attempted to develop higher practice standards, thereby moving mediation "from the margins to the mainstream" (Liebmann, 2000, p. 34).

Major Approaches to Mediation

According to Bishop and his colleagues: "In some early conceptions of mediation, approaches were often classified as being either *content* or *process* intervention" (2015, p. 70). The former refers to the substantive issue relating to conflict resolution (that is, a problem-solving approach), whereas the latter is concerned with the communicative and relational aspects of the disputed parties (that is, social and individual growth and transformation). In contemporary thought, however, the duality of meditation goals, i.e. problem-solving versus social and individual growth and transformation intervention, have taken the form of a continuum, capable of aiding "disputants determine what type of mediation they wished to undertake and what type of mediator to use" (2015, p. 71). Conceptualized as a continuum of mediation goals, varying orientations of processes and roles in the mediation program can be within the decision-making power and preference of the disputants. For example, the disputants can opt for the role of the mediator to be a "dealmaker" or "orchestrator," or the involvement of the mediator to be "passive" or "active" (see 2015, p. 71 for more information).

With reference to the contrasting types of mediation, which one would you prefer to use when helping clients to deal with the conflict? Are the two mutually exclusive? Commentators in general reckon that the dualism in mapping the approach to mediation is still dominant in much of the existing literature, but rightly point out that mediation approaches are continuing to be refined and are becoming more integrative and eclectic than the dual classification (Barsky, 2007; Jeong, 2010).

Four of the more popular approaches to the contemporary practice of mediation, including the facilitative and evaluative approach, transformative approach, narrative approach and insight approach have been identified (Bishop et al., 2015). Each of these approaches reflects the differences in terms of how mediators perceive their role and the assumptions about the parties' expectations.

- The facilitative approach places more emphasis on encouraging and helping the parties to develop a better solution that meets the needs and interests of those involved. This facilitative approach focuses more on the *process*, as opposed to the *settlement*, and very often mediators pay special attention to the emotional and relational aspects of the conflict. The evaluative approach, which is sometimes called a settlement-focused mediation, focuses on the settlement, and an evaluative mediator is expected to guide the parties in order to propose and reach an agreement in a timely and reasonable manner.
- The transformative approach, which was introduced by Bush and Folger (1994): "is based on a more 'relational' view of conflict than the facilitative and evaluative approaches are" (cited in Bishop et al., 2015, p. 75). Based on a relational model, the transformative approach emphasizes the importance of empowering individuals to make informed decisions by understanding the underlying causes of the problems, being aware of their own abilities, goals, expectations and resources, and becoming more responsive to other parties' circumstances and actions. In this regard, conflicts are seen as an opportunity for personal and social transformation, rather than a process of looking for solutions to problems. This approach is valued especially in the child protection and youth justice settings, and that will be further discussed later in this chapter.

- The narrative approach seeks to enable the parties to uncover the causes of conflicts through "storytelling" or "telling conflict stories" in an open manner. Important to narrative mediators is the assumption that these conflict stories or narratives usually reflect a long history of tension or disagreement between parties due to cultural differences, such as ethnicity, gender, social class and religious backgrounds. Whilst acknowledging multiple and complicated stories at play, this approach encourages mutual respect, active listening and meaning making of lives and relationships among all the parties throughout the mediation process. In doing so, an alternative story that brings about the resolution of disputes can be constructed by seeking the co-operation of all parties.
- In line with the transformative and narrative approaches, the insight approach focuses on relational aspects (Bishop et al., 2015, pp. 77–78). However, its key goal is to facilitate learning by engaging parties in conversation and using lines of questioning on the needs, values and interests of the parties and their subjective interpretation of the personal and social experience. Its ultimate goal is to help them be aware of their emotions, values and understanding of the conflict they are involved in, thereby gaining insights into what can be done to address to the conflict co-operatively.

It is important to note that the above approaches are not exhaustive and can be used in our day-to-day practice according to the circumstances of the conflict, the mediator's orientation and style of managing conflicts and the parties' expectation and preference of how mediation should be used.

Using Mediation in Social Work Settings

Framework of the Mediation Process

No matter which mediation approach social workers use, the framework of the mediation process includes pre-mediation, cultivating dialogue, getting into the heart of the conflict, reaching decisions and completing the process, and post-mediation (Bishop et al., 2015). While these elements may or may not work in a linear order, they provide a guidepost for the mediator to follow. Prior to the commencement, the mediator needs to be in touch with both parties to see whether everyone is ready to go to mediation. The voluntary nature of their participation is vital to ensure their commitment to the mediation process. Central to the success, the mediator needs to create an atmosphere where the parties can share their emotions and personal and social experiences freely and discuss the underlying causes of the conflict honestly.

All this will help pave a way to reaching a resolution that both parties are satisfied with. Depending upon the context of the conflict, mediators may need to follow up with the parties, either separately or jointly to see whether the settlement is continuing to be honored and has been complied with according to the terms that have been agreed.

To illustrate further how mediation can be used in practice, the youth restorative justice conference model has been chosen as an example of articulating the role of the mediator or convenor throughout the process. Restorative justice conferencing has been developed to deal with young people who are in conflict with the law (Larsen, 2014). According to Marshall, restorative justice is defined as a: "process whereby all the parties with a stake in a particular offence come together to resolve collectively how to deal with the aftermath of the offence and its implications for the future" (1998, p 32). The conference has been used across the world as an alternative to formal prosecution of, and litigation in relation to, young offenders, including youth offending teams in some areas. By bringing the young offender, victim, their families, support persons, community representatives, police and legal representatives together, the convenor or mediator will facilitate all these parties to achieve a mutually agreeable resolution with the ultimate aim of reintegrating offenders in the community and giving the victim a voice in the process (Chui et al., 2005). It is noted that, in some places, such as Belgium, mediators are often the trained social worker (Bradt et al., 2014) and in others they are accredited mediators, such as in Queensland, Australia. Despite this, Table 11.1 summarizes the role of the convenor/facilitator in the youth justice conference system in Queensland. It follows very closely the mediation framework above.

Table 11.1 Function of Convenor/Facilitator in the Restorative Justice Conferencing System. Adapted from Queensland Government (2016)

Before the conference	• To meet with each participant to:
	   – discuss the conference process
	   – discuss what that person may want to share at the conference
	   – discuss what might happen at the conference
	   – answer any questions

At the conference	• To help everyone talk about what happened, how they were affected and how they feel about it • To facilitate the negotiation of an outcome between the participants • To help the participants to determine an agreeable outcome that can help the young offender make things better and prevent him or her from further offending • To reach an agreement which is signed by the victim and the young offender, and that it becomes legally binding
After the conference	• To ensure the young offender follows through on the agreed tasks • To take further action against the young offender if he or she fails to comply

Hayes and Daly (2003) report that in most jurisdictions in Australia, evaluation studies have measured levels of satisfaction among victims and offenders in conferences as an indicator of effectiveness. On the one hand, victims of crime were more satisfied with the process than they would have expected to be through the courts, and recognized that their needs were attended to fully during the mediation process. On the other, young offenders reported that they found the facilitated meeting fair and just, thereby promoting their understanding the impact of crime on others and their willingness to stop offending behavior (Hayes and Daly, 2003). This mediation practice has proven to be transformative by promoting offenders to change and restoring the relationship between the offender and the victim. The use of mediation in other fields of social work practice can be found in *Mediation and confliction resolution in social work and the human services* (Kruk, 1997) and *Conflict resolution for the helping professions* (Barsky, 2007).

Taking the example of Elizabeth and her husband described earlier in this chapter, assuming the role as a social worker, how would you consider whether mediation is the most appropriate method of intervention? If considered appropriate, how would you prepare the disputants before they sit face-to-face with each other? What difficulties would you anticipate in having the two disputants come together? How would you tackle these difficulties, ensuring that they both would work collaboratively? Finally, what skills would you use from your social work training to achieve this? There are no straightforward answers to these questions, but these are some of the questions that need to be addressed when doing mediation.

Essential Mediation Skills

Mediation is a unique and skilled process whereby a mediator plays an important role in offering assistance of various kinds to those who are in conflict with each other. Bishop et al. believe that an ability to communicate effectively is of utmost importance, and the key attributes of a skilled mediator include: "being empathetic [*sic*], non-judgmental, tolerant fair-minded, flexible, creative, patient yet persistent, optimistic, and having a healthy sense of humour" (2015, p. 17). Moss (2015, pp. 163–165) has articulated several mediation skills that mediators should be equipped with through continuous professional training. They are:

- Active listening and clarifying – identify what the conflict is about in terms of behavior, beliefs and emotions; focus on both verbal and non-verbal cues or signals from each of the disputants.
- Interpreting and clarifying – facilitate the disputants to express themselves clearly, despite being emotional when talking about the conflicting situation; make sure that everyone has a chance to convey their interpretations clearly; seek clarification if there are doubts and unclear expression.
- Summarizing – reflect on what has been discussed and what the common goals and interests are; highlight the major points for further elaboration and clarification if necessary; provide an account of important facts and the steps toward seeking a resolution.
- Mutualizing, normalizing and reframing – recognize the common ground and interests between all the parties concerned; invite

them to co-operate with each other, despite their differences; reframe negative statements to positive ones to encourage mutual understanding and respect; facilitate looking at a situation from a different perspective.

- Looking toward a "win–win" outcome – enable each party to reach an outcome that satisfies the interests and needs of both sides.

In addition to the above, other commentators believe that a mediator also needs to be a reflective practitioner who is able to reflect on his or her actions and interactions with the client in order to engage in a process of critical thinking and continuous learning (Barsky, 2007; Bishop et al., 2015). All these skills outlined are relevant not only to mediators, but also to social workers.

Conclusion

To conclude, mediation offers an alternative social work intervention to work with two or more individuals, groups or communities that are involved in conflicts. Conflicts can be a threat to interests, relationships and identities and they cause physical pain, suffering, ill feeling and fears for those parties involved. Some conflicts are rather minor and can be solved easily, and these may not cause significant impact. However, other conflicts cannot be resolved within a short period of time and therefore the disputants get involved, on either a mandatory or voluntary basis with the mediation service in order to receive help from them. It is not surprising to note that they may not have the personal capacity to talk about their differences because of the lack of trust and a low level of problem-solving abilities. Under such circumstances, the mediator has an intermediary or a neutral third party role to play in assisting people in conflict. As discussed earlier in this chapter, in terms of values and skills, mediation practice is entirely compatible with social work practice and therefore potentially a useful tool that can be used in a variety of conflict situations.

The mediator role is an integral part of social work. Social workers are well suited to taking up this role in a wide range of contexts, such as couple conflicts, child–parent disputes and discrimination in the workplace.

Points to Ponder

1. Think of one example of conflict you have recently experienced, where you had a dispute with a close friend. What makes you define it as a conflict? How would you account for the causes and sources of the conflict?

2. Imagine that you, as a mediator, were asked to help two spouses who are seeking a divorce and have arguments over the child custody and access arrangement before going to the family court. Which approach(es) to mediation would you like to use and why?

3. What skills do you feel you would need to be a successful mediator?

Key Texts

Bishop, P., Picard, C., Ramkay, R. and Sargent, N. (2015). *The art and practice of mediation* (2nd Edn.). Toronto: Emond Montgomery.

Kruk, E. (Ed.) (1997). *Mediation and conflict resolution in social work and the human services*. Chicago, IL: Nelson-Hall.

Liebmann, M. (Ed.) (2000). *Mediation in context*. London: Jessica Kingsley Publishers.

References

Barsky, A. E. (2007). *Conflict resolution for the helping professions* (2nd Edn.). Belmont, CA: Thomson.

Bishop, P., Picard, C., Ramkay, R. and Sargent, N. (2015). *The art and practice of mediation* (2nd Edn.). Toronto: Emond Montgomery.

Bradt, L., Bie, M. B. and de Visscher, S. (2014). Victim-offender mediation and social work: Focus groups with mediators in Flanders. *International Social Work*, 57(2), pp. 121–130.

Bush, R. A. B. and Folger, J. P. (1994). *The promise of mediation*. San Francisco, CA: Jossey-Bass.

Chui, W. H., Kidd, J. and Preston, C. (2005). Treatment of child and juvenile offenders in Queensland, Australia: Alternatives to prosecution. In T. W. Lo, D. Wong and G. Maxwell (Eds.) *Alternatives to prosecution: Rehabilitative and restorative models of youth justice*. Singapore: Marshall Cavendish, pp. 171–205.

Griffiths, H. (2013). Mediation approaches. In T. Lindsay (Ed.) *Social work intervention* (2nd Edn.). London: Sage, pp 167–184.

Hayes, H. and Daly, K. (2003). Youth justice conferencing and re-offending. *Justice Quarterly*, 20(4), pp. 725–764.

Jeong, H-W. (2010). *Conflict management and resolution: An introduction*. London: Routledge.

Kruk, E. (Ed.) (1997). *Mediation and conflict resolution in social work and the human services*. Chicago, IL: Nelson-Hall.

Larsen, J. J. (2014). *Restorative justice in the Australian criminal justice system* (Research and Public Policy Series 127). Canberra, ACT: Australian Institute of Criminology.

Liebmann, M. (2000). History and overview of mediation in the UK. In M. Liebmann (Ed.) *Mediation in context*. London: Jessica Kingsley Publishers, pp. 19–38.

Marshall, T. (1998). *Restorative justice: An overview*. St Paul, MN: Centre for Restorative Justice and Mediation.

Mizrahi, T. and Davis, L. E. (2008). *Encyclopedia of social work* (20th Edn.). New York: Oxford University Press.

Moss, B. (2015) *Communication and skills in health and social care* (3rd Edn.). London: Sage.

Queensland Government (2016). *About youth justice conferences*. Brisbane, QLD: Queensland Government.

Turner, F. J. and Rowe, W. S. (2013). *101 social work clinical techniques*. New York: Oxford University Press.

12

SOCIAL PEDAGOGY

Juha Hämäläinen

Introduction

This chapter deals with the nature of social pedagogy from the point of view of social work theory and methods. The term "social pedagogy" is introduced in its complexity, and social pedagogy's contribution to social work is explored and reflected on.

Social pedagogy is a holistic term reflecting ethical principles and humanist values – for example, that each person should be treated with dignity and respect to enable them to reach their true potential and make a meaningful contribution to society (www.thempra.org.uk/social-pedagogy). The term "social pedagogy" consists of two parts, both with different connotations. The term "pedagogy" refers to "education" and "learning." The term "social" indicates that it is an approach with a community-related perspective and a society-wide responsibility.

From the very beginning, social pedagogy was introduced as a theoretical standpoint focusing on the social aspects of education instead of a limited concentration on individuals. It emphasized the importance of regarding education as a means to shape social reality in ethically justified ways. It can therefore be understood as a social work method that seeks to bring about positive change by using particular educational approaches to empower individuals, families, groups and communities to address their problems and challenges.

A Complex Term

Social pedagogy is a complex term used in different contexts (Hämäläi-nen, 2015). Historically, there is "an indisputable heterogeneity of social pedagogy" (Niemeyer et al., 1999, p. 7). The variety of contexts, meanings and understandings makes it quite difficult to use the term consistently and coherently. It refers, for example, to a:

- theoretical tradition in education, especially that of educational philosophy and educational sociology;
- field or context for social movements engaged in community development;
- theoretical framework for educational and societal development; and
- particular approach, paradigm or school of thought in social work.

As a tradition of educational theory, social pedagogy operates at the interface of society and education. In this sense, it is about reflecting on the social nature of education, combining social and educational theories, examining the underlying social context and considering the place of education in social policy and social development.

As a field for social movements and community development, social pedagogy is a set of activities combining social aims with educational means to strengthen individual/community/society relationships. Examples of civil activities based on this combination include, settlements for disadvantaged people (see Chapter 17 in this volume), activities in popular education and the educational movement for public health. The idea is to tackle social disadvantage through educational measures based on community participation as active citizens in the public interest. Such activities have often taken on an innovative pioneering character in the development of different welfare services across the public and voluntary sectors in the United Kingdom, the third sector in Europe and private market and voluntary agencies in the United States. Educational means are increasingly and widely used also in developing countries to promote well-being and social development.

As a theoretical framework, social pedagogy connects the fields of social work, social policy, youth work and education at the organizational level and provides an educational perspective and innovative tools for a range of practitioners. It has broad reach and covers all professional groups, such as social workers, youth and community workers, play workers and teachers operating in the field.

As an approach, paradigm or school of thought in professional social work, the term "social pedagogy" is used in a variety of ways and has contributed to social work becoming a holistic discipline.

From *Paideia*[1] to Social Help: A Brief Historical and Spiritual Journey

In the history of western thought, an understanding of the importance of education for social development was first conceptualized by social philosophers in ancient Greece. They considered ethical, political and pedagogical questions as preconditions for social and cultural development. For example, Plato's social philosophical opus, *The Republic*, was a study of the political and pedagogical preconditions for justice in society. Correspondingly, Aristotle dealt with these three elements in *Politics* and other social philosophical studies.

The significance of education for social and cultural development was encompassed in the Greek idea of *paideia* (see Jaeger, 1934/1937). Later this view was adopted by scholars of the Renaissance. Increasingly attention was paid – to the detriment of fatalism – to people's opportunities to influence their temporal destiny on an individual level and collectively as a society. This led to optimism during the age of Enlightenment that our understanding could be explained by logic, reason and the pursuit of objective knowledge that would enable social problems to be tackled.

Two strategies for social development were developed: political and pedagogical. Political strategies were concerned with social infrastructure, legislation, social institutions, policy and governance, while the latter aimed at social development, by influencing people, their morals, values and cultural beliefs. Increasingly, problems of social disadvantage and inequality were viewed as challenges for education to try and help solve. Historically, the social pedagogical tradition in educational theory building, policy and social work practice originates from this spiritual ground.

Along with modernization, industrialization and urbanization, the social structures of the traditional estate society broke down and new social problems came into existence. Increasingly, education was viewed as a remedy for tackling poverty, neglect, criminality and other social problems (Dollinger, 2006). Education, in theory and practice, was developed as an instrument of social assistance and social change.

Social pedagogy originates from the educational need to balance the discrepancies between individual autonomy and the demands of modern society (Reyer, 2002), particularly on children and young people (Mollenhauer, 1957). On the one hand, social pedagogy is a theory-based tradition around the socialization of the entire population; on the other hand, it is about educational help for people with special social and educational needs. In practice, these two developments intertwine.

As an educational tradition, social pedagogy can be seen to express a pedagogical dimension of social work (Hämäläinen, 2003). Representing an educational view of social and psychosocial problems, it provides educational strategies and methods of help for social work to deal with people's social needs. Moreover, it presents an education-centered concept of the individual in society and a social theory in which education is seen as a key element in the build-up of the relationships across individuals, communities and society.

Core Ideas Relevant to Social Work

It is common to introduce social pedagogy as an entity consisting of different approaches and paradigms expressing different concepts of humankind and society, diverse moral philosophies and even various worldviews and political interests (Hämäläinen, 2015). As such, it could not be *an* approach or *a* paradigm of social work, but rather a constellation or a set of approaches and paradigms shaped by country-specific political, cultural and institutional factors (Lorenz, 2008).

Generally, social pedagogy provides an educational lens for social work. Drawing on theory and practice in education, it attempts to project social work as an educational activity and reframe the aims and means of social work in terms of education. The global mission of social work and its aspiration to tackle social problems and promote social integration, participation and emancipation are seen in the context of an educational partnership. In this way, social pedagogy exerts a decisive influence on social work practice.

Social work operates with clients in difficult life situations, aiming to help them to cope with and overcome a range of practical difficulties and problems. It aims to strengthen their ability to manage problems, find solutions and generate practical changes through educational interaction. Utilizing the concept of critical dialogue developed by Paulo Freire (1972), the great Brazilian education theorist, people are empowered to develop a critical consciousness, reflect upon the nature of their problems and seek opportunities to promote social change.

We will now consider how social pedagogy can be used in work with young offenders, complement community social work, tackle discrimination against migrant children and support older people.

Social Work with Young Offenders

How can social pedagogy influence social work with young offenders? We know well that people cannot be forced to stop doing something – for example, not to commit crime. Young offenders must be helped to conclude that there is more to life than theft or vandalism. Pedagogic interaction aims to make young offenders aware of this and help change their behavior (see Chapter 5 in this volume). Furthermore, it facilitates critical reflection and the self-assessment of the aims, means and quality of social work practice. Indeed, social pedagogy is not restricted to the individual mind only, but considers people in their social and cultural context. Juvenile offending, for example, is seen as not only an individual issue, but also a cultural reality that shapes and reinforces the lives and priorities of young offenders.

Despite the complexity of the term, with its diverse theoretical bases and practical intentions, some common elements of social pedagogy can be identified, such as engaging in critical exploration, the systematic and sequential questioning of an issue which might elicit potentially different answers or an agreed way of identifying the most appropriate problem, say anger management or low self-esteem, to apply a theoretical focus. There will, of course, always be different ways of addressing such problems. This may be the most relevant starting point for approaching questions about how social pedagogy relates to contemporary social work and what it brings to the discipline.

In general, three trends in social pedagogical ways of thinking in relation to theory and practice can be identified which reflect a Nordic and northern European approach (Eriksson, 2014). The first is an *adapting trend* concerned with an individual orientation by applying community-oriented individual methods; second, the *mobilizing trend* comprises a collective orientation aimed at social emancipation through encouraging people to cooperate to ameliorate common social problems; and third is the *democracy-oriented trend* which is mostly about citizenship education in a democratic society.

In the broadest range of its use, the concept of social pedagogy combines social and educational dimensions of human existence – two fundamental aspects of life – comprehensively covering these two important contexts of human action. The social pedagogical schools of thought are representative of different worldviews concerning the concepts of the person and society. The fields of application are many and varied, regardless of the nature of individual approaches to theory and methods.

Influencing Community-based Social Work

As a discipline and a field of social work, social pedagogy deals fundamentally with the issue of social integration, focusing on the processes of human development that are necessary for an individual's growth in their social functioning, involvement and participation. It covers pedagogical activities that aim to promote these processes, as well as the problems that people have in integrating successfully in communities and social systems that are important for social development (see Chapters 15 and 17 in this volume).

Considering social work as an educational activity, social pedagogy tends to steer social work towards operating essentially at the boundary of person/community/society relationships. It is not specifically about person-to-person interaction, but working in and through communities, based on an understanding of the educational potential of those communities. It aims to promote and enable people's self-education, by making them aware of the need to take greater responsibility for community development. It is also about strengthening communities' educational potential by promoting their collective awareness of the benefits of self-development.

It is common to face the increasing problem of social exclusion in social work. The danger exists, however, of focusing narrow-mindedly on what is wrong with people for whom integration with the communities they belong to proves difficult. This also applies to the social systems important for their living, life management and quality of life, such as schooling, employment and leisure activities. Social exclusion is a relational matter, not an individual characteristic. Moreover, this raises the question of what is wrong with the communities, social networks and societal systems, which some individuals, or even groups of people, find it difficult to integrate with and become excluded from. Social pedagogy directs the social worker's attention to these relationships and systems, instead of concentrating on repairing people's imaginary personal defects.

Social Work with Older People

In social work with older people the social pedagogical perspective means that attention is paid to the social and educational needs of older persons in relation to their opportunities for human growth as members of their communities and networks. Social work programs aiming to strengthen older people's citizenship, for example, may benefit from, and be connected with, social pedagogical ideas of citizenship education (Payne, 2012). Correspondingly, social work programs aiming to improve older people's potential for personal relationships, independent life and preparing for death may utilize pedagogical ideas, theories and methods.

Discrimination against Migrant Children

Social work deals with many forms of social exclusion, such as the isolation of migrant children and families, young people's dropout from schooling, long-term unemployment and the social isolation of older people. How does social pedagogy enlighten social work in the case of extensive bullying and discrimination against migrant children at school?

Practice Focus 12.1

Adnan was a 14-year-old Syrian boy who came to Finland last year with his mother and 12-year-old sister, Asil. His father and older brother were back in Aleppo caught up in the conflict. While Asil seemed to have settled well in school and was making progress with the Finnish language, Adnan was very unhappy, and a sympathetic teacher had discovered that he was being bullied. Timo, a social worker attached to the school, offered to help using a social pedagogic approach.

Timo's first step was to establish a pedagogic relationship with Adnan, and attempt to inspire confidence by reassuring him that they were both on the same side. After gaining Adnan's trust, Timo offered support and helped him to analyze and reflect on the situation to try and find a solution. This included: enhancing Adnan's social integration by encouraging him to make new friends, take up his hobbies and other leisure activities.

Four simultaneous pedagogic strategies were used to tackle the problem of bullying:

1. Assisting Adnan to rise morally above the problem and try to see it as an opportunity for personal growth and self-education, while conveying hope and reassurance.

2. With Adnan's approval, making contact with his family to discuss the situation. Recognizing the trauma of what they have experienced in Syria, with continuing worry about the father and brother in Aleppo, difficulties associated with being refugees and adapting to life in a new cultural environment. Involving his mother (with the help of a translator) and sister to support Adnan, while offering the family intellectual, emotional and practical support. Over time access to parent education should prove helpful.

3. Working in partnership with school staff to activate the anti-bullying policy. If possible, establishing an educational

dialogue with the bullies and promoting change through constructive personal relations.

4. Establishing contact with key members of the local community to get their support to promote non-bullying lifestyles, greater understanding and tolerance towards new migrants and creating a socializing culture among the community's young people.

The main points that follow from Practice Focus 12.1 are the importance of:

1. Seeing the school as a collective learning community, and strengthening its capacity for appropriate pedagogical action.
2. Working with families – both migrant and others – to strengthen parenting skills, so that parents and children can tackle problems together.
3. Cooperation with school to tackle problems in partnership. The pedagogical influence may also extend to the residents' community, and organizations and clubs representing children's leisure interests. In general, the school, parents and residents working together offers the best prospect for achieving the desired pedagogical outcomes.

The consideration of communities' potential for self-determination in its appropriate educational context is something that can be applied to all communities. This includes families, neighborhoods, groups of friends, school classes and clubs, as well as larger communities and the wider society. Thus, social work can be inspired by social pedagogy in terms of a community-based way of pedagogical thinking.

Social pedagogy provides conceptual frameworks for social work and other social professions for theorizing about professional practice from the point of view of the qualities of clients' human relationships, communities and social networks for human development and self-education. Recently, it was introduced in the United Kingdom as a particular educational activity in childcare and youth education, by emphasizing its potential for developing communication skills that are crucially needed in these fields (Cameron and Moss, 2011). At the same time, while it has been adapted to the professional needs of social work (Hatton, 2013), it is not a concept limited to one profession or one field.

Use in Different Fields

Social pedagogy is not a set of special pedagogical methods and techniques, but, rather, a perspective on people in their appropriate social context. However, this perspective provides groundwork for the development of relevant pedagogical measures focusing on people's inherent potential for development. Social pedagogy provides both methodological principles and context-specific working methods for many kinds of educational activities, both in the fields of formal and non-formal education as well as professional social work and social care.

On the one hand, social pedagogy – as a discipline and a field of education – is seen to cover the whole life course (for example, Kornbeck and Rosendal Jensen, 2011/2012), and on the other it is seen to focus – only or particularly – on working with children and young people (for example, Mollenhauer, 2001; Cameron and Moss, 2011; Petrie, 2011; Storø, 2013). It contributes not only to the fields of early education, youth work and child and family care, but also to the education of older people (Hämäläinen and Nivala, 2015).

Considering age-specific social and educational needs, social pedagogy provides age-specific innovations to social work practice related to the challenge of social integration. In the fields of early youth and adult education, as well as corresponding areas of care work in health organizations, its tasks and methods vary according to the function of the target groups, organizations and educational challenges it is dealing with (Eriksson and Winman, 2010). When considering social pedagogy as a special field of education, the focus is on marginalized groups and people in difficult life situations. There is a wide range of such contexts, including disability, unemployment, youth offending and inability to manage in everyday life activities. In social pedagogy, the challenge is often the development of pedagogical tools for helping people face difficult life situations and strengthen their social integration skills, both as individuals and communities. These ideas are extremely relevant for developing critically reflective models of social work practice.

The meaning of social pedagogy for social work practice does not concern only case- and situation-specific activities, but also the understanding we have of social work as a professional discipline. It helps to shape professional identity and culture, and the function and legitimacy of social work in modern society (Thompson, 2016). The same client situation can be approached in very different ways by both individual social workers and social work organizations. It is not merely a question of methods and techniques, as such, but a wider orientation and understanding about the nature of social work. Social pedagogy encourages social workers and social work organizations to pay attention to educational matters in defining and fulfilling their function and tasks, as well as for quality assessment.

Social Pedagogy and Critically Reflective Practice

In general, social pedagogy contributes to critically reflective models of social work practice in many different theoretical contexts, from therapeutic and individual reformist models to those orientated towards radical social change (see Payne, 2014). It brings educational reflection to social work practice by providing an ethically sound humanitarian perspective which highlights people's educability and opportunities for developing their capacity for self-education, self-help and self-improvement. This can be achieved both individually and collectively. A good example of this concerns how Freire's ideas have been adopted in social work since the 1970s, particularly influencing the theory and practice of radical social work and community social work (see Chapter 17 in this volume).

Conclusion

Social Pedagogy Contributes to the Theory of Social Work

Social pedagogy provides a special tradition of educational philosophy to social work theory by focusing on people's relationships with their social environments from the point of view of education. The social environments that people live in are considered educational contexts that make people's human development, social and cultural involvement, participation and active citizenship possible. It aims to strengthen communities and society's educational capacity to integrate and emancipate people and provide a setting for social cohesion.

Social pedagogy represents a particular theoretical orientation in social work, despite its varied forms, that steers social workers and social work organizations to reflect upon the quality of practice on offer. It does this by applying pedagogical criteria to promote clients' capacity for social integration, participation and emancipation. In this sense, how it is accepted and utilized in social work is a broader question involving philosophy, theory and practice. Social pedagogy provides an education-related perspective for many subfields of social work (Hämäläinen, 2003). In this sense, social work theory building can benefit from social pedagogical reflections and critical exploration.

There are numerous examples of working practice inspired by social pedagogical ways of thinking in different contexts. Some fields focus on care, some on education and some on social help, and the practice procedures vary in relation to clients' needs, both between and within the care, education and social work sectors. In care, for instance, there are many examples, from kindergartens to institutional childcare, home care for older people, and long-term hospital care for different medical reasons for patients of different ages and with different social and educational needs.

Social Pedagogy Contributes to Methods of Social Work

Social pedagogical practice is often defined in terms of critical dialogue, creative methods and community-related activities. As a profession or a professional field integrated within social work, social pedagogy is connected to counseling and guidance, and therapeutic person-to-person approaches. Generally, a social pedagogical orientation is characterized by meetings with an educational focus and person-to-person interaction.

In the field of social care, social pedagogy is seen as an educational approach complementing medical and nursery care. In youth work activities that encourage young people's participation, self-determination and self-education are organized. In social work, the methods are context specific and sensitive to clients' needs.

It may be useful for social work and related professions to consider social pedagogy as a dialogue-based educational activity that strives for social emancipation (Stephens, 2013). Further, social work methods are often community-based, activity-based and experience-orientated, based on and aimed at the active participation of people (Hämäläinen and Nivala, 2015). Social pedagogy provides social work with theoretical frameworks and concepts for the development of creative working methods. These are inspired by a social pedagogical way of thinking, supported by research evidence, mobilization for collective self-development (Eriksson, 2014) and pedagogic interaction in relation to interpersonal communication (Petrie, 2011).

However, the most significant yield for social work from the social pedagogical tradition may be the opportunity to reflect and theorize and to inspire those around us to improve existing working methods and designs. Social pedagogy itself is more about educational theory linked to philosophical anthropology and social ethics than a selection of methods and techniques. It provides an ethically sound platform for critically reflective working in the fields of social work and education.

Points to Ponder

1. How do you perceive the contribution of pedagogical orientation to parent support in the field of child care with families suffering from poverty in particular?
2. How would a pedagogical orientation help social work with young substance misusers?
3. How might a pedagogical working orientation contribute alongside psychiatric assessments in residential child care?

Key Texts

Eriksson, L. (2014). The understandings of social pedagogy from northern European perspectives. *Journal of Social Work*, 14(2), pp. 165–82.
Hämäläinen, J. (2003). The concept of social pedagogy in the field of social work. *Journal of Social Work*, 3(1), pp. 69–80.
Lorenz, W. (2008). Paradigms and politics: Understanding methods paradigms in an historical context: The case of social pedagogy. *British Journal of Social Work*, 38(4), pp. 625–44.

Note

1. In ancient Greece, *paideia* referred to the rearing and education of an ideal member of the polis.

References

Cameron, C. and Moss, P. (2011). *Social pedagogy and working with children and young people: Where care and education meet.* London: Jessica Kingsley Publishers.

Dollinger, B. (2006). *Die Pädagogik der Sozialen Frage: (Sozial-)Pädagogische Theorie vom Beginn des 19. Jahrhunderts bis zum Ende der Weimarer Republik.* Wiesbaden: VS Verlag für Sozialwissenschaften.

Eriksson, L. (2014). The understandings of social pedagogy from northern European perspectives. *Journal of Social Work*, 14(2), pp. 165–82.

Eriksson, L. and Winman, T. (Eds.) (2010). *Learning to fly: Social pedagogy in a contemporary society.* Gothenburg: Daidalos.

Freire, P. (1972). *Pedagogy of the oppressed.* Harmondsworth, UK: Penguin.

Hämäläinen, J. (2003). The concept of social pedagogy in the field of social work. *Journal of Social Work*, 3(1), pp. 69–80.

Hämäläinen, J. (2015). Defining social pedagogy: Historical, theoretical and practical considerations. *British Journal of Social Work*, 45(3), pp. 1022–38.

Hämäläinen, J. and Nivala, E. (2015). Social pedagogy. In L. H. Meyer (Ed.) *Oxford bibliographies in education.* New York: Oxford University Press.

Hatton, K. (2013). *Social pedagogy.* Lyme Regis, UK: Russell House Publishing.

Jaeger, W. (1934/1937). *Paideia. Die Formung des griechischen Menschen.* 3 Vols. Berlin: de Gruyter.

Kornbeck, J. and Rosendal Jensen, N. (Eds.) (2011/2012). *Social pedagogy for the entire lifespan.* 2 Vols. Bremen, Germany: Europäischer Hochschulverlag.

Lorenz, W. (2008). Paradigms and politics: Understanding methods paradigms in an historical context: The case of social pedagogy. *British Journal of Social Work*, 38(4), pp. 625–44.

Mollenhauer, K. (1957). *Die Ursprünge der Sozialpädagogik in der industriellen Gesellschaft. Eine Untersuchung zur Struktur sozialpädagogischen Denkens und Handelns.* Weinheim and Basel: Beltz Verlag.

Mollenhauer, K. (2001). *Einführung in die Sozialpädagogik. Probleme und Begriffe der Jugendhilfe.* Weinheim and Basel: Beltz Verlag.

Niemeyer, C., Schröer, W. and Böhnisch, L. (Hrsg.) (1999). *Grundlinien Historischer Sozialpädagogik. Traditionsbezüge, Reflexionen und übergangene Sozialdiskurse.* Weinheim and Munich: Juventa.

Payne, M. (2012). *Citizenship social work with older people.* Chicago, IL: Lyceum Books.

Payne, M. (2014). *Modern social work theory* (4th Edn.). Basingstoke, UK: Palgrave Macmillan.

Petrie, P. (2011). *Communication skills for working with children and young people: Introducing social pedagogy* (3rd Edn.). London: Jessica Kingsley Publishers.

Reyer, J. (2002). *Kleine Geschichte der Sozialpädagogik. Individuum und Gemeinschaft in der Pädagogik der Moderne.* Baltmannsweiler: Schneider Verlag Hohengehren GmbH.

Stephens, P. (2013). *Social pedagogy: Heart and head.* Bremen, Germany: Europäische Hochschulverlag.

Storø, J. (2013). *Practical social pedagogy: Theories, values and tools for working with children and young people.* Bristol: The Policy Press.

Thompson, N. (2016). *The professional social worker: Meeting the challenge* (2nd Edn.). London, Palgrave. www.thempra.org.uk/social-pedagogy/

13

FAMILY THERAPY

Robert Taibbi

Introduction

Family therapy came into its own in the 1960s and early 1970s, and, like other forms of therapy, has been shaped over time by both emerging research and new clinical models. In this chapter we will look at family therapy from its foundational core, namely a family systems perspective, and begin with a discussion of some key concepts.

Process

Therapy is divided into content and process. Content is what the family talks about and often argues about: Tuesday vs. Wednesday; what the text message said; how often Sam leaves his backpack in the living room. Process is content and problems in motion: that dad always blows up when he sees Sam's backpack lying in the middle of the living room; that mom tries to dominate the conversation in the session. While the family is often trying to drag you into the content to sort and decide who is right and who is wrong, your focus is most often on the process, what unfolds in the room, in the home. This is where the problem lies, in the movement, not the facts; here in the process is where the family gets stuck in solving their own problems.

Patterns

Process solidifies into interactional patterns. In contrast to the individual pathology models that look at problems residing within the individual's psyche and past that then need to be unraveled, family systems models look at problems in the present, created by the way family members bounce off each other in set ways: Dad sees the backpack and yells; Sam yells back, dad threatens to take away his phone, Sam picks up the backpack and stomps away. Often in families the patterns are more complex. Dad yells, Sam yells back, mom tells dad to leave Sam alone, dad starts to argue with mom. Though the content changes, the pattern – of dad yelling at Sam and mom taking Sam's side – is repeated over and over. One of the goals of therapy is to detect and help the family see where problematic patterns are arising, stopping them, and helping the family change them.

Structure

The source of many problematic patterns is faulty family structure. Here we can look to Minuchin (1974) and his structural family therapy. According to Minuchin, the ideal family structure looks something like Figure 13.1.

What we see are two parents. The solid line represents their being on the same page regarding parenting rules and routines. The Cs are the children and the solid lines between them represent the fact that the children, while there is occasional sibling rivalry, are supportive of each other. The solid line separating the parents and children and the fact that the children are below the line denotes that there is a hierarchy in place: the parents are in charge, have more power, and there is a couple relationship separate from the children.

What we often see in families in therapy are skewed variations on this ideal. Instead of the parents being on the same page, they disagree and

Figure 13.1 Ideal family structure.

the children are confused or constantly split the parents. Or the parents are not connected at all, or one of the parents is below the line and allied with the children, and in fact treated like one of the kids. Or in the worst case scenario, one of the children is actually on top, running the family, leaving the parents feeling powerless and victimized.

Bowen Self-Differentiation

Minuchin's family structure gives a way of quickly assessing the family, by comparing what we see against this ideal, much in the same way your physician may assess your health by comparing your lab work against known healthy standards. A model that we can use for assessing adults is that of Bowen (1993) and his notion of self-differentiation. According to him, adults who are self-differentiated are able to regulate their emotions, and, rather than spraying them around the room, use them as information about what they need and what problems they need to solve. Those who are less differentiated tend to absorb and react to the emotions of those around them. Differentiated individuals are able to be assertive, rather than aggressive or passive, can set appropriate boundaries and let others know what they need. Finally, they are committed to their values, can be compassionate towards others, seeing them as struggling, rather than being malicious or manipulative.

In practical terms this model is similar to what is thought of in law as the "reasonable [wo]man" standard – evaluating someone's behavior against what we could expect a reasonable person to do in any given situation. In assessing families, we can make the same assessment, noting that dad constantly blows up and yells at Sam, rather than more calmly setting expectations and enforcing limits.

Learning Problems vs. Problems about Learning

This concept was articulated by Ekstein and Wallerstein (1958) in their classic text on psychotherapy. According to them we can divide problems into two broad types: learning problems, those arising because we simply lack the knowledge and skills; and problems about learning, where we have the knowledge and skills, but override them with our emotions. Discovering in which category family members fall can give us an additional way of seeing where and how clients get stuck in solving their problems.

To go back to our example, dad may be yelling at Sam because dad basically lacks parenting skills. He did not have good role models and literally doesn't know that there are more effective ways of parenting Sam besides venting his frustration and making threats. Or, it may be that dad overall does in fact have a good repertoire of skills and is generally a good father, but there is something about the backpack that simply pushes his emotional buttons and, when it does, his skills go out the window.

Looking at problems this way can be applied to a host of common family problems. Is the Jones family struggling with money because they lack skills? For example, do the parents not know how to set up and work within a budget or balance a checkbook? Or is it because they do have a budget, but blow it when dad gets angry at his wife and, rather than talking with her about it, channels his anger into rationalizing that he needs a new fishing rod?

Problems as Bad Solutions

There is yet another useful way of looking at problems, namely the concept of problems as bad solutions. What this means is that usually what others may see as a problem in another, is for that individual in fact merely a solution, albeit not always a good one, for another problem that lies beneath. Dad's yelling and threats are a bad solution to managing his frustration; cutting and other forms of self-harm are bad solutions to being emotionally overwhelmed; running away is a bad solution to internal stress; affairs are bad solutions to relationship problems. Whatever you think of as a problem, your next question is: If this is the bad solution what is the real problem beneath? Thinking about, and presenting issues in this way, help to redefine the problem, move towards its source, and change the conversation.

Look for the Holes

Therapy is about creating change, and change means helping clients move outside their comfort zones. Looking for the holes is looking for what is not in the room – what emotions are not expressed, what topics are not raised. This is similar to the concept in art of positive and negative space. Say you are painting a picture of an orange. The orange, what you focus on, would be the positive space, while the background around the orange that you don't notice would be the negative space.

By seeing what a family doesn't present, what is in the background tells us where we and they need to go. The changing of patterns and process and structure, the move toward differentiation, the solution to their problems lie here, where they are not. If what we always hear from dad is anger, we are not hearing soft emotions like worry, fear, or love and we may want to move him in that direction. If mom is always dominating the session, what we are not hearing is from others in the family, and so ask them to join in. If the parents are always focusing on what Sam does wrong, rather than what he does right, or on how Sam and they never mention his brother, Tom. We may want to ask what Sam does well or ask them to tell us about Tom.

This moving towards the negative space, the holes, changes and deepens the conversation, arouses new emotions and, with it, new perspectives and ideas. The process shifts, creating the basis for real change.

Family Concepts in Action

In order to see how these concepts may be applied, let's build on our earlier example:

The Johnson family consists of dad, Ken, mom, Cheryl, 14-year-old Sam, and 8-year-old Tom. Cheryl contacts you after Sam and Ken had a huge argument over the weekend that resulted in the police being called. Ken, Cheryl, and Sam come to the first session; Tom is absent, tied up with an after-school activity.

As with other forms of therapy you have several essential goals in those all-important opening sessions. You need to build rapport, in this case with each family member. You need to assess to determine the source of the problem and where the family struggles to solve their problems on their own. You need to offer a new perspective and ideally a preliminary intervention plan so that they have a pathway out of their problems. Finally, you want to make sure that they feel differently when they walk out than when they walked in.

Your feedback of your assessment and intervention plan will go a long way in doing this, but you also want to look for ways of changing the emotional climate in the room by drawing out new emotions and changing their experience. If you don't and they have merely replicated the problem in your office and little else, they will leave with the impression that therapy is not effective, that what they did with you they could have done at home. To avoid this danger you need to show leadership and shape the process unfolding in the room, deepening the conversation.

You start by helping the family settle and begin to build rapport by introducing yourself, touching base with each of the family members. You ask the parents about their jobs, how long they have been married; you ask Sam about school, friends, hobbies. The goal is to have each one begin to build a connection to you, albeit small.

You notice that Ken easily engages; Cheryl seems a bit shy and quiet; Sam, though slow to open up, quickly begins to warm up and answer your questions. You then turn the corner and ask what brings them in. Not surprisingly, Ken starts. He describes how he and Sam got into it again – this time about cleaning up his room, Ken telling him he couldn't go out with his friends until the room was cleaned up. Sam "copped that attitude he always has," started talking back, and both escalated. Cheryl "as usual" undermined Ken yet again; he told her to stay out of it. Both Sam and Ken started pushing each other, Cheryl called the police who told them that they needed to settle down or they would press charges. They did calm down, but the family hasn't talked to each other since. As Ken describes the events you notice that he sounds more and more frustrated and angry.

You turn to Sam. What does he think about what his dad has just said? He's always on my back, Sam says. I can't do anything right. Ken jumps in: If you would just do what I ask we wouldn't have these problems … Sam starts to argue back.

They are beginning to replicate the problem. You need to step up and stop the process; if you don't they will continue and see you as condoning what is unfolding. You call a halt. You turn to Cheryl. What do think about all this?

Cheryl, in her quiet voice, says that they do this all the time. Ken is always on Sam's back. In fact, she says, he is always on everyone's back – always critical, always controlling. Even of you, you ask? All the time; I'm sick of this, she snaps. But you're always siding with the kids, says Ken. How come I'm always the bad guy? Why don't you see what needs to be done. Why am I the only parent here? He's angry again. Do you both try and talk about this? Cheryl snaps again: I've given up.

What do we know so far? Actually a lot. Let's use our concepts as a checklist:

Process: The family is doing a good job of showing us their process and how the arguments unfold. What they are not doing which a lot of families do, is getting mired in facts or try to drag you in to take sides. They are comfortable enough to speak their minds and say what is bothering them.

Patterns: We can already see what their problematic pattern is, namely that Ken makes a demand of Sam, Sam snaps back, Cheryl backs up Sam, Ken feels undermined and gets more angry, Sam and Ken escalate. Also, the fact that none of them has spoken to each other, circled back to try and repair the relationship and solve the problem, gives a clue as to why the problems persist.

Family structure: Cheryl and Ken are clearly not working as a team and are not on the same page regarding expectations for the children. The result is that Ken always feels like the "bad guy" who has no support from Cheryl, leaving Cheryl undoubtedly looking to the kids to be easier and less demanding; we could guess that the kids probably ask for permission to do things when Ken is not around.

And Cheryl herself too feels Ken's criticism and control. We could imagine that she identifies with the kids, rather than feeling equal with Ken; she is below the line of hierarchy and Ken stands there lonely and alone.

Differentiation: What can't Ken do that a "reasonable" man would do? Well, we know that. He would control his temper and channel it towards solving the problems with Sam. He would try and have calm discussions with Cheryl about the kids and expectations, as well as try and understand better why and how she sees things differently. Rather than seeing Sam as defiant and malicious and always copping an attitude, he would try and be more compassionate towards him.

And Cheryl? She too would speak up and, if feeling criticized and controlled and like one of the children, have an adult conversation with Ken about this so that he can better understand what she needs, rather than giving up and then allying herself with Sam.

Finally Sam. We need to consider his age, the teenage ability to push back and the greater difficulty with self-regulation. That said, we wonder why he so quickly angers and digs in.

Learning problems: Is Ken struggling with skills? Certainly could be since he is described as always controlling and critical. Does he need to learn other ways of controlling his emotions as well as dealing with a teenage son? Or does he carry around a lot of stress that override his skills and cause him to fall into the problematic pattern with Sam? Does the couple lack good communication skills overall and so can't have those calmer conversations?

Problems as bad solutions: Are Ken's arguments with Sam an emotional outlet for other emotions that Ken cannot handle? He seems isolated from his family – is this the only way he has of connecting, albeit unhelpfully? Has Sam learned to take the negative attention that Ken gives him, rather than getting no attention at all? And what about the younger brother? Just as parents get polarized, so too can siblings. If Tom is the good kid, he can be a tough act for Sam to follow.

Holes: What's not in the room? We see and hear Ken's anger and frustration but no soft emotions so far. Cheryl is speaking up, but at home seems to struggle being assertive overall with Ken. We don't know as yet if there are any positive communication and experiences to balance out all the negative.

Where does this all leave us, what do we need to do? We have several avenues to explore as part of our further assessment, but also know paths that can lead towards a deepening of the conversation. Here are some questions we can now begin to ask:

> Ken, Cheryl and Sam see you as critical and controlling. Do you see your behaviors and actions differently? Why was cleaning the room so important? What are you most worried about for Sam? Do you ever feel lonely in your own family, like it's you always against them with no one in your corner?
>
> Sam and Ken, do you both ever have good times, do things together? If not, why not? Is that something you would both like?
>
> Cheryl, how do you explain to yourself why Ken is the way he is? What do you think makes Ken tick? Tell me about good times you and Ken have had together as a couple.
>
> Sam, what do feel your dad doesn't understand about you? How do you get along with your brother? Does he have the same problems with your dad? If not, why not?

What these questions hopefully do is not only give us more information to help to shape a preliminary intervention plan, but also change each person's narrative and, we hope, the emotional climate in the room. If Ken opens up about indeed feeling lonely or worried, his family is seeing a side of him different from his anger and control. If Sam can talk about wanting to spend quality time with Ken or about how hard he actually does feel he tries to make his dad proud of him, Ken can begin to be more compassionate towards his son. And even if Cheryl struggles to talk about positive times with Ken, it opens the door to work they may need to do as a couple to get reconnected. You can't control the outcome of this conversation, but you are helping them talk in different ways.

How does all this help us shape a preliminary intervention plan? What most motivates people are problems and one of the challenges of family therapy is helping the family work on everyone's concerns rather than arguing over whose pain is greater. Ken wants Cheryl to step up and Sam to have a better attitude. Cheryl and Sam want Ken to be less critical and angry and Cheryl wants to feel more like an equal partner. Both Ken and Sam may want to build their relationship in positive ways, rather than falling into negative ones.

All these are possibilities. Our emphasis is on changing the problematic patterns: Cheryl and Ken as a team, Ken regulating his emotions so he is not always the bad guy. We talk about process and patterns and how it is easy for families to fall into emotional ruts. We let them know that our job is to help them change those patterns because this is certainly one thing that they all agree needs to be changed. We use the rapport that we have created, as well as our leadership, to let them know that we can help guide them towards better ways of solving problems.

And then we offer options:

- A session between Ken and Cheryl on overall expectations for the children to repair the family structure, linking it to what they both want.
- A session between Sam and Ken to work out expectations they both can agree on and concrete ways to improve their relationship as a couple.

- A session with Ken to help him learn self-regulation techniques, so that he is not so easily triggered.
- A family session including Tom to see what he would like changed. We offer and see what direction they are willing to move.

Any of these options will go a long way to changing the patterns and make them more effective. We see what the family members are most motivated to do, help them create success experiences, further motivating them to improve their relationships.

Conclusion

Family therapy can seem overwhelming for many new clinicians, for several reasons. One is that it is easy to feel overloaded by so much content; one feels pressure to have to sort through all the stories, connect all the dots. There is also the pressure of feeling that one has to fix all the problems in the room – Ken's, Cheryl's, Sam's – and it's difficult to sort through priorities and decide on a course. Finally, there is the challenge of managing all the people, their stories, and most of all, their emotions.

It is to be hoped that our discussion has helped allay some of these fears. Worry less about facts and content, and instead focus on process and patterns. Realize that all the problems are interconnected, and that beginning to change some patterns and behaviors will ripple across to others. Understand that you don't have to have all the answers, but instead need to ask the hard questions, move towards where the family is not, ask them what is the problem under the problem. Work as a leader in guiding the process, but also as a teammate helping them battle and put to rest their own problems. Offer options and help the family decide what next steps they want to take. Finally, realize that you don't have to have grandma and the dog in the room to do family therapy, but that family therapy is a way of thinking – about problems, about relationships, about how to help people better run their lives.

Points to Ponder

1. What types of family problems would be most difficult for you to help with? What do you need to feel more confident in handling such problems?

2. Looking back on your own personal problems, did they turn out
    to be bad solutions to other problems you were struggling with?
3. What for you are your own learning problems as opposed to
    problems about learning?

Key Texts

Bowen, M. (1993). *Family therapy in clinical practice*. New York: Jason Aaronson.
Ekstein, R. and Wallerstein, R. (1958). *The teaching and learning of psychotherapy*.
    New York: Basic Books.
Minuchin, S. (1974). *Families and family therapy*. Cambridge, MA: Harvard University
    Press.

References

Bowen, M. (1993). *Family therapy in clinical practice*. New York: Jason Aaronson.
Ekstein, R. and Wallerstein, R. (1958). *The teaching and learning of psychotherapy*.
    New York: Basic Books.
Minuchin, S. (1974). *Families and family therapy*. Cambridge, MA: Harvard University
    Press.

14
GROUP WORK
Mark Doel

Key Ideas that Inform Group Work

The key ideas underpinning group work are delightfully simple to understand, yet rather more complex to achieve. In this opening section let us consider, in turn, the ideas of mutuality, solidarity, giving voice and belonging.

Perhaps the best-known notion in group work is that of mutuality: individual people coming together to provide mutual aid for a common purpose (Steinberg, 2004). This purpose might be relatively inward looking, such as mutual support, or more outward looking, such as mutual action: the two do not exclude each other. At the level of a colloquialism, it is a question of "all in the same boat" (Doel, 2014).

At a philosophical level, group work has much in common with collective traditions, such as the social contract and communitarianism, in which the connections between individuals and their wider society are emphasized (Rousseau, 1998 [1762]). The community is not seen as the sum of its individuals, rather as what defines those individuals. Individuals are born into and raised by existing communities whose values shape them; they are not the free-standing independent beings of classical liberalism. Almost a century ago, Tawney expressed it powerfully thus:

> Few tricks of the unsophisticated intellect are more curious
> than the naive psychology of the business man, who ascribes his
> achievements to his unaided efforts, in blind unconsciousness of
> a social order without whose continuous support and vigilant
> protection he would be a lamb bleating in the desert.
>
> (Tawney, 1926, p. 264)

Group work is about solidarity as well as mutuality. Solidarity implies an ability to stand with others, even when your mutual situations are different. When coal miners marched in solidarity with striking nurses they did so knowing that they would not themselves benefit from any improved pay and working conditions achieved by their actions. It was a show of solidarity with an entirely different group of workers with whom they shared common values.

Group workers are sometimes surprised when they find "miners" and "nurses" together in their group; in other words, people who have different identities. In these circumstances group workers must help the members to find their common values (even if this is the value of respecting different values) in order to grow solidarity in the group. At the level of a colloquialism, it is "united we stand, divided we fall."

A group is a place where people can find their *voice*, at first individually and then collectively (Fleming and Luczynski, 1999; Pollard, 2007; St Thomas and Johnson, 2002; Steinberg et al., 2011). It is hard to exaggerate the isolation that some people feel about their own particular circumstances, and the extraordinary liberation they can experience when they are heard and, even more liberating, the discovery that they are not alone. This process of finding and sharing voice often requires skilled facilitation; individuals need to discover not just their voice but also their ear, so that they can learn how to listen to others' stories and come to know the value of listening. Sometimes it is enough for these voices to be heard within the confines of the group and other times a common voice is amplified beyond the group to provoke social change.

Finally, a key idea in group work is the central need for humans to *belong*, colloquially "one of us." If you already have affiliations where you feel at home (a family, a social group, a club, a sports team) you might take for granted the deep sense of satisfaction that derives from this sense of membership. For those people whose circumstances deny them this opportunity, social group work can provide a new experience of membership as well as the social learning that accompanies it. In groups we learn about the relationship between self and other. Problem solving ("two or more heads are better than one"), planning, achieving successes, having fun – all of these experiences enhance the feeling of belonging (Maidment and Macfarlane, 2009).

The Broad Significance of Group Work

Group work is the active use of group process in order to bring a collection of individuals towards a common belonging and, usually but not always, a common purpose. Some have seen this as a specialized activity; others see group work as having much broader scope and import. It is my belief that, as human beings, we are all group workers, some more skilled than others. Some have an innate capacity to inspire people to come together, yet do not necessarily see themselves as "group workers;" we have much to learn from them. Others learn these skills through practice and experience and put themselves into roles that are labeled "group worker." However, there are positions that do not carry the group worker tag, yet rely heavily on group work skills: for instance, team leader; coordinator of inter-professional networks; chair of a local community meeting. A knowledge of group work is of huge benefit in any situation where three or more people are gathered together.

The case has been made in many texts for the wide significance of group work, not confined to what happens when groups are created by professionals (Doel, 2006; Thompson, 2017). It *can* be a practice specialism, but we all theorize in and about groups, small and large, much of the time.

An interesting question, which we have space to explore only partially, is whether our theorizing about very large groupings can be construed alongside theorizing in respect of much smaller ones. For example, following the 2016 UK Referendum to decide membership of the European Union (EU), there has been theorizing about the two "groups" of voters, those who rejected membership and those who wanted to remain members (less is theorized about the third group who did not give voice). What similarities and differences are there between the ways we theorize about those enormous groups and the kind of social work group we will visit later, where perhaps a dozen parents come together for help and support in relation to their children's behavior? The former groupings might at first seem to have no *agency* in the way that the latter do, yet if agency is the power to effect change, the group of people who voted "Brexit" can be seen as the most powerful agency possible (for a discussion of Brexit, see Stepney, 2016). The notion of "membership" can, then, be applied to an entity as large as the EU, as it can to a small group of people sitting in a circle.

At one level the answer to the perennial group work question: when is a group (not) a group? (Doel, 2012) is an existential one: if you feel you belong, if you feel membership, then you are a group. This raises the question that people in the same group might experience this differently: undoubtedly, this was true of the experience of being a member of the EU. A group must achieve a certain *meaningfulness* to its members: in this sense, the two groups in the UK Referendum are groups. There are undoubtedly many complex reasons why each person voted the way they did, but it was a binary choice between two opposing "belongings," and subsequent discourse has hardened this awareness of belonging to one group or the other, us or them. Membership of the third group, the non-voters, is nebulous and, to that extent, it is not a group; for instance, it has no name, unlike Brexiteers and Remainers.

Group work has, then, an extraordinarily wide arc of relevance, not just in the small group facilitation that most professionals like social workers find themselves in, but in the much broader political discourse. It is interesting, then, that knowledge of group dynamics is not acknowledged as crucial, and it does not sit alongside English, Maths and Science in the core educational curriculum.

Theorizing and Hypothesizing in Group Work

The success of group work is dependent on an especially wide range of factors and the scope for theorizing is thus similarly broad. Added to the obvious theorizing about the nature of human interaction in group settings are the contextual factors that support group work. For instance, a group for women with severe learning disabilities using day care facilities was a great success in terms of the social and communication improvements for its individual members. The two co-leaders happily wished to continue to facilitate further groups, there were more women in the day center who could benefit from such a group, and the resources were available for further groups. One might hypothesize that the day center would wish to run more of these groups on the back of this success. Nevertheless, when the first group came to an end no more were started.

Given these facts, what hypotheses might be offered? It seems a mystery, until we discover that the very success of the group sparked an institutional jealousy in which other workers felt resentment at their colleagues' success, the manager of the day center being unwilling or unable to bring a resolution to these conflicts other than to foreclose any opportunity for further groups (Doel, 2006, pp. 117–18).

"Institutional jealousy" is a *construct*, and constructs are the bricks with which we build theories. How useful this particular construct is, needs to be tested. How commonly or rarely might *institutional jealousy* help to explain situations that otherwise appear baffling? And how commonly do you use or create these kinds of construct in order to find meaning in situations? In our current inquiry, these constructs are intended to bring meaning to our group work, within groups or outside them. We all hypothesize – make up meanings that might help to explain a set of observations: when we start to use constructs, perhaps create them, we are moving this hypothesizing to a conscious level, disciplining it into a kind of theorizing. Perhaps we will enquire whether others have explored this construct and, if so, what they have discovered about it. When one construct starts to be associated with others, we have the beginnings of theory building – in this case, theory building that derives from the experience of practice. Practice-based evidence becomes possible.

Theorizing from practice is made easier when that practice is disciplined – that is, it follows a recognizable structure that makes one instance of practice comparable to another. The discipline of "social work methods" once formed the backbone to teaching and learning practice; they provided what was distinctive about social work practice. Indeed, one of these practice methods, task-centered practice, came exclusively and directly from research into direct social work practice (see Chapter 6 in this volume). Others, like group work, were shared with, and borrowed from, other disciplines.

Co-leading

My own research over ten years revealed that co-led groups were more likely to be successful than single-led groups, at least in the setting of a large social services department. I measured success using Peake and Otway's (1990) simple but effective device of "voting with their feet" – that is, attendance. Unless required to attend a group, perhaps mandated by a court order, people are likely to come to a group that they feel meets their needs and stay away from those that do not. For this measure of success, I gathered the statistics for planned groups that reached fruition. Of the 68 planned groups in the project, 54 (79%) started successfully. Although only 13% of the groups were sole led, 36% of the groups not reaching fruition were sole led. Co-leading, certainly in this project, had a significant impact on the likelihood of planned groups reaching fruition. Interestingly, if a planned group did achieve the starting line, it had a 100% chance of continuing; none of the groups that started folded.

What might one do with this information and how might it help your theorizing about co-leadership and created groups? Some, indeed most, sole-led groups were also successful, so how do we theorize about the particular circumstances by which some came to fruition and others did not?

Theorizing in Direct Practice

Put yourself in the position of having the opportunity to observe a group session from the inside. Not quite a fly on the wall because you are sitting amongst group members; you are *in* the group but not quite *of* the group. This is the privileged position that I have found myself in as an external person to help the group evaluate itself.

Picture yourself in a group for parents experiencing behavioral difficulties with their children, such that there is a risk of the children being received into care ("accommodated"). Of the twelve members, five are couples and two are single parents. One couple and one single parent are there because of a Parenting Order issued by the court, so they are obliged to attend. It is the fifth of twelve weekly two-hour sessions and the members have discussed and agreed your involvement and its purpose, to help the group evaluate progress to date. You will attend the whole session and lead an evaluation slot towards the end.

Your preparation for this involvement will lead you to hypothesize about how the group's consent was achieved and the possible impact of your presence. If you know the group workers, you have a sense of your confidence in their ability to have achieved a meaningful consensus, and trust in the impression your presence might have. All of these processes are summarized in Shulman's (2009) notion of "tuning in."

Might you hypothesize whether you will be able to tell which three people are present in the group as a result of a Parenting Order (that is, involuntarily) and, if so, what indications might you expect and why?

As a stranger entering an established group, these are some of the questions you might have:

- What are the "norms" of this particular group and how might these be influenced by the fact that this is a closed, time-limited group?
- What rituals does the group have? Are these explicit or implicit and what impact do they have on the group?
- Have any widely held assumptions developed within the group – "myths"? Myth is not intended to suggest their truth or otherwise, but they can be untested beliefs that solidify into "groupthink" (Turner and Pratkanis, 1998).
- Are there any taboo topics? Is there a culture of confronting or running from these topics?
- How participative is the group and how is participation distributed among group members? How is the leadership perceived?
- Do the biographies of individuals in the group reflect the wider society in terms of gender, ethnicity, class, employment, sexuality and so on?
- Does the group feel itself to be *a group*?

What Do You Make of That?

As a colloquialism, theorizing from direct experience can be summed up as: "what do you make of that?" Let us return to the parenting group. The members agreed to a suggestion that you re-visit six months after the group finishes. You make contact via the group leaders. Half of the participants respond, of whom just one couple agree to meet up with you. What do you make of that?

You meet Melody and Ben, the parents of 12-year-old Callum. They greet you in a relaxed mood and, after the pleasantries, you explain that you have various questions to help understand the impact of the group now that water has flowed under the bridge. You ask them to think back to the group and discuss whether it was helpful and, if so, how. At the conclusion of several very positive comments you ask if they could rate the group on a scale of one to ten (not at all helpful to extremely). "Definitely a nine, maybe even ten," they say. This concurs with their descriptive comments.

"And Callum's behavior, can you remember how you scored it at the time of the group?" They both agree that, with ten being the worst, they had given his behavior an eight or nine. "And now?" After a pause, "Oh, at least as bad, isn't it?" "Oh, yes." "If it was an eight then, it's at least that now – even a nine?" "Definitely!"

What do You Make of That?

The rating is completely at odds with Melody and Ben's glowing tributes for the group and the relaxed interactions between them. The only way to make any sense of this is to find out the story behind it and you share your own observation. "To be honest, I'm confused because you've given such high praise for the group, and you seem very relaxed, yet you've scored a 'nine' for Callum's behavior … It doesn't sound like the group made any difference at all."

"But now we can handle it. It doesn't bother us, and we know we can weather it and we both trust it will get better. And the group did that for us."

As the story unfolds, Melody and Ben describe how their marriage was on its last legs at the point that they joined the group. "It's no exaggeration to say that that group saved our marriage. Really. Our relationship is so much better now."

What do You Make of That?

One immediate conclusion might be that quantifiable information is misleading. Yet, without the request to quantify Callum's behavior, the rich information about Melody and Ben's relationship might not have been exposed. We might theorize that quantified knowledge needs contextualizing and this is enabled through qualitative discourse. A standalone tick-box questionnaire, with results fed undigested into a research study or into the agency's statistics, would have been severely damning for the group: no returns from 83% of the participants and a score deteriorating from eight to nine for the behavior of the only child for whom there is data six months on. It is unlikely there would have been a question: Did this group save your marriage/relationship? and who knows whether Melody or Ben would have mentioned it under "Any Other Comments?"

Emphasizing Groupness or Individuality?

Whether you see a group as potentially emphasizing one's connection with other people or an opportunity to express one's individuality is largely dependent on the wider social context. The findings from a global group work project tentatively suggest that small group work in collectivized societies where individual expression is difficult or frowned upon provide a safe place for just this kind of personal discovery (Cohen et al., 2012). Conversely, those who are steeped in a more individualized western tradition of group work might assume without question that group work is about mutuality. What these group works have in common is an implicit notion of group work providing some kind of counterbalance to the broader cultural hegemony.

Theorizing about the cultural relevance of group work must, therefore, be framed by a broader understanding of the social context from which the group is drawn. If all our theorizing takes place within the parameters of a particular paradigm (for instance, that group work is about mutual purpose), then we unwittingly exclude a universe of other possibilities.

Models and Philosophies to Help Theorize

Tuckman's (1965) model of group development is well known, but the "forming, norming, storming, performing, (mourning)" rhyme is too often taken as a reliable linear sequence, rather than a broadly useful sketch; phases of group development are dependent on too many variables specific to each different group. Papell and Rothman's (1966) focus on group purpose – reciprocal, remedial and social goals – is a useful characterization of different group types. Doel and Sawdon's "Continuum" (1999, pp. 73–4) provides a universal structure for group workers to understand the components of groups as an aid both to planning and to practical theorizing.

Thompson (2017) considers existentialism as a philosophy that is relevant to theorizing about group work. Its emphasis on perception and meaning sits well with the notion of a group as somewhere people can find a sense of belonging and meaning in an interpersonal context. "Finding oneself" is not a singular, individual path to enlightenment, rather a discovery of shared meaning and the interconnectedness of people and their existence. This also means discovering the differences in the way we each see the world, and negotiating the conflict that can arise from these different perceptions. From this can grow empathy, emerging from a willingness to enter other people's worlds.

The tide of broad, political events is revealing how binary choices (this or that, but nothing else) can become socially divisive, with identities cast strongly in seemingly mutually opposed camps. Group work seeks not to avoid or deny conflict, far from it, but to help people take more control by understanding and coming to terms with other people's realities alongside their own.

Points to Ponder

1. When facilitating and leading groups, how best can you ensure a balance between expertise in the *topic* of the group (mental health, youth offending and so on) and expertise in *group work* as a method of practice?

2   How best can you ensure that successes in the group are shared with and by people who might not be members of the group – for example, family members of group participants; colleagues of group leaders; the wider community?

3   How best can you collect and reflect on the group's own theorizing – the explanations, beliefs and hypotheses that it constructs during its lifetime to help bring meaning to the experience of the group *as a group*?

Key Texts

Doel, M. (2006). *Using groupwork*. London: Routledge/Community Care.
Doel, M. and Kelly, T. (2014). *A-Z groups and groupwork*. Basingstoke, UK: Palgrave Macmillan.
Gitterman, A. and Salmon, R. (Eds.) (2009). *Encyclopaedia of social work with groups*. New York: Routledge.

References

Cohen, C., Doel, M., Wilson, M., Quirke, D., Ring, K. and Abbas, S. A. (2012). Global group work: Honoring processes and outcomes. In A. M. Bergart, S. R. Simon and M. Doel (Eds.) *Group work: Honoring our roots, nurturing our growth. Proceedings of the XXXI international symposium of social work with groups* (Chicago). London: Whiting and Birch, pp. 107–27.

Doel, M. (2006). *Using groupwork*. London: Routledge/Community Care.

Doel, M. (2012). When is a group not a group? In G. J. Tully, K. Sweeney and S. Palombo (Eds.) *Groups: Gateways to growth. Proceedings of the XXIX international symposium of group work* (Jersey City). London: Whiting and Birch, pp. 129–38.

Doel, M. (2014). All in the same boat – but where is the flotilla? In C. Lee (Ed.) *Social group work: We are all in the same boat. Proceedings of the XXXIII international symposium of social work with groups* (Long Beach, CA). London: Whiting and Birch, pp. 1–10.

Doel, M. and Sawdon, C. (1999). *The essential groupworker*. London: Jessica Kingsley Publishers.

Fleming, J. and Luczynski, Z. (1999). Men united: Fathers' voices. *Groupwork*, 11.2, pp. 21–37.

Maidment, J. and Macfarlane, S. (2009). Craft groups: Sites of friendship, belonging and learning for older women. *Groupwork*, 19.1, pp. 10–25.

Papell, C. and Rothman, B. (1966). Social group work models: Possession and heritage. *Journal for Education for Social Work*, 2.2, pp. 66–77.

Peake, A. and Otway, O. (1990). Evaluating success in groupwork: Why not measure the obvious? *Groupwork*, 3.2, pp. 118–33.

Pollard, N. (2007). Voices talk, hands write: Sustaining community publishing with people with learning difficulties. *Groupwork*, 17.2, pp. 51–73.

Rousseau, J-J. (1998 [1762]). *The social contract*. Ware, UK: Wordsworth Editions.

St Thomas, B. and Johnson, P. (2002). In their own voices: Play activities and art with traumatized children. *Groupwork*, 13.2, pp. 34–4.

Shulman, L. (2009). *The skills of helping individuals, families, groups, and communities* (6th Edn.). Belmont, CA: Brookes/Cole.

Steinberg, D. M. (2004). *The mutual-aid approach to working with groups: Helping people help one another* (2nd Edn.). New York: Haworth Press.

Steinberg, D. M., Tully, G. and Salmon, R. (Eds.) (2011). *Voices from the classroom: Students speak. Social Work with Groups*, special issue, 34, pp. 3–4.

Stepney, P. (2016). To leave or not to leave: A social work perspective on the EU referendum debate, *Professional Social Work*, June, 28–9.

Tawney, R. H. (1926). *Religion and the rise of capitalism*. Harmondsworth, UK: Pelican.

Thompson, N. (2017). *Theorizing practice: A guide for the people professions* (2nd Edn.). London: Palgrave.

Tuckman, B. (1965). Developmental sequence in small groups. *Psychological Bulletin*, 63, pp. 384–99.

Turner, M., and Pratkanis, A. (1998). Twenty five years of groupthink research. *Organizational Behavior and Human Decision Processes*, 73.2, pp. 105–15.

15

ECOLOGICAL THEORIES

Aila-Leena Matthies and Kati Närhi

Introduction

This chapter discusses theories that help us understand how the environment is an integral part of social work and how social workers can apply this understanding to practice. Since the early historical days of social work, the environment has been embedded in it. First, social work emerged in western societies at the end of the nineteenth century as a response to new social needs arising from the social consequences of the new industrial forms of using natural resources in production and accumulating economic resources. The enormous volume of natural resources used in the economy has also influenced the structure and the relationship between human communities and their environment (Besthorn, 2003; Coates, 2003; Haila and Dyke, 2006).

For the second, the constellation of the person-in-environment indicates one of the fundamental principles in social work practice and theory. The idea of the person-in-environment argues that the situation of a person cannot be understood and changed by social workers without taking her or his environment into account. It also makes a basic difference to several other professions, such as the medical and nursing professions in health, which may address people in person-focused settings detached from their environment. However, social work has applied the framework of the person-in-environment primarily to intrapersonal and social interactions in a way that mainly addresses the social environment of a person. Not enough attention has been paid to professional functions related to the policy context of practice and to interactions with the built, physical and natural environment (Gray et al., 2012; Kemp, 2011).

This dichotomized way of understanding the environment in social work can be traced back to the early years of social work as an emerging practice and discipline, especially in the thinking of Jane Addams (1910) and Mary Richmond (1917, 1922). Both these pioneers of social work emphasized the importance of environment for human well-being, but in different senses. Mary Richmond, who developed social casework, focused on a holistic view of an individual's social environment and social situation, in the sense of social interaction. Jane Addams, who developed community work and social research in social work, contextualized social work within entire urban settlements, which included not only the social environment but also the physical and built environment. She also applied political and economic considerations to frame interventions in social work (Närhi and Matthies, 2016a).

Decades after the seminal work of these two important pioneers of social work, the two different theoretical directions of ecological social work can still be identified and remain influential (Närhi and Matthies, 2001; Gray et al., 2012; Peeters, 2012).

- *A systems theoretical approach* in which the main emphasis is on the social environment and holistic thinking (Germain and Gitterman, 1980). For example, Greene and Schriver (2016) give a comprehensive illustration of an approach that draws on ecological systems theory in social work practice. Theories on the interdependence between human behavior and the social environment are used to cast light on various systemic contexts of clients (see also Henriques and Tuckley, 2012).
- *The ecocritical perspective* which focuses on the impact of the natural and built environment on people's well-being and the issues of sustainable development in social work. It transformed the influence of ecological movements and the profound ecological criticism of modern industrial society in social work at large. Dominelli's *Green social work* (2012) is one example of this critical

ecological thinking in social work at political and global levels that has roots in anti-discriminatory practice. Boetto (2016a) has provided a comprehensive example of a framework that indicates how to integrate the built and natural environment within casework practice. Furthermore, the increasing research and practice of social work, contributing to local and global sustainable development, reflect social work's interconnection with the environment today (Matthies and Närhi, 2016).

The eco-systems approach highlights the significance of the social environment as a key framework for human behavior, growth and well-being. The word "systems" refers to the way of seeing that individuals and groups are in a relationship linked together across different parts of a system. For instance, families, schools and social communities can be seen as interconnected systems. The environment of these subsystems consists of dynamic relationships containing interdependencies, power and complementarity (Henriques and Tuckley, 2012).

Social relationships and social functioning are regarded as analogous to biological-natural processes. Used in practice, a systems-theoretical approach constructs a holistic picture of the significant social relationships, of the person as part of an eco-system and helps social workers to understand better how people's problems and resources relate to their social networks and environment.

The ecocritical perspective in social work questions more comprehensively the mainstream model of our modern societies that pursues continuous economic growth. It does this by exploiting natural and human resources and, in the process, increases social inequality. This perspective challenges social work to reflect on its own role within its technological-economic and bureaucratic-professional contexts. The status of social work in this context means that it becomes dependent on the economic system, which in turn causes ecological and social crises (Närhi and Matthies, 2016b). The term "ecosocial approach" is used for such actions and models of practice, which are enhancing and supporting people's own "natural" resources (Matthies et al., 2001). It addresses the quality and resources of the entire living environment and aims to enable people to get connected with their natural environment as a source of well-being. It also aims to create such service settings that are protecting, re-cycling or up-cycling environmental resources. The following practice focus offers an example of using both ecological theories to theorize practice.

Practice Focus 15.1

A new local network of multiple stakeholders from the public and private sectors invites social workers as experts to bring their knowledge to a new project, in particular to support an application for a nationally funded program. The aim of the program is to integrate young unemployed people back into society by improving job creation and social inclusion. European, national and local institutions report an alarming increase in the social exclusion of young people who neither have access to the labor market, nor are they participating in further training.

In the year 2016, an average of 18.6 per cent of young people under 25 were registered unemployed in Europe, while in some countries, such as Greece, it was as high as 46 per cent (Statista, 2016). Almost eight million young Europeans are not in work, education or training. Social workers know that this precarious situation creates serious problems: being an outsider may cause mental health problems, conflicts in the family, financial challenges and the risk of getting involved in anti-social behavior and crime, which can be seen as a threat to mainstream society. At the political level, critical voices are concerned about the missing economic contribution of young people to national wealth. Labor market policies require young people to display more agility, mobility and transferability of skills. What kind of concrete measures and interventions can ecological theories of social work contribute to the project proposal?

Methods Applied to the Practice Focus: Systems-theoretical Work with Youth Unemployment

Social workers with the *systems-theoretical understanding of ecological social work* suggest a comprehensive program of individual and family-related support for the young people in their social environment. It will include:

1. engagement of the participants;
2. assessment of their life situation in their social environment including family relations;
3. a plan of a systematic intervention and its application; and
4. evaluation.

Starting from the basic assumption that human behavior is conditioned by the social environment (Greene and Schriver, 2016), a comprehensive analysis of the social relationships of each young participant needs to be developed. This assessment will be done by developing the ecological model according to Bronfenbrenner (1979) alongside drawing an ecomap (Henriques and Tuckley, 2012, p. 173). As a first pre-condition, the project funding will bring capacities for additional time resources for social workers to have face-to-face meetings with each individual young participant. In these meetings, the young people will draw an ecomap and discuss it step by step with the social worker. It will help to identify those environmental impact factors that cause stress and either help or hinder the mobilization of the young people's resources for more effective job seeking or further training. Furthermore, sources of strength, valued experiences and motivation will be analyzed.

The ecological model includes micro (home, friendship, networks, social media), meso (school and job experiences, use of services, organized engagements), macro level (national and local policies, programs, labor market) and exo-fields (physical environment, institutions, bureaucracy) (see Henriques and Tuckley, 2012, p. 167).

Consequently social workers will have additional time to focus on each individual young person and their living environment, in order to be able to co-create realistic new perspectives starting from the micro-level of the young people's living environment. Social workers will apply outreach methods, similar to detached youth work, to meet the young people in cafés, clubs, street corners, shopping malls and the informal parts of the community. Further, they will make home visits and learn about the physical environment of the individual young people, especially those most disadvantaged. The ecomaps will be used to analyze, with the young people themselves, what are the supportive dimensions in their social systems and micro-level networks, what kind of contacts they have and the quality of these relationships. For instance, excessive addiction to social media or social isolation can have negative effects, and need to be discussed together, and tools of relevant harm reduction need to be created.

Social workers will also use the ecomap to analyze individually, what kind of experiences and intentions each young person has in relation to educational pathways, use of welfare and other services, as well as job seeking. Visual drawing of network maps and analyzing the different system levels will be helpful, especially if young people may have challenges with language skills and in talking about their personal problems.

Systems analysis will help the young people to discover interconnectivity across different zones of challenges in their everyday life. For instance, having problems with housing or private space at home may bring obstacles for starting a training course that demands concentration on homework. Having health-related problems or challenges of mobility may cause a barrier to enter the labor market as jobseekers. Also, the impact of the macro-level factors, such as current economic development in the region and national programs related to job creation, are important to be taken into consideration. Such macro factors determine the labor market opportunities of young people in the community, probably as much if not more than their own behavior and motivation.

In the phase of planning and maintaining intervention, targeted individual strategies will be developed to eliminate any personal bias and problems caused by the interaction between the young person and his or her social environment. Access to individual interventions, such as counseling, therapy or targeted training will be included in the project's budget. The interventions can also include joint group activities to offer a new platform and social environment that is designed to strengthen self-esteem and promote empowerment skills to face new challenging social situations. These interventions are seen to be preconditions for improved employability and motivation for further training, which will be assessed in the final evaluation of the project.

The social workers apply an anti-discriminatory approach (Thompson, 2016) by respecting the diversity of the individual life circumstances and culture of the young people, with their empowering focus on the young people's own capabilities instead of oppressing them just to seek jobs. They also consider the discriminatory structures of the recruitment practices at the labor market office regarding young jobseekers without previous job experiences. This will include giving support and creating methods to improve their well-being and self-esteem in the case of disappointments.

Ecocritical Work with Youth Unemployment

In the frame of the *ecocritical perspective* social workers want to contextualize the project aims and activities in a global context and critical development of the labor market. In Europe, where productive work appears not to be available for all people in the future, the nature of work is going to change. Climate change and the need to reduce the use of natural resources must be taken into consideration. On the other hand, the perspectives of smart green growth, job creation in nature-based projects, the new local exchange economy and social entrepreneurship all provide potentially promising solutions (Elsen, 2016; OECD, 2011).

While starting the planning process, social workers will invite a group of young people facing unemployment to discuss their own wishes in relation to such a project and identify their future work aspirations. Some of the young people may say: "We actually don't want to contribute to this polluting economic system any more. But we would rather have a place, like an old farm, where we could just make our own living, renovate it and grow our own food." It transpires that some of the young people were already involved as volunteers in a group called "Re-(f)-Use," which has been running a social restaurant based on the use of waste food. It offers a more participatory alternative for the charitable delivery of food, which they do not like to visit, even though they are sometimes hungry and in need of free food (Kortetmäki and Silvasti, 2016). Other young people suggest that it could be possible to creatively develop the recycling workshops and second-hand "charity shops" of their region.

Social workers respond by devising a plan to establish a social enterprise or collaborate with an existing one. Regarding the special needs of young participants, with, say, social phobia and low self-esteem, social workers can use animal-assisted methods and nature-assisted tools of social work and interventions based on the concept of "green care" (Gallis, 2013). The ideas and arguments from the planning phase will feed into a regional systematized plan, which can be evaluated against the need to create a new local economy, in harmony with the environment and resource limits of the earth. In this new radical way, the anti-discriminatory approach means in this case not just an equal delivery of services to the young unemployed people, but also promotes their equal opportunity to contribute themselves to the activities they want to develop. In this way, it helps to define the content of their own agency in diversity.

Conceptual Discussion

Both the systems-theoretical and ecocritical traditions underline the interactive relationship between humans and the environment. As demonstrated through the practice case, both ecological traditions can be applied to the strong roots of anti-discriminatory practice that is committed to equality, diversity and social justice (Thompson, 2016). It achieves this by the means of a participatory approach and co-creation of the project. But there also remain significant differences between the two traditions. The systems theory approach understands the person as a part of a holistic system, including micro, meso and macro systems. The ecocritical approach views the individual as a part of nature, which, in turn, is itself a part of the holistic system of the planet. In the ecocritical approach, the environmental crisis not only concerns nature and the environment, but also encompasses human beings and their relationships, values and cultural assumptions. Systemic theorists are inclined to see ecological issues as disturbing factors in the system. But they do not take an overt political stand in relation to the economic and political structures that produce these disturbances.

While exploring the various conceptualizations emerging in the global debate around the ecocritical tradition in social work, we can identify the following approaches: ecosocial; deep-ecological; eco-spiritual; green; social ecological and environmental. What all of these approaches have in common is that they challenge mainstream social work to broaden its focus and share the critical notion of humans being a crucial part of nature (Närhi and Matthies, 2016a). This deepens the idea of the person-in-environment from a different perspective than previously identified. In our view, the theoretical and practical implications of eco-logical social work can be promoted by starting with the shared dimensions of the current debates.

Research Evidence

There are a number of studies that show evidence in adopting ecolog-ical social work theories in practice. Gray et al. (2012) provide exam-ples, including work with drought-affected families and young offenders, and preservation of "green" space in city areas. There are also social work practices that involve nature and wilderness therapy (Gallis, 2013), food security (Kortetmäki and Silvasti, 2016), community development (Sayer et al., 2016), and animal-assisted social work (Risley-Curtiss, 2010).

Boetto (2016b) has formulated five social work strategies for ecosocial practice. In our eyes, her approach successfully combines the ecocritical tra-dition of ecological social work with practice with individuals and families, and not only at community and structural level of social work. First, social workers need to develop personal growth towards connectedness with the natural environment, which means increasing your knowledge and action about environmental issues in your personal life. Second, social work needs to continue to develop a holistic approach to human well-being. In the context of ecological social work, it means understanding human well-being from the perspective of sustainable ways of life. Third, social workers can develop communities of practice that promote organizational change. This means collaborating with like-minded workers, organizing environ-mentally oriented groups and building alliances with inter-professional groups with environmental scientists and planners, for instance. Fourth, social workers can use community-based approaches in order to enable the mobilization of local resources to develop community-based sustainability initiatives (see Chapter 17 in this volume). Finally, social work can arrange social action to facilitate economic and political change – that is, organize collective social action and advocacy groups for people who share similar environmental and social disadvantage (Boetto, 2016b).

A systematic literature review by Nöjd (2016) focused on actual social work practices considering environmental and sustainability issues. She found that such practices are improving the living environment, infrastruc-ture and facilities, as well as ensuring greater participation and the influence of people. Ecological social work is also promoting environmental justice, increasing awareness of environmental issues, assessing the effects of these, negotiating what issues to address and gathering the resources with partners, as necessary, to address these issues. The efforts are community based, local and often multidisciplinary. Many of the activities are adapted from mainstream social work, but accommodated to social work considering issues related to the bio-physical environment (Nöjd, 2016).

Conclusion: Challenges Associated with the Theory and Practice of Ecological Social Work

We argue that both Mary Richmond's and Jane Addams's contributions emphasized the importance of the environment in social work, although in different ways. The common factor in systems theoretical and ecocritical perspectives is their shared view about the imbalance in the relationship between humans and the environment. When it comes to the present day, we should no longer talk about social works relationship with nature, but understand social work as a part of nature that is shaped by humans. Drawing along the historical line of ecological social work, a similar development can be identified, as Mark Doel describes in Chapter 14 in this volume.

Ecological social work has shifted historically from a strong individualistic focus with psychodynamic thinking towards a larger, social scientific perspective by systems theory and, towards a critical sociopolitical perspective by the ecocritical tradition. But, we can also learn from our history that the best opportunities for people in oppressive circumstance can be developed by social work if both traditions can be combined. Then, both the diversity of individual challenges and resources and the sociopolitical and environmental factors at the level of communities, societies and the earth come together. This provides the unique context for people to live and for social work to play its role.

Understanding the politicization of nature (Haila, 2000) in social work practice leads to examining and developing a kind of knowledge and practice that expands the holistic person-in-environment perspective in social work. In pursuing the goal of challenging the mainstream paradigm of social work, ecological social work shares much in common with the critical, structural, radical, feminist and participatory approaches in the profession. They all reflect an understanding of the person-in-environment and the dynamics of power in transactional processes (Coates, 2003; Kemp, 2011).

We agree with Kemp (2011) who argues that never has the need for social work to revitalize its environmental commitments been more urgent. Some studies tell us that it might be worthwhile to consider complexity theory, evolution theory or even neuroscience, which might provide a new understanding of the relationship between people and their environments. Social workers might then focus on affecting the climates that can sustain the conditions (social, ecological, biological, economic and political) that are essential for human well-being (Green and McDermott, 2010). Therefore, it follows that a global and local ecological framework is needed in social work education, both as a theoretical perspective and as a critically reflective model of practice (Närhi and Matthies, 2016a).

Points to Ponder

1. How do social problems and everyday challenges of your clients interlink with problems in their social, built and natural environment?

2. What kind of nature-based solutions could you develop together with your clients for strengthening their well-being and participatory social inclusion?

3. Which of the methods of intervention and settings in your social work practice contribute to sustainability?

Key Texts

McKinnon, J. and Alston, M. (Eds.) (2016). *Ecological social work: Toward sustainability*. London: Palgrave.

Matthies, A-L. and Närhi, K. (Eds.) (2016). *Ecosocial transition of society: Contribution of social work and social policy*. New York: Routledge.

Greene, R. R. and Schriver, J. M. (2016). *Handbook of human behavior and the social environment. A Practice-based approach*. New Brunswick: Transaction Publishers.

References

Addams, J. (1910). *Twenty years at Hull House*, with autobiographical notes. Re-published 2004. Whitefish: Kessinger Publishing.

Besthorn, F. (2003). Radical ecologisms: Insights for educating social workers in ecological activism and social justice. *Critical Social Work* 3(1), pp. 66–106.

Boetto, H. (2016a). Developing ecological social work for micro-level practice. In: McKinnon, J. and Alston, M. (Eds.). *Ecological social work: Towards sustainability.* London: Palgrave, pp. 59–77.

Boetto, H. (2016b). A transformative ecosocial model: Challenging modernist assumptions in social work. *British Journal of Social Work.* DOI: https://doi.org/10.1093/bjsw/bcw149.

Bronfenbrenner, U. (1979). *The ecology of human development: Experiments by nature and design.* Cambridge, MA: Harvard University Press.

Coates, J. (2003). *Ecology and social work: Towards a new paradigm.* Halifax, NS: Fernwood Press.

Dominelli, L. (2012). *Green social work: From environmental crises to environmental justice.* Cambridge, UK: Polity.

Elsen, S. (2016). Community-based economy and ecosocial transition. In Matthies, A-L. and Närhi, K. (Eds.). *Ecosocial transition in society. Contribution of social work and social policy.* New York: Routledge, pp. 54–70.

Gallis, C. (2013). *Green care: For human therapy, social innovation, rural economy, and education.* New York: Nova Science Publishers.

Germain, C. B. and Gitterman, A. (1980). *The life model of social work practice.* New York: Columbia University Press.

Gray, M., Coates, J., and Hetherington, T. (Eds.) (2012). *Environmental social work.* New York: Routledge.

Green, D. and McDermott, F. (2010). Social work from inside and between complex systems: Perspectives on person-in-environment for today's social work. *British Journal of Social Work* 40, pp. 2414–2430.

Greene, R. R. and Schriver, J. M. (2016). *Handbook of human behavior and the social environment. A Practice-based approach.* New Brunswick: Transaction Publishers.

Haila, Y. (2000). Ekologiasta politiikkaan. Kurinpitoa vai solidaarisutta. *Tiede ja Edistys* 25(2), pp. 80–96.

Haila, Y. and Dyke, C. (2006). Introduction: What to say about nature's "Speech". In Haila, Y. and Dyke, C. (Eds.). *How nature speaks. The dynamics of the human ecological condition.* Durham, NC: Duke University Press, pp. 1–48.

Henriques, P. and Tuckley, G. (2012). Ecological systems theory and direct work with children and families. In Stepney, P. and Ford, D. (Eds.) *Social work models, methods and theories.* (2nd Edn.). Lyme Regis, UK: Russell House Publishing, pp. 166–180.

Kemp, S. P. (2011). Recentring environment in social work practice: Necessity, opportunity, challenge. *British Journal of Social Work* 41(6), pp. 1198–1210.

Kortetmäki, T. and Silvasti, T. (2016). Charitable food aid in a Nordic welfare state: A case for environmental and social injustice. In Matthies, A-L. and Närhi, K. (Eds.) *Ecosocial transition in society. Contribution of social work and social policy.* New York: Routledge, pp. 219–234.

Matthies, A-L. and Närhi, K. (Eds.) (2016). *Ecosocial transition of society: Contribution of social work and social policy.* New York: Routledge.

Matthies, A-L., Närhi, K. and Ward, D. (Eds.) (2001). *The eco-social approach to social work.* Jyväskylä: Sophi.

Närhi, K. and Matthies, A-L. (2001). What is the ecological (self-)consciousness of social work? Perspectives on the relationship between social work and ecology. In Matthies, A-L., Närhi, K. and Ward, D. (Eds.) *Eco-social approach in social work.* Jyväskylä: Sophi, pp. 16–53.

Närhi, K. and Matthies, A-L. (2016a). Conceptual and historical analysis of ecological social work. In McKinnon, J. and Alston, M. (Eds.) *Ecological social work: Toward sustainability.* London: Palgrave, pp. 21–38.

Närhi, K. and Matthies, A-L. (2016b). The ecosocial approach in social work as a framework for structural social work. *International Social Work*, pp. 1–13: DOI: 10.1177/0020872816644663.

Nöjd, T. (2016). *A systematic literature review on social work considering environmental issues and sustainable development.* Master's Thesis, University of Jyväskylä, Finland. https://jyx.jyu.fi/dspace/handle/123456789/52488.

OECD (2011). *Towards green growth.* OECD Publishing: http://dx.doi.org/10.1787 /9789264111318-en.

Peeters, J. (2012). The place of social work in sustainable development: Towards ecosocial practice. *International Journal of Social Welfare* 21(3), pp. 287–298.

Richmond, M. (1917). *Social diagnosis.* Philadelphia: Russell Sage Foundation. Reprinted 1964.

Richmond, M. (1922). *What is social case work? An introductory description.* New York: Russell Sage Foundation. Reprinted 1939.

Risley-Curtiss, C. (2010). Social workers and the human-companion animal bond: A national study. *Social Work* 55(1), pp. 38–46.

Sayer, Th., Grazillo, Ch. and Elsen, S. (2016). *Cities in transition: Social innovation for Europe's urban sustainability.* London: Routledge.

Statista (2016). *Youth unemployment rate in Europe* (EU member states) as of October 2016. https://www.statista.com/statistics/266228/youth-unemployment-rate-in-eu -countries/.

Thompson, N. (2016). *Anti-discriminatory practice: Equality, diversity and social justice* (6th Edn.). London: Palgrave.

16

ACTIVISM AND ADVOCACY

Donna Baines, Emma Tseris and Fran Waugh

Maya is an experienced social worker who has just started a new job in risk reduction at a local women's shelter. After a few weeks on the job she realizes that, though the program is funded to do risk reduction, the Executive Director favors abstinence and takes negative actions against clients who cannot maintain sobriety. Maya has been working closely with a very isolated, recent immigrant, Senzie. Senzie has a bad week and is found in bed one night, passed out and clearly under the influence. The Executive Director starts eviction procedures against her. Senzie is terrified of being homeless and tearfully asks Maya for help.

Maya consults with co-workers and her supervisor, who all support risk reduction, but find they have little room on the job to promote this framework. Maya's supervisor recommends that Maya unobtrusively accompany Senzie to the Tenants' Rights Advocacy Board to see if they can stop the eviction. The workers also want to quietly call a meeting of all the women in the shelter to make sure that they know their rights as tenants. In addition, Maya and the supervisor want to read over the details of the risk reduction funding contract to see if there may be a way to pressure the Executive Director to let them do risk reduction work and end the evictions. One of Maya's co-workers is a member of SWAN (Social Work Action Network). She encourages the workers to attend a meeting and join their campaign against austerity and evictions. Maya's supervisor agrees to go to the meeting and recommends that everyone also join the union to give them back up if they need it further down the road.

This vignette, based on a real situation, highlights some of the ways that social work is more than just a profession of nice, caring people who want to help others. In today's context of workplaces that are frequently underfunded and organized like top-heavy, private-sector corporations, the only way to enact caring and respectful relations is to stand alongside clients and communities to defend their rights. In other words, high quality, effective social work practice needs to extend beyond good communication and casework skills to consistently include advocacy, campaigning and social activism.

Anti-oppressive practice (AOP) theory is a useful frame for analyzing the vignette above (Baines, 2017; Kennedy-Kish et al., 2017). Rather than viewing policies and practice as distinct areas, AOP emphasizes the way that they shape each other. In this case, the more progressive risk reduction policies are not being enacted in the workplace because of the Executive Director's personal convictions. As a result, the workers are experiencing difficulty practicing social work in a way that is ethical and supports vulnerable clients.

AOP theory is critical of neoliberalism, an approach to social, economic and political life that views the private market as the source of all solutions to life's problems. Consistent with neoliberalism, the Executive Director in this vignette operates like the head of a private corporation, rather than the leader of a non-profit caring organization. She has too much power and single-mindedly enforces the policies and practices she prefers. This approach excludes workers from policy and program development, and means that sometimes they are part of processes that they find deeply oppressive and harmful (such as the eviction).

AOP encourages social workers to think of their work as extending beyond the agency to the larger community and society, to find ways to meet the needs of clients as well as to challenge the policies, cultures and practices that oppress them. This often means being involved in advocacy and campaigning, like the workers in the vignette. AOP theory recognizes social movements and advocacy groups as natural allies in a shared social work venture for social justice and fairness. AOP also encourages workers to develop effective advocacy skills and to join and support social justice organizations and actions.

Though participation may vary depending on commitments to family and care, as Baines (2017) notes: "social justice organizing and advocacy are not something that a person undertakes once or twice and then puts away for the rest of one's life" (p. 79). Instead, social workers are encouraged to: "think of collective social change and individual advocacy as central to one's career as well as integrated into everyday life" (Baines, 2017, p. 70; see also Kennedy-Kish et al., 2017).

The drive for social justice can come from a number of sources: individual values, shared values, religious beliefs, political commitment, human rights legislation and some professional codes of ethics. For example, The International Federation of Social Work's *Global standards for the education and training of the social work profession* (IFSW, 2014) states that: "social work is a practice-based profession and an academic discipline which promotes social change and development; social cohesion and the empowerment and liberation of people. Principles of social justice, human rights, collective responsibility and respect for diversities are central to social work."

This ethical standard confirms that it is not outside the profession of social work to undertake advocacy and social activism. Instead, it is central to it.

Human Rights

Human rights often motivate people to challenge unfair and oppressive situations in the workplace and larger society, and can be the basis for social justice-based social work theory and practice (Ife, 2012). Human rights are generally defined in formal ways, such as state-based Human Rights legislation or global rights, such as those detailed in the United Nations Universal Declaration of Human Rights.

At the level of everyday practice, rights take on an interactive dynamic between clients and workers. For example, power is often expressed in who is seen as having the "right" to define social problems, to diagnose individual issues, to determine what options will be offered to individual clients and to decide the resources that will be provided or withheld.

> Lily is a social work student who wants to work with people experiencing mental health issues, a drive that has arisen whilst caring for a close family member with a mental health diagnosis. Lily believes that universal access to mental health care is a human rights issue, and she is passionate about identifying the need for more frontline mental health services to support people experiencing acute distress.
>
> On placement at a mental health organization with a high level of client-led consultation, Lily meets a number of clients who are engaged in critiquing conventional mental health services, arguing that the support that they have received has been overly coercive, undignified and not attuned to the needs of people with a diagnosis of a mental illness. "We do not simply want more mental health services," they tell Lily. Rather, they want access to alternative types of support outside of the hospital system, as well as enhanced opportunities across a range of areas, including access to safe housing and meaningful education and employment. Instead of a focus on mental health services developed by mental health "experts," they want to play an active role in new and innovative forms of service design. As a result of these interactions with clients, Lily becomes aware of the hazards of attempting to speak on behalf of clients, and the need to avoid arriving too quickly at assumptions about what their needs might be. Furthermore, she learns that her own view of human rights in the area of mental health – while not incorrect – may not go far enough towards representing the breadth of perspectives held by people who are on the receiving end of human service interventions.

This short vignette, drawn from a real situation, demonstrates that the pursuit of human rights is not always a straightforward task, and social workers cannot presume that they fully understand the needs and hopes of clients. Claims about social justice and human rights are often contested, complex and fraught (North, 2006). Critical and AOP theory asserts that it is essential that social workers take a grassroots approach to understanding the views of clients. This can be achieved through engaging in mutual exchange with clients and always being open to new ways of thinking (Fook, 2016). Rather than seeing their role as "helping" those with less power, social workers should re-conceptualize their role towards engaging in collaborative discussions with clients, where learning can occur bi-directionally, and then supporting clients as allies within social justice and human rights movements. Drawing on the lived experiences of clients to form a holistic view of human rights issues is extremely useful in expanding social work skills and challenging negative or problematic attitudes (Dorozenko et al., 2016).

Critical and AOP theory also argues that when working towards human rights, it is necessary for social workers to foster an awareness of their own values and life experiences and how these can impact on the assumptions made within practice (Pease et al., 2016). Lily had an experience of caring for a family member with a mental health diagnosis, and this was highly beneficial in driving her passion towards studying social work and understanding gaps in service systems. However, she had not fully considered the need to speak with a diverse range of clients about their experiences before arriving at a place of certainty about her role as a social worker. Being open to the partiality of her perspective allowed Lily to identify that people who have been diagnosed with a mental illness may want increased access to sufficient traditional services, but at the same time they may want the space to challenge conventional understandings of how mental well-being can be understood and achieved.

The pursuit of human rights is central to social work values (Steen et al., 2017) and AOP theory (Kennedy-Kish et al., 2017). In practice, social workers can respect human rights by using their professional status strategically to question conventional service provision and to elevate the voices and perspectives of clients, who might otherwise be ignored by those in power. Additionally, social workers can act within agencies to challenge policies and practices that fail to reflect human rights principles, including respect for human dignity and freedom. Working towards the genuine participation of clients at all levels of human service agencies means that social workers will be attuned to the views of the people who are most adversely affected by oppressive systems. In this way, social workers can avoid a top-down version of human rights that imposes ideas onto clients and does not recognize the knowledge or voice of people with lived experience.

Advocacy

Advocacy is a particular set of skills aimed at defending the rights of clients and to challenge larger systems of inequity and injustice. Though the example below is not situated in an industrialized country, the skills and process mirror those used in similar situations in the global North.

> Xie is the coordinator of a social work center in a clothing manufacturing area in a large city. The area is characterized by older-style, unregulated dense housing, chaotic traffic, open storm-water canals, air and water pollution and limited basic amenities for the collection of refuse. The social work center, part of a non-government organization, employs eight social workers and has a number of volunteers. It is a drop-in center for children aged 5–15 years whose parents work 12–13 hours per day, six to seven days a week in the clothing industry. Between 40 and 60 children attend the drop-in center each day to engage in the various activities. Typically, families live in one or two rooms near the parents' workplace. These families have re-located from rural areas in search of employment. Parents need to make the difficult choice of either having their children live with them in the city where they will need to pay for their children's education and health services or leaving them in their rural hometown with their grandparents or other relatives where the children will receive free education and health services. In the first year of establishing the children's drop-in center there were reports of children drowning in the open storm-water canals.

As argued earlier in this chapter, within an AOP framework, advocacy is seen as central to social work practice (Baines, 2017). Based on the vignette presented above, it is evident there were multiple areas and stakeholders to engage with in order to defend the rights of clients, namely, the children and their families. What are some of the skills and qualities Xie needed to draw on to foster effective advocacy?

Using a critical social work theory frame, Fook (2016, pp. 191–193) has suggested that advocacy needs to focus on both the *outcomes* and the *process* aspects. What are the agreed *outcomes* that are being worked towards? Who has the power to define these? How does the social worker ensure that the voices of the clients are heard when developing outcomes? What are the *process aspects* which may need to be considered in this vignette, namely, what are the multiple points of contradiction, alliance, complexity and resistance (Fook, 2016, p. 192)?

With this in mind, Xie drew on her professional skills and qualities to gain an understanding of the multiple dimensions of this situation, underpinned by respect for diversity and difference. The skills Xie and her colleagues drew on, and the links to theory are noted below.

1. Communication that is clear and respectful involving interpersonal (listening, questioning, understanding non-verbal space, cultural sensitivity, openness to feedback (Weber and Pockett, 2011, p. 201) and written skills. Depending on how the situation unfolds, communication may include one or more of the following: lobbying, negotiating, persuading, persisting, confronting, resisting and withdrawing (Connolly and Harms, 2015, p. 125), with stakeholders who have the power to influence or create change resulting in the achievement of the desired outcomes.

2. Assessment that is ongoing because of the changing dynamics in the situation. The assessment is based on the social workers' critical thinking and critical analysis of the cultural, political, social, economic, policy contexts in which injustices and inequities are located. Social workers need to be confident they are drawing on sound intelligence – based on the emotional, social, political, cultural positions which are operating within the micro and macro systems (Pease et al., 2016).

3. Teamwork that provides a safe place for generating and fostering creative strategies, support, challenges, discussions and decisions about the different roles and responsibilities of the team members in the *process aspects* of advocacy. It is important that the social

worker is not the lone crusader, assuming they know best, but that they work in partnership with clients, other team members and other organizations that share similar concerns about particular inequities and injustices (Baines, 2017).

4. Networking with stakeholders in organizations known to share a similar position about inequities and injustices and with organizations with the potential to influence change such as government officials and politicians. In terms of theory, this networking involves working collaboratively to build strong alliances based on respect and trust, and focusing on commonalities, to work towards addressing the inequities and injustices (Pease et al., 2016).

5. Ethical decision making in deciding on agreed *outcomes* as well as in the *process aspects* of *advocacy*. Engaging with the framework of critical reflection (Fook, 2016) is a useful way for social workers to be transparent about the assumptions and principles underpinning their decisions, strategies, priorities, available resources and actions.

6. Knowledge and understanding of the interdependence of research, policy, practice and theory in social work practice to ensure all advocacy is informed by current and relevant information.

7. Flexibility and openness in order to be responsive to alternative assumptions and changes in the situation.

This is an advocacy story that has a happy ending, as many do. Drawing on some of the above skills, Xie and her team have advocated effectively and continue to do so on a number of levels. Understanding the cultural and political context has been especially important for addressing inequities and injustices, as it was important that the clients were not further disadvantaged through the struggle for social change. Outcomes to date include:

- All canals now having safety guard rails to prevent children from drowning.
- Alternative education for children whose parents cannot afford to pay, though it is minimal. Continued policy and legislative changes are under review.

- Holiday programs for children visiting from rural areas while their parents work in the clothing industry.
- A public campaign led by the social work agency in partnership with the clients to raise awareness about the environment issues – such as water pollution and the collection of refuse.

Campaigning

Campaigning is a strategy undertaken by groups of people over longer periods of time. Campaigning weaves people together around shared concerns in order to improve the conditions of people's lives. In the social work world, campaigning almost always involves social workers and frequently clients and other concerned individuals. It may deliberately try to draw in specific regions or communities such as the western part of Sydney where poor, diverse and racially and ethnically marginalized groups of people live. Or campaigns may work to attract people with access to political power, such as elected government representatives or members of social movements with some size and clout, such as the union or environmental movement. Many campaigns draw specific groups of clients and their communities together to assert their dignity and rights in a world that too often runs roughshod over those with less economic, social and political power.

In New Zealand, the Government is contemplating privatizing out-of-home and foster care to a large, multinational corporation with a dismal record of human rights violations in private prisons and profit gouging in the many contracted-out services they provide across the Anglo world (NZ Net, 2016). This change dovetails with policy changes made a few years ago that vilified clients and introduced funding cuts for all services and supports to families involved in the child welfare system (*The Australian*, 2016). This policy direction viewed families involved in child welfare services as "feral" and "evil," rather than as people struggling with poverty, abuse and, frequently, racism (Beddoe, 2015). Social workers found that these changes further victimized people who were already deprived and marginal, and intensified the distress and harm experienced by vulnerable families.

In 2015, the Public Service Association (one of the main New Zealand unions representing social workers) joined with social workers and social work professors to establish the New Zealand Social Work Action Network (SWAN). SWAN also has active branches in the UK and Ireland (see the internet for local groups). Defending social workers whose jobs were changing in ways that felt profoundly unethical, SWAN campaigned alongside the union to demand a voice in government inquiries and to promote a positive, social justice vision of child welfare. They held meetings, wrote briefs, organized conferences, stood by workers when they refused to practice in ways that felt unethical, defended clients' right to have a voice, attended rallies and lobbied politicians to vote against regressive government policy. University-based educators started a blog and a twitter strategy in conjunction with this campaign to add their research, analysis and ongoing commentary to the campaign. SWAN members and academics also spoke regularly to the media and tried to replace negative images of clients with more humane and realistic ones.

AOP argues that it harms society and clients to view unjust policy as something that we just have to accept and work within. Instead, AOP theory argues that social workers ought to seek like-minded colleagues in their workplaces, discuss their concerns, develop a shared critique and analysis and join with allies, such as advocacy groups, unions and social change movements to challenge unfair and oppressive policies (Baines, 2017). This calls for "moral courage" (Briskman et al., 2009, p. 8) which, as noted above, can come from personal or professional values, political convictions or religious beliefs. Organizing to stop harmful policies and to promote liberating ones has a long history in social work, dating back to the settlement house movements in the 1880s (Kennedy-Kish et al., 2017; Morrison, 2016). Drawing on this history and critical theory, Morrison (2016) notes that: "there has been a constant stream of social workers ... who have advocated for strong engagement in politics and activism" (p. 286).

In the vignette presented at the beginning of this chapter and in the one discussed above, unions are viewed in AOP theory as natural allies who can provide social workers with skills, resources and organizational structures within which to build social change efforts. In this vignette, the union worked with members and non-members to build a new organization, SWAN, which drew together a broader cross-section of social workers, clients, activists and academics to oppose harmful policies and propose an empowering alternative.

Ross (2017) uses AOP to theorize that social work activism should be understood as a broad tent that involves many ways of individually and collectively pushing back at policies and practices that harm people and rob them of their hope and dignity. The vignette above highlights the cooperation between groups and the creativity they developed to engage with an important struggle in a myriad of tactics and approaches. Though the struggle described above continues, many social workers have found new knowledge and liberating practices through their experience in this campaign as well as deep friendships and a renewed sense of social justice ethics and values.

Conclusion

This chapter has shown how advocacy, human rights and campaigning are pivotal parts of everyday, ethical, engaged social work practice, and how theory can be used to deepen our understanding of these central practices. As such, they are part of a process of transforming social work and larger social life in more socially just and equitable ways.

Points to Ponder

1. What knowledge, skills, and values are required for effective activism and advocacy in social work practice, and how does theory fit with this?
2. What might be some of the challenges involved in activism and advocacy, and how might these be addressed?
3. How can social workers be sure that the voices of clients are being respected and prioritized within advocacy and activist efforts?

Key Texts

Baines, D. (Ed). (2017). *Doing anti-oppressive practice: Social justice social work* (3rd Edn.). Halifax: Fernwod.

Kennedy-Kish, B., Sinclair, R., Carniol, B. and Baines, D. (2017). *Case critical: Social services and social justice in Canada.* Toronto: Between the Lines.

Pease, B., Goldinjay, S., Hosken, N. and Nipperess, S. (2016). *Doing critical social work: Transformative practices for social justice.* Melbourne: Allen & Unwin.

References

The Australian (2016). NZ shows Turnbull the way forward for welfare reform. Retrieved December 12, 2016. www.theaustralian.com.au/national-affairs/treasury/nz-shows -turnbull-the-way-forward-for-welfare-reform/news-story/bb66c69e3bf4a807c 909cefb4a0d9c90.

Baines, D. (Ed.) (2017). *Doing anti-oppressive practice: Social justice social work* (3rd Edn.). Halifax: Fernwod.

Beddoe, L. (2015). Making a moral panic – "Feral families," family violence and welfare reforms in New Zealand: Doing the work of the state? In V. E. Cree (Ed.), *Moral panics in theory and practice: Gender and family*. Bristol: The Policy Press, pp. 31–42.

Briskman, L., Pease, B. and Allan, J. (2009). Introducing critical theories for social work in a neo-liberal context. In J. Allan, L. Briskman, and B. Pease (Eds.) *Critical social work: Theories and practices for a socially just world* (2nd Edn.). St. Leonards: Allen & Unwin, pp. 3–14.

Connolly, M., and Harms, L. (2015). *Social work: From theory to practice*. Melbourne: Cambridge University Press.

Dorozenko, K. P., Ridley, S., Martin, R. and Mahboub, L. (2016). A journey of embedding mental health lived experience in social work education. *Social Work Education*, 35(8), pp. 905–917.

Fook, J. (2016). *Social work: A critical approach to practice*. London: Sage.

Kennedy-Kish, B., Sinclair, R., Carniol, B. and Baines, D. (2017). *Case critical: Social services and social justice in Canada*. Toronto: Between the Lines.

Ife, J. (2012). *Human rights and social work: Towards rights-based practice*. Cambridge: Cambridge University Press.

IFSW (2014). *Global definition of social work*. Retrieved December 12, 2016. http://ifsw .org/policies/defintion-of-social-work/.

Morrison, J. (2016). Taking it to the streets. Critical social work's relationship with activism. In B. Pease, S. Goldinjay, N. Hosken, and S. Nipperess (Eds.) *Doing critical social work. Transformative practices for social justice*. Melbourne: Allen & Unwin, pp. 286–297.

North, C. E. (2006). More than words? Delving into the substantive meaning(s) of "social justice" in education. *Review of Educational Research*, 76(4), pp. 507–535.

NZ Net (2016). New Zealand's private prisons: Profiting from incarceration. Retrieved December 12, 2106. www.wakeupnz.net/new-zealands-private-prison-profiting -incarceration/.

Pease, B., Goldinjay, S., Hosken, N. and Nipperess, S. (2016). *Doing critical social work. Transformative practices for social justice*. Melbourne: Allen & Unwin.

Ross, M. (2017). Social work activism within neoliberalism: A big tent approach? In D. Baines (Ed.), *Doing anti-oppressive practice. Social justice social work*. Halifax: Fernwood, pp. 304–321.

Steen, J-A., Mann, M., Restivo, N., Mazany, S. and Chapple, R. (2017). Human rights: Its meaning and practice in social work field settings. *Social Work*, 62(1), pp. 9–17.

Weber, Z., and Pockett, R. (2011). Working effectively in teams. In A. O'Hara, and R. Pockett (Eds.) *Skills for human service practice: Working with individuals, groups and communities* (2nd Edn.). New York: Oxford University Press, pp. 274–295.

17

COMMUNITY SOCIAL WORK

Paul Stepney

Introduction

As a distinct method of practice community social work (CSW) is still relatively young, but its origins can be traced back to the nineteenth-century Settlement movement. It emerged in the UK in the wake of the development of community work and community action, following the rediscovery of poverty and urban deprivation in the 1960s. In the US community practice has always complemented social casework following the pioneer work of Mary Richmond in the 1920s (see Richmond, 1922) and more recently developed as community social casework (Hardcastle and Powers, 2004). In Canada it is associated with macro or structural social work (Mullaly, 2007), and in Australia located within a critical social work tradition (Gray and Webb, 2013). Hence, wherever it is practiced in the world CSW is viewed as part of a radical tradition challenging oppression, reducing inequalities and committed to social justice.

CSW is primarily concerned with working alongside clients and community members to develop more preventative local services, together with creating and enhancing informal networks of support. None the less, its change agent role means that it is sometimes criticized for being more overtly political than mainstream practice. This tension reflects a paradox at the heart of CSW. On the one hand, it has sought to promote greater social responsibility revealed in its commitment to social justice and establishing new and more inclusive local services. On the other, it is working in agencies where opportunities for working in this way have become quite limited and submerged by the pressure of responding to everyday problems. Hence, CSW remains contested and its popularity has waxed and waned during the past 40 years or so.

In many European countries it has migrated from the state to the voluntary or third sector where the scope for doing preventive work is assumed to be greater. Thus, as the late David Sawdon (1986) once said, its development has often been littered with high hopes, modest achievements and some messy failures, something that still very much applies today.

Interest in CSW and the need for community-based intervention has never diminished, despite official ambivalence, and has revived in recent years. There are two main reasons for this. First, concerns about effectiveness, managing risk and how to balance prevention with protection are occupying the minds of policy makers once again. Second, it is a response to growing professional dissatisfaction with the commodified, consumerist and marketized approach to public services. This has led to proposals for more effective partnership working and collaboration between health and social work professionals to tackle common problems, especially in the high-profile areas of child protection and mental health.

The problem is that practitioners now operate in a policy paradox where the need for community support and prevention must be balanced against strict procedures for risk assessment, protection and control (Stepney, 2014). This has been well illustrated by the way child welfare services in the UK, in the post Baby Peter era (see Chapters 2 and 3 in this volume for details of the Baby Peter case), have developed, concentrating on early intervention, but governed by a framework of child protection and risk management (Featherstone et al., 2014). In the process the need for community and family support has been compromised. The following practice focus highlights the problem:

Practice Focus 17.1

Jenni was a single parent with two children, 3-year-old Steve and baby Suzi, and lived in a basement flat in a run-down inner city neighborhood. The family have been struggling since Jenni's partner left three months ago and, when she confided in her doctor that she was emotionally drained and couldn't cope, the family were referred to the Children's Services Department. Developmental checks on the two children revealed problems, with Steve being withdrawn and showing signs of possible neglect; and baby Suzi underweight and seemingly malnourished. After that the family were visited by a stream of professionals checking on the children and voicing concerns. Jenni became quite isolated and came across as bewildered, inconsistent and not understanding what exactly she needed to do. She had already fallen out with the nurse, who reminded her of her own overbearing mother. She believed the social worker had already given up on her and was trying to persuade her to consider giving up the children for adoption. Jenni had been set some targets for improvement which she feared would be impossible to meet.

This case reveals a contemporary problem in that, with few family support services and without a strong commitment to prevention, the practitioner's early intervention role is dominated by child protection concerns. And one can predict the likely outcome of where such defensive practice will lead, consistent with UK national trends which have seen increases in applications for care orders, year on year, to remove children "at risk" in the wake of the Baby Peter case. This has echoes of mistakes made in the past, following many child abuse scandals, where social workers have over-reacted to public criticism after being accused of indecision and not seeing dangers that were allegedly obvious with hindsight. The impact on practice has been dramatic, with an increase in early intervention linked to child protection and neglecting the community support role (Featherstone et al., 2014). But it does not have to be like this.

As welfare policy has become more prescriptive, target driven and underestimates the impact of growing social inequalities, there is an urgent need to find creative community-based solutions. In Jenni's case the absence of community and family support services is highly significant and something a CSW approach would tackle. The fact that there are other families like Jenni in the neighborhood only reinforces the need for an alternative approach, utilizing the resources of the community.

The Contested Concept of Community

In the literature the term *community* is a slippery concept and frequently applied to a range of professional activities, which can be confusing. The term has been used to denote:

- a geographical area or spatial location;
- an organizational unit, network or group based upon ethnicity, faith, interest or occupation where communal interaction take place; and finally
- something that signifies emotional identity, togetherness or attachment with a shared spirit of purpose.

Thus the task of defining community is far from straightforward, as many sociologists have found. Raymond Williams notes it is a: "warmly persuasive word ... that never seems to be used unfavourably" (1976, p. 66). The problem reflects an enigma that: "the term is as much an aspiration as it is a reality" (Stepney and Popple, 2008, p. 7). For this reason, we can approach the question of community in three complementary ways. First, we can look back to an earlier time or bygone age and idealize about how things used to be. Such reminiscing about the communities of the past conjures up memories of a "golden age," in keeping with Young and Willmott's (1957) classic study of Bethnal Green in London in the late 1950s. Here community spirit was strong, children played out in the street until dark and people never bothered to lock their doors at night, even if things were never quite like this.

Second, we can look ahead and construct an idealized notion of the community of the future – based upon consensus and solidarity, and where everyone has a stake in the future. This is likely to offer a comforting image in an otherwise unpredictable world and an antidote to our fears about globalization. Third, we can consider the community of today, even if it is contested, diverse and socially divided (see Stepney and Popple, 2008, pp. 8–9). Looking back and then looking forward may help us address the important challenges we face today.

It would seem that the loss and fragmentation of community are not just a nostalgic issue, but affect everyone and are particularly germane to social work. Many disadvantaged urban neighborhoods and impoverished rural areas, from Manchester to Melbourne and from Houston to Helsinki, have witnessed a decline in infrastructure facilities and services. Local shops, banks, pubs or bars, cafes, schools, welfare agencies have closed down in recent years, replaced in part by global coffee chains, charity shops, convenience stores and new business ventures. The good news for CSW is that these problems come with opportunities to reclaim buildings for community use.

The focus of this chapter is on CSW, acknowledging that it draws upon knowledge and skills from other disciplines. The aim is to explain its key ideas and core theories, demonstrating how these can be applied to both Jenni and a variety of practice situations. It will be argued that CSW is a core method of practice that every social worker should be equipped to use, developing what has been called a "patch" approach.

Development of the Patch Approach

Following the development of a universal approach to the delivery of welfare services in the UK in the early 1970s, the Barclay Committee (1982) recommended that CSW should become a central feature of social services provision. In arguing that formal services should be integrated with informal networks of support, the Committee underestimated that those in greatest need frequently had inadequate or non-existent support networks (Abrams et al., 1989) or low levels of social capital (Putnam, 2000). Ironically, there is often a greater need for CSW in such disadvantaged communities.

The Barclay Committee recognized that the majority of community care is provided informally by women, and by 2014 the governmental saving had risen to an estimated £61.7bn per year (Popple, 2015). Consequently, a challenge for CSW was to develop a non-exploitative approach not driven by cost-saving imperatives. One way to achieve this was to reorganize services into patch teams serving populations of 15–20,000 people. Patch teams were set up in a number of UK towns and typically included two or three professional social workers, occupational therapists, unqualified community care workers, as well as local people employed as family carers, street wardens and home helps. These are exactly the kind of resources that could help Jenni to cope before making any decision regarding the long-term future of the children. In the

US community social casework has been influenced by the UK patch model, underpinned by a range of theories and these will be explored in the next section.

Community Social Work Theory

CSW is informed by a number of theoretical approaches, including systems theory, community networking, community work, empowerment and socio-spatial analysis derived from human geography. It also encompasses psychosocial models of human behavior and group work found in mainstream social work practice. Given this diversity it is the main theoretical ideas that I shall concentrate on here.

Systems Theory

Systems theory has wide applicability to practice and an eco-systems approach is especially relevant to working in the community (see Chapter 15 in this volume). Briefly, an eco-systems approach suggests that many problems can be tackled by improving the fit between a person's environment and their needs, capacities and aspirations through the life course (Gitterman and Germain, 2008). This suggests working with clients in a holistic way and recognizing that positive change in one part of a system will often lead to change in another. For example, strengthening Jenni's support network is likely to have a positive impact on the micro system based within the home and around care of the children. If every part of a system is inter-connected (Henriques and Tuckley, 2012), then the application of eco-systems theory means we must embrace the theory of networking.

Networking Theory

In very general terms a network is: "a system or pattern of links between points which have particular meanings for those involved" (Seed, 1990, cited in Payne, 2014, p. 202). A preliminary step is to assess a client's informal network and the underlying systems of primary and secondary support. Jenni, like many single mothers in her neighborhood has a very fragile, almost non-existent support network. However, even if some support exists, it is the quality of the relationship between people in the network that is important, not just the number involved. And drawing an eco-map of a client's network will be helpful and revealing.

Community Work

There is an inevitable overlap between CSW and the community work role even if this is carried out by workers from voluntary agencies or community projects. However, community work is broadly concerned with "tackling injustice and inequality by organising people to promote policy change at the local level" (Stepney and Popple, 2008, p. 113). The theoretical base of community work is wider and incorporates approaches concerned with change and empowerment.

Community Empowerment

This is a central part of CSW. Empowerment is a contested concept concerned with structural change, as well as personal change and control. But, of course, exercising some control does not always equate with feeling empowered, especially if services are commodified and marketized. Professionals can make a difference, especially if they are committed to the mutual empowerment of every citizen. Empowerment theory offers a challenging framework for practice and raises questions about social justice, diversity and equality in the community (see Lee, 2001).

Socio-Spatial Awareness

Human geographers have helped us to appreciate the need for a new socio-spatial awareness of how our communities are characterized by social divisions, segregation and inequalities. This is reinforced by the impact of unplanned migration throughout the globe. The organization and use of physical space reflects social, economic and political priorities often reflecting the interests of the global market. The challenge is to incorporate this analysis as part of a wider commitment to spatial justice, creating services that promote human rights alongside tackling community problems (Soja, 2010).

The approach proposed here is to start with the precise practice situation, then theorize using the above theoretical framework as a guide. The ideas of Freire (1972) and Gramsci (1986) are relevant here, as they offer a "critical context for practice," linking ideology, inequality and power (Stepney and Popple, 2008). We will now look at how CSW theory might be used in practice, and focus on Jenni's situation to illustrate this.

Community Social Work in Action

The following is an eight-phase process model that has been adapted principally from the work of Stepney and Popple (2008) and Hardcastle and Powers (2004), and can be applied to Jenni as well as clients in different community settings.

The eight phases are as follows:

1. Initial assessment of community and analysis of patch – this is the familiarization stage of walking around to get a "feel" for the neighborhood, gathering baseline data to understand what kind of community it is and the nature of its problems. The community in which Jenni lives is disadvantaged, the housing is old and it has high levels of poverty, unemployment and social exclusion.

2. Refine and develop analysis – this comes from undertaking a more in-depth analysis and assessment of community needs and resources, alongside engagement with key local people. At this stage the client's situation is considered and initially assessed. Jenni's neighborhood is fragmented and has multiple problems, with refugees living alongside an older white working-class population. In Jenni's part of the community are a number of single mothers living in flats of poor quality and challenging circumstances.

3. Assessment of client's problems, strengths and support systems – drawing on relevant theory, as well as psychosocial models, to provide a more complex analysis of client's problems. Identify informal support networks and possible support systems (family, neighbors, friends) using an eco-map. In Jenni's case she is experiencing loss of her partner, has financial problems and is struggling to meet the children's physical and emotional needs. She has no local support system and her older mother lives in another town some distance away. But Jenni is desperate and willing to try anything if it will help. The SMARRT system of objectives (specific, measurable, acceptable, realistic, results orientated, and time specific) could be a useful problem-solving strategy to tackle the issues in an understandable way so that Jenni is clear about

what is required and has a checklist for evaluating progress (see Hardcastle and Powers, 2004).

4. Build or rebuild support networks – this is a crucial phase because it is important to create networks of potential support and then work to sustain them. In Jenni's case it means identifying (with colleagues) other single mothers in the area, and organizing to bring them together in a support group to discuss mutual problems and address child care issues. Allied to this is to identify what resources are needed, who can help (local family aid worker), and location for group meetings. Offer Jenni one-to-one support to address issues of loss, isolation and meeting the children's needs.

5. Access resources and develop partnerships – this involves advocacy, modeling and even teaching skills alongside mainstream social work skills. The SMARRT objectives may help Jenni see what the support group can do to help, what she needs to do herself and what resources might be needed. Involve health staff in group sessions to give advice and monitor child development. In short it will give Jenni a sense of what progress she is making with the children and check that she herself is feeling empowered.

6. Evaluate goals and objectives (modify if necessary) – it is likely that, in CSW, as with any approach, not all will proceed smoothly and unforeseen problems may arise. Change in one part of the system affects other parts and sometimes things might deteriorate before getting better. In Jenni's case the impact on the children should be positive, but will need careful monitoring (checking that Steve is healthy and baby Suzi is gaining weight), and worries about the future may be an underlying source of concern. Further, there could be tensions in the single mothers' support group that will need addressing. Goals may need modification to reflect the fact that progress often brings additional problems.

7. Support social networks to become effective – this is a wider role concerned with supporting networks for both Jenni and other clients in the community (support group for older people, a tenants group and so on). The long-term health and sustainability of networks in the neighborhood are the priority and to this end resources to establish a family center should be considered.

8. Monitoring and evaluating – client empowerment is the aim and a time comes when this must be evaluated. Again, the SMARRT objectives or similar can act as a guide. Does Jenni feel she has taken appropriate responsibility for her children's welfare? If CSW intervention has been successful then Jenni will be less dependent on professional staff, better at managing her own affairs and can access help as and when needed. CSW, in partnership with health professionals, can also contribute to a broader commitment to research-informed and evidence-enriched practice.

Research Evidence of CSW's Effectiveness

A literature review by Ohmer and Korr (2006) found that effective practice improved "the psycho-social aspects of communities, influencing citizen participation ... in terms of increasing self-awareness and self-esteem" (Ohmer and Korr, 2006, p 142). However, the impact on the economic and physical environment was mixed. These findings are consistent with UK research. For example, Barr (1997) found very few examples of CSW solving the problems of disadvantaged communities, but many cases of it increasing the self-confidence, self-respect and skills of local people.

Partnership work is a key ingredient in CSW, particularly between statutory services, voluntary agencies and informal carers. Research by the UK Children's Society demonstrates that CSW is preventive – preventing crisis through strengthening communities, as well as cost effective in terms of reducing the number of statutory interventions (Holman, 1995). Featherstone et al. (2014) call for a return to patch working, pointing out that "staff are too often tethered to their computer stations with direct contact a time limited project" (p. 1743). Further, research by Stepney (2014) suggests that prevention strategies, including community and family support, allied to protection plans, are an essential ingredient of high-quality practice.

Conclusion

CSW continues to be a distinct and highly relevant method of practice, in a societal context increasingly scarred by social divisions and inequalities. As practice has become more defensive, risk adverse and protection minded, as evidenced by the way children's services in the UK have developed (Featherstone et al., 2014), there is a danger of it bearing down heavily on marginalized clients like Jenni from disadvantaged communities.

In the US community social casework's strength is its clarity of objectives, its flexibility to integrate clients into appropriate support networks and its overall commitment to client empowerment (Hardcastle and Powers, 2004). In the UK many practitioners wish to practice in this way to complement their care management role. In the Nordic countries and other parts of Europe CSW remains popular and receives support from municipal agencies, both for individual work with clients and for regenerating communities in ecologically sound ways (Matthies and Närhi, 2016). In Finland it is now the approach increasingly used in work with refugees and new migrants to strengthen their local communities.

In this chapter I have argued that CSW has much to offer. There is an urgent need to develop a range of preventive community-based services that offer family support to children and families at this time. The strength and capacities of clients can be harnessed, rather than practitioners becoming preoccupied with deficits, risks and vulnerability. Similar issues can be found in adult services and mental health where the need for community support and prevention is equally strong (Stepney, 2014). CSW, with its emphasis on patch working and creating informal networks of support, offers a reliable way of combining prevention with protection, to ensure that decisions are informed by sound judgement, local knowledge and high-quality evidence.

Points to Ponder

1. How would you undertake an analysis of a community or patch that you are familiar with (through placement, previous knowledge or work experience)? What data could you access and which local people might you speak with?
2. What specific prevention strategies might be incorporated in your future work with vulnerable clients and how can these be balanced alongside the need for protection?
3. Pause for a few minutes and reflect on the community of your childhood, when you were, say, 8-years old. What key features

do you remember? You might like to draw a plan of your living room, the street outside and identify who were the important people in your life at that time. How does this picture differ from the community that children live in today?

Key Texts

Stepney, P. and Popple, K. (2008). *Social work and the community: A critical context for practice*. Basingstoke, UK: Palgrave Macmillan.

Hardcastle, D. and Powers, P. (2004). *Community practice: Theories and skills for social workers* (2nd Edn.). New York: Oxford University Press.

Featherstone, B., Morris, K. and White, S. (2014). A marriage made in hell: Early intervention meets child protection. *British Journal of Social Work*, 44, pp. 1735–1749.

References

Abrams, P., Abrams, S., Humphrey, R. and Snaith R. (1989). *Neighbourhood care and social policy*. London: HMSO.

Barclay Committee (1982). *Social workers: Their role and tasks*. London: Bedford Square Press.

Barr, A. (1997). Reflections on the enigma of community empowerment. *Scottish Journal of Community Work and Development*, 2, pp. 47–59.

Featherstone, B., Morris, K. and White, S. (2014). A marriage made in hell: Early intervention meets child protection, *British Journal of Social Work*, 44, pp. 1735–1749.

Freire, P. (1972). *Pedagogy of the oppressed*. Harmondsworth, UK: Penguin.

Gitterman, A. and Germain C. B. (2008). *The life model of social work practice: Advances in theory and practice* (3rd Edn.). New York: Columbia University Press.

Gramsci, A. (1986). *Selections from prison notebooks*. London: Lawrence and Wishart.

Gray, M. and Webb, S. (2013). *Social work theories and methods* (2nd Edn.). London: Sage.

Hardcastle, D. and Powers, P. (2004). *Community practice: Theories and skills for social workers* (2nd Edn.). New York: Oxford University Press.

Henriques, P. and Tuckley, G. (2012). Ecological systems theory and direct work with children and families, In P. Stepney and D. Ford (Eds.) *Social work models, methods and theories* (2nd Edn.). Lyme Regis, UK: Russell House Publishing, pp. 166–180.

Holman, B. (1995). *Putting families first*. Basingstoke, UK: Macmillan.

Lee, J. A. B. (2001). *The empowerment approach to social work practice: Building the beloved community* (2nd Edn.). New York: Columbia University Press.

Matthies, A-L. and Närhi, K. (Eds.) (2016). *The eco-social transition of societies*. London: Routledge.

Mullaly, B. (2007). *The new structural social work* (4th Edn.). Ontario, Canada: Oxford University Press.

Ohmer, M. and Korr, W. (2006). The effectiveness of community practice interventions: A review of the literature. *Research on Social Work Practice*, 16(2), pp. 132–145.

Payne, M. (2014). *Modern social work theory* (4th Edn.). Basingstoke, UK: Palgrave Macmillan.

Popple, K. (2015). *Analysing community work: Its theory and practice* (2nd Edn.). Maidenhead, UK: Open University Press.

Putnam, R. (2000). *Bowling alone: The collapse and revival of American community*. New York: Simon and Schuster.

Richmond, M. E. (1922). *What is social case work? An introductory description.* New York: Russell Sage Foundation.

Sawdon, D. (1986). *Making connections in practice teaching.* London: Heinemann & NISW.

Seed, P. (1990). *Introducing network analysis in social work.* London: Jessica Kingsley Publishers.

Soja, E. (2010). *Seeking spatial justice.* Minneapolis, MN: University of Minnesota Press.

Stepney, P. (2014). Prevention in social work: The final frontier? *Critical and Radical Social Work,* 2(3), pp. 305–320.

Stepney, P. and Popple, K. (2008). *Social work and the community: A critical context for practice.* Basingstoke, UK: Palgrave Macmillan.

Williams, R. (1976). *Keywords.* London: Fontana/Croom Helm.

Young, M. and Willmott, P. (1957). *Family and kinship in East London.* London: Routledge.

CONCLUSION

Social work, by its very nature, is a challenging undertaking, mainly because, if the situations we deal with were not difficult and complex, they would not be landing on our desk. Social work is therefore for those of us who like a challenge, and not for people who are looking for an easy life. The challenges come from the nature of the work itself, from the wider political and social policy context, from organizational cultures and dynamics, and even from within ourselves sometimes. But, wherever the challenges come from, our professionalism demands of us that we do our best to rise to them. Therein lie the rewards and satisfactions that balance out the challenges.

Social work is for people who want to make a positive difference. To be able to make a difference we need to be well equipped in terms of knowledge, skills and values. The social work theory base provides us with a strong foundation of knowledge from which we can continue to develop our understanding over time. Methods related to, and deriving from, social work theories provide us with tools and frameworks around which we can develop our skills. And, of course, underpinning both the knowledge and the skills are values, the ethical principles that, on the one hand, ensure that we are practicing safely, and, on the other, motivate and sustain us.

This book, across its 17 chapters, has aimed to provide a solid foundation of knowledge for you to build on with a view to equipping yourself well for the various challenges that social work presents. Trying to do social work without the knowledge and understanding you need is potentially a recipe for disaster. However, it is important for us to re-emphasize the book's subtitle, "The Essentials." We chose that subtitle to make the point that what we have covered is, in effect, just the basics – there is so much more to learn. But, of course, you have the rest of your career to learn it. Continuing to learn, develop and grow (continuous professional development, to use the technical term) is another example of what our professionalism demands.

So, now that you have reached the end of the book, you should not be assuming that your journey is coming to an end. In fact, it is much wiser to see it as the end of just one small part of your learning pathway, a pathway that should lead you to an ever-growing knowledge base, with the greater confidence and effectiveness that comes with that knowledge.

We wish you well on that journey and hope that what we have presented you with in this book will stand you in good stead for rising to the challenges and reaping the rewards.

INDEX